IRELAND'S ECONOMIC CRISIS

TIME TO ACT

Editors **Joe Mulholland** and **Finbarr Bradley**

A Carysfort Press Book

First published as a paperback in Ireland in 2009 by
Carysfort Press Ltd
58 Woodfield
Scholarstown Road
Dublin 16
Ireland

ISBN 978-1-904505-43-3

© 2009 MacGill Summer School

Typeset by Carysfort Press Ltd

Printed and bound by eprint limited
Unit 35
Coolmine Industrial Estate
Dublin 15
Ireland
Cover design by eprint

Acknowledgements

We wish to express our gratitude to Donegal County Council, Forfás, IBEC, Postbank and Hewlett Packard Ireland without whose generosity this publication could not have been produced. We hope it justifies their belief that the proceedings of the 2009 MacGill School merited being made available as widely as possible.

We are also indebted to Carysfort Press and in particular Dan Farrelly, Lilian Chambers and Rachael Kilgallon as well as Margaret Hamilton and Barry O'Brien of eprint limited for their commitment, courtesy and overall professionalism to which, we feel, this work bears testimony. Our gratitude is also due to our photographers in Glenties, Mary Ita Boyle and Michael O'Donnell, and to Fiona Mulholland whose photo embellishes the cover.

Loyal friends of the MacGill School have always been available to put their shoulders to the wheel when required as did, on this occasion, Charles Byrne, Nuala Naughton, Michael Norris and Joe and Cathy Carroll. We thank them. We are also grateful to the MacGill Summer School committee for their loyalty and support and especially its Secretary, Mary Claire O'Donnell and Chairman, Michael Gallagher.

Finally, as we have said on previous occasions, there would not be a MacGill School at all, and consequently no volume such as this, without the generosity and public spirit of the contributors whose edited essays are contained within these covers. All are very busy and involved people in public life and it is to their credit that they devoted so much time to travelling to Glenties and sharing their most valuable insights into and concerns about the economic crisis in which Ireland finds itself.

Ár mórbhuíochas dóibh go léir.

CONTENTS

Foreword

Joe Mulholland and Finbarr Bradley

'We have always known that heedless self-interest was bad morals; we now know that it is bad economics.' – US President, Franklin D. Roosevelt

We met in extraordinary times and the words of the 32nd President of the US had special resonance. There was an air of crisis at the twenty-ninth MacGill Summer School. The feeling, though, was not one of despondency but rather of shock and anger that the economy had been so mismanaged. The spectre of the report of An Bord Snip Nua loomed large with the School taking place within days of its publication. Chairman Colm McCarthy spelt out to our audience what had happened to the economy to bring us to the point where we are borrowing over €400 million per week for day-to-day expenditure. At the time of putting this book to bed, hovering over the debate is NAMA and its future, though in Glenties in July it appeared that NAMA was accepted as a *fait accompli*. Ireland's foremost banking academic, Patrick Honohan, Governor-Elect of the Central Bank, was with us and he outlined his alternative and creative NAMA 2.0 proposal.

The party is definitely over. Having lived through good times, are we now ready to live through bad times? The country that had come out of the dark years of the 80s and decades of depression to become one of the most attractive locations in the world for foreign direct investment is no more, at least for the next number of years. Now we are suffering from the worst recession of any advanced country since the 1930s. The controversial article by Nobel laureate, Paul Krugman, in the *New York Times* in April, *Erin Go Broke*, appeared, in fact, to get it right. Krugman wrote that in the third freest economy in the world behind Hong Kong and Singapore what was especially free was the banking sector 'which used its freedom to finance a monstrous housing bubble'. Krugman went on to describe how Ireland, like its near-namesake, Iceland, 'had jumped with both feet into the brave new world of unsupervised global markets.' Fridrik Baldursson of Reykavjik University was with us in Glenties to tell from direct experience, having been involved in the crisis, what had brought about the collapse of their banking system with no European Central Bank to turn to and how, in some ways, they have better prospects than Ireland of getting out of their crisis.

It was and remains obvious, as will be evident from these pages, that Ireland is in deep trouble. Our disastrous downturn has happened at the same time as the world recession but, to make matters worse, we will find it difficult to take advantage of the upturn which appears to be in its infancy in some of the big economies and notably in the US. Burdened with a chaotic situation in the banks which, as was pointed out by several speakers at MacGill, we have managed to survive only because of the injection of funds of the order so far of €130 billion by the European Central Bank as well as the nationalization of Anglo-Irish Bank, the Government is in a political strait-jacket when it comes to taking steps to re-invigorate the economy. Add to this difficult situation a steadily increasing budget deficit, growing unemployment, falling domestic activity due to the collapse of the construction sector and the subsequent diminution of domestic consumer spending as well as the serious erosion of the competitiveness of the country's exports and you get a clear picture of just how serious our economic crisis is. How we allowed ourselves to get into it is, at this point, somewhat academic, apart from the lessons to be learned about regulation and about the ability of our political system as well as the institutions of the state to run the economy so that a crisis of this dimension is avoided in the future or at least minimised.

Audiences were aghast as speaker after speaker, with extensive experience in Irish public life, described how and why the economy went so awry. Eamon Gilmore, for example, said the economy had been hijacked 'by speculators and developers'. It is true that many of our problems are due to overdependence on house building. By 2007, construction accounted for 13.3 per cent of employment, the highest in the OECD. Very strong growth in public spending was financed by revenue generated largely from taxes on property which could not possibly be sustained. As Karl Whelan illustrated, a substantial slowdown was looming for Ireland by 2007 but evidence was ignored even though this was obvious as far back as 2002. Of course there was plenty of blame to go around but, characteristic of the School, we did not over indulge in looking back. The thrust was what road now needs to be followed, what choices need to be made in terms of economic policy, public services, and of course, the regulation of financial institutions, in order to reinvigorate our economy and society. We must equip ourselves for setting out on the path to recovery and this was very much on the agenda in Glenties. Competitiveness is key and as Peter Bacon and others stated, wages and salary cuts of 10-15 per cent are essential in this process.

As is also clear from these papers, Ireland faces not just an economic crisis, but a political, social and moral crisis as well – a whole confluence of circumstances built up during the Celtic Tiger and indeed decades before. The Irish celebrated materialism, affluence, consumerism, and self-indulgence with gusto, according to Rowena Pecchenino, evils Pope John Paul II warned against on his 1979 visit. In Pecchenino's words, 'hard work and sacrifice were not in the Irish lexicon' during those heady years when, as we all know, it was difficult to find native tradesmen willing to do handiwork at a reasonable price, with Poles, Latvians, Lithuanians, and others preferred for work of all kinds.

The Official Opening speech by Michael McLoone raised the question of whether Ireland's political and social institutions have the capacity not alone to decide what has to be done but the will and competencies to do so within a timescale that gets us out of the hole quickly but without doing serious damage in the process. During the boom, critics claim the well off got richer while the poor were left behind and the numbers living at the margins of society continued to grow. However, according to Minister for Finance, Brian Lenihan, everyone benefitted from the Celtic Tiger, including those on social welfare payments. Economic success was not achieved without cost. In the headlong pursuit of prosperity, there were negative impacts on the natural environment and a sense of community which, in many people's opinion, dented and weakened the social and cultural fabric of the nation. In the Ninth Annual John Hume Lecture, Dr Diarmuid Martin argued the need for a strong civil society. Self-interest alone, he said, no matter how enlightened, cannot be the sole measure for evaluating relations within society. Ireland needs not just a revival of social partnership, but an even wider model of social participation.

While there was a sense of resignation at the sorry state of our finances, the consensus was that the time for action is now and to gear ourselves for recovery – whenever it comes. There was deep concern about the slow pace of change and inadequate governance in the public sector. Reform is essential although if one is to judge from the remarks of one of our most distinguished former civil servants, Brendan Tuohy, it is far from being a given. Perhaps it was the need to maintain social partnership and consensus that slowed down the reform process and prevented the necessary radical measures being taken. He painted a bleak picture with report after report over the years analysing the effectiveness, efficiency and value for money in the public sector. Yet, either they were never implemented at all or only partly implemented. Results, not more reports, are needed now. Here is the challenge: deliver public services that are lean and efficient, not self-serving, expensive and ultimately unaffordable.

The private sector has fared no better. It has become obvious in quite a dramatic and terrible way that not enough attention was paid to what the bankers and developers here and elsewhere were up to. Obviously, those in positions of responsibility were not paying attention either. Is it any wonder we are in a crisis when, as David Murphy points out, Irish banks insisted time and again in 2007 and 2008 that they were in fine fettle with sufficient capital to meet the worst scenarios that could be envisaged. Eugene Sheehy, then Chief Executive of AIB, stated in October 2008 then he would rather die than raise new capital! Its former Chairman, Dermot Gleeson, admitted at Glenties that serious mistakes were made; loans were given out which should not have been. Dan Boyle maintains that banking practices varied from the incompetent to the morally suspect to the illegal. He believes we can learn best from Canada, a country which stands alone in not having had a banking crisis, due largely to having a system of regulation more interventionist and more stringent in standards applied to its banks.

As to the state of the economy now, our choice, as Colm McCarthy bluntly puts it, boils down to either raising taxes or cutting spending. Brian Lenihan maintains that the only path to recovery is to have sustainable public finances, regain competitiveness and repair our banking system. But George Lee says it is a mistake to correct the catastrophic imbalance in public finances at the pace now proposed. Unless the global economy, as he puts it, 'experiences the fastest revival since Lazarus got up out of his bed and walked', then the burden of fiscal adjustment placed on the public may be too great. It is a perspective with which David Begg concurs. Wage and public spending cuts, he argues, will impart a further dangerous deflationary shock to the demand side of the economy. Conventional perspectives on competitiveness are a questionable concept, he added.

As a society we are going to have to do more with less in order to limit the damage to our living standards and return to a path of sustainable economic growth. Despite a painful adjustment, Danny McCoy is in no doubt that reduction in unit labour costs, delivered through public pay reform, will strengthen our long-term competitive position. But will Mary Coughlan's call at Glenties to protected professions, who have yet to reduce high fees, continue to fall on deaf ears? References from the floor pointed to the exorbitant fees of doctors with medicines costing far more than in other member states of the EU.

We have to move forward, and quickly. The question is: can we rebuild a damaged economy as well as a damaged society? Yes we can, provided the right measures are now taken. Examples were given by those in positions to know what this might imply in practice. Jim O'Hara, CEO, Intel Ireland, supported the current strategy of strong investment in 4th level education but urged that the focus be on how to get more research from the same budget and achieve greater commercialization of that research. He stressed that young people must be imbued with the vision, ambition and confidence to create start-ups and believe that they can grow our own Irish Nokia or Google. Martin Murphy, who heads up HP Ireland argued that as an open economy on the periphery of Europe, excellence has to be our trade mark – both to attract further investment to this country and crucially to build an indigenous global enterprise culture of our own. The objective is to deliver a better service at a lower cost through innovation. The aim is to think smart, work smart and buy smart.

Of course, many other issues were discussed at Glenties such as education, energy, Lisbon, the all-island economy and how Ireland's distinctive cultural resources contribute to competitiveness. In summary, there is, as is vividly illustrated in these pages, an urgent need for an invigorated national strategy and sense of purpose. Some politicians and business leaders make powerful contributions on this theme. Fine Gael Leader, Enda Kenny, says 'Our political culture is discredited. We cannot fix our economy or create a just society unless and until we also fix our politics'. He calls for fundamental reform arguing that the findings of An Bord Snip Nua are an absolutely damning indictment of the way that Government has been run for the past decade.

Ireland's fundamentally changed circumstances require a radical transformation in its policymaking. The development model must be founded on harnessing national innovative capability, focusing on social cohesion and proper regulatory oversight. Contributions from the podium and floor in Glenties ranged from policy, vision and context to practical suggestions on how the country can emerge from its present crisis. Bleak though the prognosis was, spirits were neither dampened nor was good humour absent. Debate, reflection and, as ever at MacGill, courteous disagreement, was stimulating and lively. The papers in this volume, we feel, make a valuable contribution to the debate about Ireland's future economic welfare. Policy-makers, business leaders, academics, opinion formers, students and all those interested in the future of this nation will gain invaluable insights by reading and studying their contents.

Tá súil againn go mbainfidh tú taitneamh as iad a léamh!

Official Opening of MacGill Summer School

Michael McLoone

Manager, Donegal County Council

Born Ballyshannon, Co. Donegal. Trainee Health Inspector (1962-6), Health Inspector, Sligo Co. Council and Senior Health Inspector North-West Health Board (NWHB) (1966-75). Personnel Officer, Midlands Health Board (1978-81). Programme Manager NWHB (1981-8). Chief Executive, Beaumont Hospital (1988-94). County Manager, Donegal Co. Council since 1994. Appointed Chairman, Irish Blood Transfusion Service in 2001. Chairman, Letterkenny Institute of Technology since 1996. Member Western Development Commission (1996-2001). Chairman, Donegal Enterprise Board since 1994.

Over the past 29 years the Patrick MacGill Summer School has provided a forum for presentations and debates on the contemporary issues that were shaping life in Ireland. In the 1980s the School explored issues around employment, enterprise and immigration. The single market in the Europe of Maastricht introduced the European dimension in the 1990s. Northern Ireland was an all-pervasive theme as Orange and Green representatives to the school tracked the pathway to the recent historic events, culminating with the establishment of the Northern Ireland Executive. During this present decade the school went in search of the soul of Ireland – our identity, our literary and artistic culture, our value system – and how much it was being battered by the greed and avarice, crassness and vulgarity that can sometimes accompany affluence and overindulgence in alcohol and drugs.

The underlying assumption in recent times was that we had fixed the economy. We could now turn our attention to how the economy could better serve our society. We were experiencing annual growth rates in GDP of 4 per cent, 5 per cent or 6 per cent. But 2007 and 2008 changed all that. It was an economic crash of gigantic proportions – there was no soft landing.

The 8 per cent swing in the economy from 6 per cent growth

Ireland also had the unenviable distinction of being the first Euro area economy to record a recession, being the first to have two consecutive quarters of negative economic growth.

in GDP in 2007 to 1.8 per cent contraction in 2008 had never been experienced over such a short period before, with a predicted further contraction of 4 per cent to 5 per cent in 2009. All this is unprecedented in its speed and depth. According to the OECD economic outlook 2008, the downturn in the Irish economy was the most severe of any experienced by an OECD member state with the exception of Iceland. Ireland also had the unenviable distinction of being the first Euro area economy to record a recession, being the first to have two consecutive quarters of negative economic growth.

In order to bridge the gap between government expenditure and income, the country is borrowing over €400 million every week to keep afloat. A Professor of Economics at UCD, Morgan Kelly, has predicted that the country is on an 'unstoppable drift into national bankruptcy'.

The MacGill Summer School Programme 2009 has changed gear and has brought a high-powered group of speakers to confront the key questions on what went wrong with the Irish economy and how we can fix it. The National Economic and Social Council[1], in its analysis of what went wrong, proposes that this is a five-part crisis facing Ireland – Banking, Fiscal, Economic, Social and Reputational – and that the only way of fixing it is to address all of these interdependent crises in a coordinated and synchronized manner. This is a useful framework of analysis.

If the economy is to recover it needs the banks. If the banks are to recover the international as well as the national dimensions of the banking crisis need to be resolved. This week may shed further light on the international banking crisis. How did sub-prime borrowers in the U.S. get loans with loan to value rations of over 100 per cent? Why did Wall Street bankers approve these loans without proper credit ratings of borrowers i.e. evidence of the ability to repay the loans? deal with defaults and no adequate insurance cover to cover high risks? How could the Federal Reserve/Central Banking System/International Regulator allow our International financial system be built on a house of cards?

The programme confronts all these dimensions of the crisis and a number of others including the capacity of our political institutions to deal with them.

How could the Federal Reserve/ Central Banking System/International Regulator allow our International financial system be built on a house of cards?

Does the fixing of the Irish Banking crisis depend on the fixing of the global problems in international imbalances, capital and regulation of capital and control of credit? What about the problems caused by the Irish Banks? Were the banks to blame for borrowing money cheaply on international markets and lending it long term to developers and house purchasers to create the worst property bubble ever and by creating all this credit created an unsustainable tax base for which we paid ourselves too much?

Or were we all to blame for generating a competitive frenzy amongst the banks? What about the European dimension and the requirement to meet the target to reduce the Government deficit to 3 per cent of GDP by 2013. And how will we fix the problem of bad/toxic debts and get credit flowing again to sustain business? Will NAMA work?

How will we sort out the fiscal crisis? The gap between what the government spends (over €50 billion per annum) and what it takes in (just over €30 billion) has grown enormously. Unsustainable tax revenues from the property bubble are drying up. Do we cut public spending à la the McCarthy menu or cut public pay or both, in order to bridge the gap? And can we transform the public service in a way which allows us to reduce costs and improve services, i.e., through productivity gains. My own Council is facing up to the new economic reality with the loss of over 200 jobs because we cannot renew temporary contracts. It will be a major challenge to maintain services at existing levels.

And what about the economy? How can we create sustainable jobs to deal with the employment crisis? If we have 500,000 or more unemployed by year-end, can we find some short-term solutions in moving people from welfare to work through retraining, back to education schemes or public works schemes? Will the Smart Economy strategy and support for indigenous entrepreneurs get us back to sustainable export-led growth? Can we restructure the economy away from the high dependence on construction to a more balanced economy which uses our natural resources, our arts, heritage and culture, our potential for wave and wind energy to gain us competitive advantage again? In Donegal, where unemployment has risen by over 80 per cent to 18,000 people, we are very interested in exploring these options. We have been hit disproportionately by the drop in retail sales, not alone as a result of the contraction in the economy but by the

Do we cut public spending à la the McCarthy menu or cut public pay or both, in order to bridge the gap? And can we transform the public service in a way which allows us to reduce costs and improve services, i.e., through productivity gains.

euro/sterling exchange rate movements. Ask any retailer in Donegal. The drop in retail sales is putting huge pressure on business and, in turn, business is putting pressure on Local Authorities to reduce their charges e.g. rates, commercial water charges.

The social crisis manifests itself in many ways. Couples without jobs with high mortgages which depended on growth in property prices to justify the leveraging they did with the banks now cannot repay the loan. They are in negative equity to the tune of 20 per cent to 30 per cent or more. What happens to them? What attitude should banks and the government take? And what about social welfare payments and the minimum wage? Should either or both be left untouched by the cuts in public spending? Do we need to address the cost to benefit ratio of our welfare state i.e. the levels of contribution and the levels of benefits particularly as between public and private pensions and in the funding of health and education services? Do we need, for example, to pay more for our social services or use an insurance-based system for all to ensure more equitable access?

Then there is the reputational risk. Can we deal with our European and International partners and lenders in ways which will give them confidence in our ability to fix the economy so that the cost of borrowing/government bonds is cheaper for us. For others the regaining of our reputation will require for them the removal of those responsible for creating or presiding over the creation of many problems, as for example, Directors/Senior Managers of banks who engaged high risk or reckless lending, financial regulators, etc.

These are the kinds of questions that will be addressed this week along with many more. The Summer School will be providing a unique forum at which the key players from the economic, political, academic, banking, cultural, artistic, social, community and other sectors of our society can present, debate, question and challenge the analysis of the underlying causes of the crisis and the pros and cons of optional pathways to recovery. It is we, the people, who

For others the regaining of our reputation will require for them the removal of those responsible for creating or presiding over the creation of many problems, as for example, Directors/-Senior Managers of banks who engaged high risk or reckless lending, financial regulators.

have to understand the need for and implications of these recovery options in the interest of this and the next generation. We, the people, also need to know whether our political and other social institutions have the capacity not alone to decide what has to be done and within a timescale that gets us out of the hole quickly but without doing us serious damage in the process.

This week may well go down as one of the most important ever MacGill Summer Schools in terms of both its timing and the relevance of what will be discussed for the future of the Irish economy. That this should be so, is a tribute to Dr Joe Mulholland, Director of the Summer School in the year he has been honoured by his native County as Donegal Person of the Year. It is not an exaggeration to say that only he could have fielded the team of outstanding speakers who are presenting at Glenties this week. It is a great honour for me to open such a prestigious 2009 MacGill Summer School.

We Need A Strong Civil Society

Ninth Annual John Hume Lecture
Most Rev. Dr Diarmuid Martin
Archbishop of Dublin

Born in Dublin and educated at Oblate Fathers, Inchicore and De La Salle School, Ballyfermot. Studied philosophy at UCD and theology at Holy Cross College, Clonliffe. Ordained in 1969. Studied moral theology at Pontifical University of St. Thomas Aquinas. Served as curate in parish of St. Brigid, Cabinteely. Entered service of Holy See in 1976. In 1986, was appointed Under-Secretary of the Pontifical Council for Justice and Peace. In 1998, was appointed Titular Bishop of Glendalough and in 2001 elected to rank of Archbishop. Permanent Observer of the Holy See at several international agencies including the UN. Succeeded Cardinal Connell as Archbishop of Dublin in 2004.

I was struck by the phrase of Franklin D. Roosevelt quoted in the introduction to the programme for this year's MacGill Summer School: 'We have always known that heedless self-interest was bad morals; we know now that it is bad economics.' Joe Mulholland's conclusion is that while FDR realized the truth of that phrase in 1936, today we can all say in chorus: '*Don't we just know it!*' The problem is that I am not so sure that as yet we have fully understood what the phrase of FDR really means.

I suppose it goes back to my natural suspicion and perhaps to my diplomatic training, that I have a particular disquiet about adjectives. So the first word that I began to look at in FDR's phase was the word *heedless*. We would all agree that heedless self-interest is immoral. But what do we mean by *heedless* or better still what would we consider to be the opposite of *heedless* self-interest?

There are those who would say that *enlightened* self-interest is not just acceptable but in the long term is an attitude which is in fact favourable towards, and indeed vital for, economic growth and the generation of wealth. Again we would have to examine what sort of a package of *enlightenment* would be at the basis of

Self interest alone, no matter how enlightened, cannot be the sole measure for evaluating relations within a society or in a global world.

such an affirmation.

Certainly enlightened self-interest is a strong motivating factor which gives human creativity and innovation a particular edge. The fundamental question we should be asking however is: is 'self' really the dominant notion on which to base our motivation for action in the economic sphere? The economy has a social function. Catholic social teaching defends the right to private property, but asserts also that all property is subject to a social mortgage. I saw this dynamic play out, for example, in the World Trade Organization(WTO) debates surrounding intellectual property and access to medicines for HIV/AIDS. In all probability we will see it again around the response to the swine-flu virus. Protection of intellectual property rights will encourage research, but that research belongs within the broader responsibility of the protection of health globally. The ownership of knowledge also bears a social mortgage. Self interest alone, no matter how enlightened, cannot be the sole measure for evaluating relations within a society or in a global world.

The fact of mutual interdependence which is the essential starting place of globalization means that no individual, no individual business enterprise, no individual country, no individual sector in society can go it alone. In today's world the concepts of entitlement and self-interest or indeed group-interest or sectoral–interest, with whatever adjective we may wish to add, have to be twinned with the concept of solidarity, which defines the responsibility side of the equation regarding any economy.

As we look at the current economic situation on the national and global level I believe that we have to generate new parameters for defining and putting into practice that twinning process. Our economy needs to balance its books and to do so in a way which is sustainable. But that sustainability will be determined not just by simply cutting back on spending and getting the sums right, but by optimizing all spending in such a way that the overall objectives of an economy at the service of society can best be realized. Cut-backs should never lose sight of the long-term objective to be achieved. But that sustainability will be determined not just by simply cutting back on spending and getting the sums right, but by optimizing

Our economy needs to balance its books and to do so in a way which is sustainable. But that sustainability will be determined not just by simply cutting back on spending and getting the sums right, but by optimizing all spending in such a way that the overall objectives of an economy at the service of society can best be realized.

all spending in such a way that the overall objectives of an economy at the service of society can best be realized. Cut-backs should never lose sight of the long-term objective to be achieved. To do this we have to re-define the word heedless and more closely identify the factors – human, economic and social – to which we should be paying heed.

I have stressed on various occasions my conviction that Ireland today urgently needs a poverty strategy. A poverty strategy is not a luxury for times of prosperity, but an essential demand in leaner times. By a poverty strategy I do not mean simply providing essential social security, much less hand-outs. I mean focussed attention on ensuring that, in the lean years, human potential and talent are fostered and that a response to disadvantage in realizing such talent be prioritized. A poverty strategy in times of cut backs has to look at investment in education and in fighting disadvantage with lenses which do not just focus on the broad percentages of cut backs. Even in times of tightening-up, there are areas where the wide-focus lens is the only appropriate one.

Let me come back to FDR's affirmation that heedless self-interest was bad morals. The second word of FDR's phrase which I felt needed closer examination was *morals*. The term morals is a word open to many interpretations, more so than ever today when there is on a global level and in our own society no longer a fundamental agreement on where morality is founded and thus where pragmatism or utilitarianism or indeed self-interest can come to dominate our thoughts. For many, morality in business is about not breaking the norms of fair competition, honesty and transparency, and not being involved in deceit or corruption. This is a job-description written very much in negative terms of 'not breaking', but would that we were even there!

For others, morality in business would focus on respect for the protagonists of economic activity, people with their rights and their entitlements. There are others who would stress that morals mean delivering to the shareholders, remembering that the shareholder may well be not just the speculator or the professional investor, but may be people's life-savings, or investment to guarantee certain social benefits, such as pensions, or even the production of social goods such as medicine and health care. We see here again another dimension of how the economy always has a social function which must always be heeded.

Morals are not primarily about immorality. The moralist is not primarily the one who criticizes, who points the finger, who judges others, very often sitting in a comfortable armchair on the sidelines observing and judging those who have to make daily and difficult decisions.

Morals are not primarily about immorality. The moralist is not primarily the one who criticizes, who points the finger, who judges others, very often sitting in a comfortable armchair on the sidelines observing and judging those who have to make daily and difficult decisions. In the past, it was ecclesiastics who took with gusto to moralising in that sense. Today they have been joined and indeed superseded by a wide range of secular pundits.

Morals must be rescued from such negativity and move towards a *morality of proposing*, of setting out indications of the framework in which moral imperatives about the good and the truth in society can be marked out and put into practice. In this context I would like to pay tribute to John Hume, in whose honour this annual lecture is held, who in the midst of the crisis of society in Northern Ireland of the late 1960s and in the years that followed had the clarity and determination to identify things to be criticized and rejected, but who never lost sight of his underlying forward-looking vision of a different Northern Ireland, a different Ireland and a different relationship with Ireland's nearest neighbour and Ireland's European roots and hopes. In facing the problems of our economy today the only solution is the long-term solution. Pragmatic decisions have to be taken, but they will never be truly pragmatic without 'the vision thing' also, to quote another US President.

What went wrong with the Irish economy? There is an abundance of analysis and abundant attribution of blame, of short-sightedness and of heedlessness and there is ample space for the old fashioned negative moralizing about which I have spoken. To answer the second question posed to this summer school – How will we fix it? – we need much more *morality of proposing* and vision.

What is the contribution to this fixing process not just of the extraordinary pool of technical talent and wisdom that is gathered here this week, but also of morals? What sort of ethical framework might be needed to ensure that we can truly 'fix it'? What are the fundamental moral choices that have to be made, what sort of society do we need to foster and what sort of people must we be in order to achieve this? These are not simply technical questions.

Indeed I would immediately take issue with the term 'fix it'.

> **What are the fundamental moral choices that have to be made, what sort of society do we need to foster and what sort of people must we be in order to achieve this? These are not simply technical questions.**

I believe that for too long now in Irish politics we have lived in a 'fix-it' mode and that perhaps the day has come for one of those occasional quantitative and qualitative leaps which have also characterized the history of Irish politics. I believe that the challenge today is not just to fix it, but to change it and to change our ways of carrying out politics and to change ourselves as individuals and as a society. A climate of uprightness can only be generated by people who are upright. I quote the latest Encyclical of Pope Benedict XVI *Caritas in veritate*:

> Development is impossible without upright men and women, without financiers and politicians whose consciences are finely attuned to the common good (n.71).

Pope Benedict in his first Encyclical *Deus Caritas Est* surprised some by stating that it is not the task of the Church to create a just society, but the task of politics.

> Building a just social and civil order, wherein each person receives what is his or her due, is an essential task which every generation must take up anew. As a political task, this cannot be the Church's immediate responsibility. (n.28)

> ... The Church cannot and must not take upon herself the political battle to bring about the most just society possible. She cannot and must not replace the State. Yet at the same time she cannot and must not remain on the sidelines in the fight for justice. She has to play her part through rational argument and she has to reawaken the spiritual energy without which justice, which always demands sacrifice, cannot prevail and prosper... A just society must be the achievement of politics, not of the Church. Yet the promotion of justice through efforts to bring about openness of mind and will to the demands of the common good is something which concerns the Church deeply. (ibid.)

At a moment when there is a certain disillusionment with politics, a moment in which many young people do not even vote, the Pope's endorsement of the centrality of politics is striking. When I speak of a qualitative leap in Irish politics I must be the first to say that part of any qualitative change must involve the relationship between Church and State, between Church and politics in a changing Ireland. There are many aspects of the relationship between Church and State in Ireland which are, as I said recently in the debate about schools, part of a hangover of our particular historical past.

There are many aspects of the relationship between Church and State in Ireland which are, as I said recently in the debate about schools, part of a hangover of our particular historical past.

When I speak of the changing role of the Church, I would not want to give the impression that it is all about being more compliant and more tolerant towards today's open-mindedness. I am not giving, as some would claim, a sort of blessing to a more secular vision of Ireland and nowhere more than in Ireland does secularism paradoxically like being blessed. Nor am I favouring the more radical response of those who would tell me: thanks for coming, now you can go off back to Drumcondra or to your sacristies or to your historical past and keep your historical hangovers out of our lives!

The Church in Ireland has to move away from any temptation to maintain an attitude of dominance. But no one wants a Church which just gives a moral veneer to the ways of society. The Church has its mission, to preach the Gospel of Jesus Christ, and that Gospel is not the Gospel of a comfort zone. But many sectors of secular Ireland also have to find new ways of addressing their own historical hangovers about faith and learn to relate in an adult way with the place of religious belief in society. A vital democracy must find ways in which the values, including the religious values, of all are welcomed and cherished.

You may think that I have drifted away from the theme of this Summer School on the Irish economy. I believe that the idea of moving from the hangovers of our historical past regarding the role of the Church opens up some areas of reflection on a new vision of politics and the economy in Ireland. Certainly a situation in which a Church took over day to day responsibility for the running of most of the school system and of our hospitals was – and still is - an anomaly. But the answer, I believe, is not simply handing everything over to complex State bureaucracies whose efficiency has certainly yet to be proven. Pope Benedict's Encyclical speaks about 'cross-fertilization between different types of business activity, with shifting of competences from the 'non-profit' world to the 'profit' world and vice versa, from the public world to that of civil society, from advanced economies to developing countries'. Market mechanisms can be used to deliver social goods, while a non-profit model can provide certain services in a more efficient way than business or the State.

Underlying many of the key insights of Pope Benedict's

Encyclical is the application of the principle of subsidiarity to a modern economy and the creation of a model of government and economy with a much wider participation of intermediary subjects. A State which simply delegated a wide part of its social responsibilities to a Church had gotten it wrong; a State which takes over the entire package is on equally dodgy ground. Monopolies of ideas can be as dangerous as monopolies in the business sector and the result could easily be a society which is passive and in that sense impoverished and less a free society. To use the 1972 words of an anti-conformist Italian song writer, Giorgio Gaber, who were he still alive might be surprised to be quoted by a Churchman: *'la libertà è partecipazione':* freedom is participation.

Without clear political leadership, the current economic crisis and the challenges of globalization might actually undermine some of the foundations of democracy.

Ireland needs today not just a revival of social partnership, but an even wider model of social participation. Civil society is not a totally separate third force, distinct from State and market. Civil society is not a cheap alternative or a fire brigade for social emergencies. Civil society and the values which are characteristic of it should also be seen as a protagonist of the economy, both in terms of the goods and services it can provide, but also as regards its basic inspiration and value system which has a different view of profit. There are various types of business enterprise which do not simply fit into the traditional clear distinction between 'private' and 'public'. There are economic actors of various types which, again to quote Pope Benedict:

> without rejecting profit, aim at a higher goal than the mere logic of the exchange of equivalents, of profit as an end in itself (*Caritas in veritate*, n.38)

The profound concept of *gratuitousness* is an essential antidote to consumerism and a narrow market-focussed mentality. As a person I can and must offer my neighbour not just goods and services, but also something of myself. It is a concept which if embraced will inevitably lead to a new way of understanding business since 'investment always has a moral as well as an economic significance' (n.40). Economic growth and solidarity are not two parallel tracks. For Pope Benedict 'solidarity and reciprocity can also be conducted within economic activity and not only outside or after it'.

For this vision to work, we need more than ever today real

Many organs of government and financial regulation, national and international, watched by heedlessly as the evident signs of 'heedless self-interest' flourished and grew. And indeed, the organs of civil society and intermediate groups – joined the heedless euphoria of the years of wealth.

political leadership at local, national and international levels. This is needed especially in the light of the process of globalization. Without clear political leadership, the current economic crisis and the challenges of globalization might actually undermine some of the foundations of democracy. The current economic crisis poses a real challenge to government institutions. After years of calling for 'small government', many of the more strident proponents of small government are looking for government to bail them out, much to the annoyance of ordinary citizens. But Government must also take its share of responsibility. Many organs of government and financial regulation, national and international, watched by heedlessly as the evident signs of 'heedless self-interest' flourished and grew. And indeed, the organs of civil society and intermediate groups – including many aspects of the media – joined the heedless euphoria of the years of wealth.

Solidarity is not a luxury addition to the way society works. In poorer times in Ireland it was the basic network of community solidarity which kept society together and enabled people to hope. Whatever happens on the political level that sense of true community solidarity will remain necessary – indeed even more necessary – in the years to come. We need a strong civil society. There is in the long-term no real answer to the challenge of violence in Ireland other than a vibrant community spirit which takes a stand. Political institutions and political parties have to the forefront of fostering a true sense of community participation and ownership of social policy. The media have a special responsibility to bring abuses of power and trust to light, but the media must also be on the side of an ethics of proposing, of constructive support for those who are out there day after day facing the front-line risks of attempting to change society. I say that not as one who believes that the media and civil society are essential to the future of Irish politics and the economy. We need more people who heed, and who heed not just their own interest, but that of society and who are prepared to stand up and get involved. There is no way to address the future of the Irish economy or of Irish society which does not involve a real politics of participation.

My role as a Bishop is not to propose how to address the

economic challenge of cutbacks but to witness to the message of a God who reveals his love in Jesus Christ, a God whose inner life is sharing and who reaches out in love and encourages his followers to do likewise.

Michael McLoone

Bríd Rodgers

Dr Diarmuid Martin

Brian and Anne Friel

Prof. Rowena Pecchenino

Prof. Karl Whelan

Dermot Gleeson

Prof. Fridrik Baldursson

David Murphy

Alan Dukes

Prof. Patrick Honohan

Dan Boyle

Dr Joe Mulholland, Eamon Gilmore TD,
Brian Lenihan TD and George Lee TD

Brian Lenihan TD

George Lee TD

Eamon Gilmore TD

Dr Peter Bacon

Jim O'Hara

Seán O'Rourke, Martin Murphy, Enda
Kenny TD and Dr Joe Mulholland

Michael Fitzgerald

Mary Coughlan TD

Enda Kenny TD

Martin Murphy

Michael O'Sullivan

Chapter 1

HOW AND WHY DID IT ALL GO WRONG?

HARD WORK AND SACRIFICE WERE NOT IN THE IRISH LEXICON
Rowena A. Pecchenino
Professor and Head of Dept. of Economics, NUI Maynooth

POLICY LESSONS FROM IRELAND'S LATEST DEPRESSION
Karl Whelan
Professor of Economics, University College Dublin

MISTAKES MADE AND REMEDIES NEEDED
Dermot Gleeson SC
Former Chairman, AIB Bank

DIFFERENCE BETWEEN IRELAND AND ICELAND
Fridrik M. Baldursson
Professor of Economics, Reykjavik University

Hard Work and Sacrifice were not in the Irish Lexicon

Rowena A. Pecchenino[2]
Professor and Head of Dept. of Economics, NUI Maynooth

Has a BA in Economics from Cornell University, an MSc in Economics from the London School of Economics and a PhD from the University of Wisconsin, Madison. Former professor and chair, Department of Economics, Finance and Accounting at Michigan State University. Also worked at Geary Institute, UCD (2006-7), CERGE-EI, Prague, Czech Republic (2005), Health Economics Research Unit, University of Aberdeen (2002), UCD (2001), London School of Economics (1999), Federal Reserve Bank of St. Louis (1995-9), ICER, Turin, Italy (1994 and 1997), Murdoch University, Perth, Australia (1993).

In the beginning

In 1979 Pope John Paul II warned the Irish people of the challenges of life in the late 20th century: materialism, affluence, self-indulgence and consumerism.[3] Yet, the Irish were among the poorest in Europe. Materialism, affluence, consumerism, and self-indulgence were all things more dreamed of than experienced. Ireland was the sick man of Europe. The statistics are staggering. GDP per capita was 69 per cent of the European average. Personal income tax rates were extortionate. Government debt exceeded 100 per cent of GNP. The cost of servicing that debt was 13 per cent of GNP. In 1985 the real interest rate was 10.5 per cent; unemployment 17.3 per cent; inflation 5.4 per cent. The exchange rate for the first half of the decade was significantly overvalued. During the 1980s 10 per cent of the population emigrated, seeking a better life for themselves and for those they left behind. The Church's admonitions notwithstanding, those Irish who had not yet abandoned hope yearned for a better quality of life.

New Ireland was a prosperous country. It attracted migrants from every continent on the globe who came in pursuit of a better life. It was characterized by fiscal rectitude.

The Miracle of Lazarus

When the boom ended in the early 2000s the Government faced significant policy challenges. The demographic effect was spent, skilled workers were among the most expensive in Europe, other countries had improved their success in attracting FDI, EU subsidies disappeared as wealth rose, the Single Market effect was a one off, and Ireland, now in the Euro area, had no independent control over its currency.

From the ashes of the 1980s there arose a New Ireland. The miraculous transformation began around 1990. By 2000 Irish GDP per capita was at the European average; by 2003 it was 136 per cent. New Ireland was a prosperous country. It attracted migrants from every continent on the globe who came in pursuit of a better life. It was characterized by fiscal rectitude. It was a country of peerless, export-led growth. It was becoming a more secular, materialistic, and self-indulgent country. It was affluent. It was envied and emulated. These sociological and economic changes were swift and pervasive. There was indeed a New Ireland. It did not mourn the Old Ireland. No whiff of the grave clung to this exuberant, self-confident country.

The resurrection of Ireland has been attributed to a number of factors, among which were sensible government policies, falling interest rates, the openness and flexibility of the economy, favourable exchange rates, European Union subsidies, the European Single Market, FDI, a ready supply of highly skilled workers, competitive wages, a surge in labour force participation rates, and Social Partnership. The miraculous growth was fuelled more by increased inputs than by increased productivity of existing inputs, but it was miraculous nonetheless. Government policies were instrumental in marshalling these resources. But the unique confluence of events that had made it possible could not be duplicated.

When the boom ended in the early 2000s the Government faced significant policy challenges. The demographic effect was spent, skilled workers were among the most expensive in Europe, other countries had improved their success in attracting FDI, EU subsidies disappeared as wealth rose, the Single Market effect was a one off, and Ireland, now in the Euro area, had no independent control over its currency. All it had was taxation and expenditure policy to entice additional FDI and spur growth and Social Partnership to promote social harmony and industrial peace and to 'reinvent' Ireland.[4] The practice and rhetoric of Social Partnership suggests that all, unions, employers, government, as well as representatives of the Chambers of Commerce, Small and Medium Enterprises, farmers, and community and voluntary groups including representatives of the Church, were in this project together. While only the government, unions and employers were directly involved in wage negotiations, the other groups lent their voices to discussions on social and economic policies. This meant that the triennial Social Partnership agreements and the infiltration of Partnership into all aspects of Irish life represented a joint project in the development of New Ireland and defined what was special about the New Irish Model. The government was central to this since it could agree to public sector wage packages, thereby setting the tone and parameters for private sector agreements. Furthermore, it could influence the possible outcomes via its taxation and expenditure policies. It could also keep the community and voluntary sector engaged by listening and responding to their wants and needs. All this was possible as long as tax revenues continued to grow at a healthy rate.

This process of wage and socio-economic policy determination was one of inclusion. It was collaborative, us and us, rather than adversarial, us vs. them. Its goal was to make everyone better off. It represented what was right and good about the Irish Model. Social Partnership made the Irish economy and the New Ireland different, an exemplar of what could be in the globalized, cut-throa competitive world economy of the 21st century.

The Irish people embraced New Ireland wholeheartedly. Ireland had finally met Mammon and liked what she saw. The materialism, affluence, consumerism, and self-indulgence that Pope John Paul II had warned against were celebrated.

Eat, Drink and be Merry

The Irish people embraced New Ireland wholeheartedly. Ireland had finally met Mammon and liked what she saw. The materialism, affluence, consumerism, and self-indulgence that Pope John Paul II had warned against were celebrated. Conspicuous consumption became the norm. Profligacy was the order of the day. The Irish leaped onto the property ladder and then added to their property portfolios. New cars choked the roads, and new roads were demanded to accommodate them. Banks financed these acquisitions even when a borrower's current income would not, in less bountiful times, have justified the loans. The boom was a rising tide that lifted

While the government appeared to be fiscally prudent, its policies, like the current boom, were unsustainable.

Times were still good and the Government could continue to support policies beloved of the Social Partners, to appear fiscally prudent, and to disparage those voices urging restraint as well as those threatening Armageddon.

all boats. Real incomes were growing across the income distribution.[5] The poor were made rich. Those who had never had money to spend now had money, a good job and good prospects. The Irish were materially better off than they ever had been before. Past poverty was forgotten. As the influence of Mammon increased, that of the Church fell. It was mired in child abuse scandals and so found it difficult to articulate a message from the moral high ground. It was unable to effectively argue against the value of wealth in this life, since wealth was accompanied by better health and well-being even if spiritual sustenance was no longer sought at its door. For too long had the Irish been promised the treasures of heaven to compensate them for the material deprivations of their lives here on earth. The treasures of earth, now finally enjoyed, were not to be discarded. The Church, an important feature in Ireland's past, was not a major player in New Ireland.[6] It no longer spoke to or for Ireland.

Voices in the Wilderness

In the early 2000s, although the source of growth changed from exports to property, growth continued, this time fuelled by low interest rates, an international liquidity glut, generous lending by banks, and generous tax relief on property investment. Initially exchange rates were favourable, buoying up the export sector, but the euro soon strengthened. Economic growth kept tax revenues growing, and expenditures increased accordingly. While the government appeared to be fiscally prudent, its policies, like the current boom, were unsustainable.

The economic situation at the turn of the century should have raised concern. Average real hourly wages had risen by 20 per cent over the decade of the 1990s outstripping productivity growth. By 2002 Irish workers were the third most expensive in the EU. The housing bubble led to substantial GDP growth, but it hid the reality that productivity gains were an artefact of the bubble not of increases in productive efficiency. The construction sector was crowding out the export sector, degrading worker skills as young people opted for high income in construction rather than for higher education. It also hid significant problems in the tax code. Revenues from transaction taxes, such as capital gains and stamp duty, were growing at a rate that allowed for further cuts to income tax rates and increases in tax relief. With gains and stamp duty, were growing at a rate that allowed for further cuts to income and increases in tax relief. With tax revenues climbing and the economy growing, the impetus for change was weak. Times were still good and the Government could continue to support policies beloved of the Social Partners, to appear fiscally prudent, and to disparage those voices urging restraint as well as those threatening Armageddon. The day of reckoning could be deferred.

Those questioning the sustainability of government policy and economic growth were not sanguine. Early warnings came in 2001 from both the European Commission and the European Central Bank.[7] They reprimanded Ireland for an overly inflationary fiscal policy. But, then Finance Minister McCreevy refused to alter the budget. The benchmarking exercise that increased public sector wages by about 9 per cent above the increases agreed in the Social Partnership negotiations was also questioned. The concern expressed was that these extraordinary wage increases would further diminish Irish competitiveness.[8] These warnings were largely dismissed. The time was not yet ripe for hard decisions.

The National Competitiveness Council (NCC) reminded the Government that to sustain growth productivity had to continue to rise.[9] It suggested a means to achieve this end. But, as its analysis was not uniformly negative, it was the positive that was seized upon.

Also dismissed as unduly negative were the ever more strident warnings that the construction bubble was unsustainable and that banks were overexposed to the property market.[10] Those voicing these opinions were admonished for scaremongering and talking down 'a robust and fundamentally sound economy'. The Government did have supporters in high places, such as the IMF or the OECD.[11,12] This support allowed for hard decisions to continue to be deferred.

The Government did have supporters in high places, such as the IMF or the OECD. This support allowed for hard decisions to continue to be deferred.

Day of Judgement

Fianna Fáil was returned to power in 2007 as the party best able to shepherd the economy into the future. Continued, if slower, growth was promised. The property sector would make a soft landing. Electioneering over, the Irish economy, perhaps less exposed to world financial woes, was found to be critically over-exposed to itself. This economy that had boomed by exporting to the world had again boomed by selling houses to itself, houses now in excess supply. Moreover, the world economy was in dire straits. The world financial system was closed for business.

The Government was in a fix. The tax revenues it relied upon had plummeted. Had it prepared for the inevitable rainy day while the sun was shining by improving the tax code, increasing income tax rates on corporations and individuals, introducing a value-based property tax, reducing reliance on transactions taxes, and/or imposing productivity enhancing work rules on civil and public servants, its problems would have been fewer. But there had not been the will. What was missing was not the desire to ensure a better future, but the willingness to do the hard work and make the sacrifices needed to get there. Hard work and sacrifice were not in the New Irish lexicon.

The Government had to face the crisis. It did so with the presumed support of the Social Partners. The Government declared that New Ireland was strong and resilient enough to ride out this storm. Things were bad, but they had been bad before. The Irish had survived. They would survive again. But, initial stumbles, such as revoking medical cards of the over-70s, strained the fabric of Social Partnership. Further strains rent the fabric as private sector workers took pay cuts and lost jobs while public sector workers were sheltered from the economic realities. Pension levies on the public sector carried little weight since private sector wages had already fallen and the viability of many pension systems questioned. The social fabric is now in shreds as the reality of the McCarthy Report sinks in. While the Government still calls on the Social Partners to work together for a better future, what had underpinned Social Partnership is already lost. There is no longer a common purpose had there ever been one. With ever larger surpluses having turned into ever larger deficits, Social Partnership has collapsed leaving all the Partners looking out for number one.As the economy staggers, the Church, which has fallen from great heights of power and prosperity and still struggles to stand, counsels charity. Preaching from its humbled and diminished Ireland that may finally take the hard, long-deferred decisions and choose to embrace a sustainable model of economic, social and spiritual prosperity in the mature knowledge that life, of an individual or a nation, does not consist in the abundance of one's possessions.

Policy Lessons from Ireland's Latest Depression

Karl Whelan

Professor of Economics, University College Dublin

Obtained PhD from MIT in 1997. Worked for over ten years in central banks, first at Federal Reserve Board in Washington and then at Central Bank of Ireland. Research generally concentrated in applied macroeconomics and published in leading journals such as the American Economic Review, Review of Economics and Statistics, Journal of Monetary Economics, and Journal of Money, Credit, and Banking.

1. Introduction

I suspect that grim finger pointing is what most people would expect my talk to be about. I think, however, that a fair analysis would show that both wide-eyed optimism and recrimination fuelled hindsight contain some truths, half-truths and falsehoods. Blame storming sessions can be cathartic but learning usefully from our mistakes will require a careful assessment of both what has gone right in the past, as well as what has gone wrong lately.

I am going to provide a selective review of Ireland's economic performance of the last twenty years, from the early days of the Celtic Tiger, through the housing boom and recent slump, and then attempt to draw a few lessons. I will argue that a substantial slowdown was looming for Ireland by 2007, independent of what was going to happen in the global economy, and much of this evidence was ignored in the implementation of economic policy. The result was a range of policies based on unwarranted over optimism which left Ireland terribly exposed to the international downturn. That said, I also emphasize that some of the criticisms that are widely aired have little merit.

> **I will argue that a substantial slowdown was looming for Ireland by 2007, independent of what was going to happen in the global economy, and much of this evidence was ignored in the implementation of economic policy. The result was a range of policies based on unwarranted over optimism which left Ireland terribly exposed to the international downturn.**

2. Good Times: 1987-2000

By the late 1980s, Ireland's economy was in crisis with unemployment of 17 per cent and a public finance problem that appeared out of control. However, at a time when few had much hope, something remarkable happened – economic growth returned. Slowly enough at first, by the mid-1990s Ireland appeared to have a full-scale 'economic miracle' on its hands. In truth, the Celtic Tiger was perhaps less miraculous than it looked. Patrick Honohan and Brendan Walsh's 2002 paper 'Catching up with the Leaders: The Irish Hare' pointed out that by the mid-1970s, Ireland had many of the policies in place that could work together with our native economic advantages to foster strong economic growth. However, a decade of poor fiscal and monetary policies had failed to provide the necessary stability for these factors to deliver the expected economic growth.

When the late 1980s saw Ireland stabilize its precarious fiscal situation – thanks in large part to a short, but crucial, period of cross-party consensus – the Irish economy was finally ready for growth. As Honohan and Walsh put it:

> inappropriate fiscal and perhaps monetary policies held Ireland back in earlier years, with the result that convergence, when it occurred, was telescoped into a short period.[13]

Luck also was a factor, as Ireland's commitment to the EU began to pay off more than could have been expected. GDP growth can be broken into three parts: a part due to higher population, a part due to having a higher fraction of the population at work, and a part due to getting more output from the average worker. All three of these factors contributed over time to Ireland's boom but there are interesting stories to be teased out of how these contributions changed over time.

As house completions went from 19,000 in 1990 to 50,000 in 2000 to a whopping 93,000 in 2006, construction became a dominant factor in the Irish economy.

2.1. Employment and Productivity

By the early 1990s then, Ireland had an enormous capacity to grow far faster than it had been doing. Perhaps the clearest way to illustrate how much room Ireland had to grow is to show how underemployed its people were. In 1989, only 31 per cent of Ireland's population was at work, the lowest in the OECD and fifteen percentage points below either the UK or the US. Ireland's underemployment partly reflected its exceptionally high unemployment rate.

However, it also reflected demographic factors. Ireland's baby boom occurred in the 1970s and peaked in 1980, so the depressed Ireland of the 1980s was supporting a very large population below working age. This demographic factor gradually unwound over time so that by the late 1990s, Ireland had a higher fraction of the working age population than either the US or the UK.

By 2007, construction accounted for 13.3 per cent of all employment, the highest share in the OECD.

With good fundamental policies in place, the combination of macroeconomic stability and a starting point of severe underemployment meant that the Irish economy became an incredible employment creating machine. Employment rose steadily from 1.1 million in the late 1980s to 2.1 million in 2007. In addition to getting more people employed at a rapid pace, the 1990s saw a strong productivity performance. Productivity growth averaged just under 3 per cent per annum during the 1990s. The exceptional capacity for growth unleashed during the 1990s had profound implications for Irish fiscal policy. After stepping away from the brink of a debt disaster in 1987, rapid economic growth allowed successive governments to achieve the fiscal holy grail of cutting taxes, raising spending and also achieving substantial reductions in the debt-GDP ratio.

The landing was almost certainly going to be bumpy.

3. Housing Boom and Inevitability of Slowdown

By the start of the new millennium, there was every reason to expect that the Celtic Tiger period was coming to an end. The unemployment rate was extremely low by international standards, GDP per capita had caught up with the EU average and the employment to population ratio was only just below the levels recorded in the US and UK. While there was still some limited additional growth potential left from demographic factors such as young workers coming into the labour force and a still somewhat low level of female labour force participation, these factors would only be capable of providing a more limited boost to future growth.

3.1. Housing Boom

Even by the early part of this decade, Ireland still had a relatively small housing stock, the smallest stock per capita in the EU. Our higher incomes and lower unemployment rates were bound to lead to smaller average household sizes, as younger people started to be in a position to buy their own homes at a younger age. The result was an extraordinary construction boom. The total stock of dwellings – which had stood at 1.2 million homes in 1991 and had gradually increased to 1.4 million homes in 2000 – exploded to 1.9 million homes in 2008. As house completions went from 19,000 in 1990 to 50,000 in 2000 to a whopping 93,000 in 2006, construction became a dominant factor in the Irish economy. By 2007, construction accounted for 13.3 per cent of all employment, the highest share in the OECD. With the exception of Spain and Portugal, Ireland's share of construction employment exceeded all other OECD member states by almost five percentage points.

One might have expected the huge increase in the supply of housing to have cooled off house prices. Most likely, if the economy had not had the substantial supply response, house prices would have gone higher. However, the supply response was still not able to keep up with the growing demand and the increase in ability to pay generated by income tax cuts and the low interest rates regime that came with our membership of the Euro. The result was an astonishing combination of rising house prices and an increasingly construction-dependent economy.

3.2. Slowdown was Coming

Any reasonable analysis of the economic circumstances in early 2007 would have suggested that a substantial economic slowdown was imminent. The factors underlying the long expansion in our employment-population ratio had run out. Labour force participation rates had reached high levels and further growth was unlikely. Unemployment could hardly go lower. Demographic factors were no longer working in our favour. The composition of recent growth had fundamentally changed: productivity growth had slacked off during the later construction-dominated years of the boom, as the room for catch-up growth fell off. Both house prices and the level of housing activity were

The long boom that preceded 2008 had allowed successive Irish Governments a freedom from the normal fiscal constraints faced by governments around the world. There were sizable increases in public expenditure, income tax rates were cut and yet the debt-GDP ratio had gradually tumbled to one of the lowest in Europe.

unsustainable. With house prices very likely to fall, much of the development and construction business was going to become unprofitable leading to the sector shrinking. The economy was going to have to be re-oriented away from construction and such economic re-organizations are rarely easy to undertake quickly.

The landing was almost certainly going to be bumpy. However, despite this economic background, Fianna Fáil was re-elected to government in 2007 on the basis of an election manifesto whose underlying assumptions were based on 4.5 per cent average growth in nominal terms over the five-year period. Opposition political parties largely agreed with this assessment. This endemic over-optimism was, I believe, the fundamental source of a range of different policy mistakes which left Ireland badly placed for coping with the economic slowdown to come. Then we had a global financial crisis and the most severe global recession since the Great Depression.

> **The construction boom generated huge tax revenues in the form of stamp duty, capital gains taxes and VAT.**

4. Consequences of Over-Optimism

The over-optimism about economic growth that prevailed during the period leading up to 2007 was responsible for a number of serious policy errors. I will discuss fiscal policy first and then banking and credit policy.

4.1. Fiscal Policy

The long boom that preceded 2008 had allowed successive Irish Governments a freedom from the normal fiscal constraints faced by governments around the world. There were sizable increases in public expenditure, income tax rates were cut and yet the debt-GDP ratio had gradually tumbled to one of the lowest in Europe. However, by the later years of the boom, fiscal policy as well as the rest of the economy had become distorted by the housing boom.

While tax revenues had continued to rise, the composition of these revenues had substantially changed. Income tax rates, which had been very high in the 1980s, were repeatedly cut. The substantial increases in income meant that the income tax take still rose every year but income taxes as a share of GNP fell from 20 per cent in 1988 to around 13 per cent in the later years of the boom. In addition to rate cuts, exemption points were raised to a level that took significant numbers out of the tax net altogether. The result was that the income tax burden was exceptionally light, particularly for those on low to middle incomes. Despite this erosion of the income tax base, the Government's coffers remained buoyant due to revenue earned from other sources. In particular, the construction boom generated huge tax revenues in the form of stamp duty, capital gains taxes and VAT.

4.2. Banking and Credit Policy

The other key aspect of Ireland's current economic problems is the banking crisis. It is undeniable now that in Ireland, as with elsewhere, there were substantial financial regulatory failures. However, we should be wary of false equivalences between the banking collapse in Ireland and events elsewhere. Rather than mortgages or complex financial instruments, the demise of the Irish banks stemmed from their loans to property developers. The value of Irish houses is down significantly from their peak level; with housing activity at minimal levels, the value of much of the speculative development land bought near the peak is now close to zero. With the widespread belief that the housing market was heading for a soft landing, insufficient attention was paid to the extreme concentration of property development risk that could cause huge losses. And since the development loans that are causing the most problems for the banks are the substantial quantity that were lent out during the final years of the boom, an intervention even as late as 2005 to cool development lending could have prevented the upcoming meltdown.

And since the development loans that are causing the most problems for the banks are the substantial quantity that were lent out during the final years of the boom, an intervention even as late as 2005 to cool development lending could have prevented the upcoming meltdown.

5. Conclusion

If, as I believe likely, economic growth resumes at significantly lower average rates than in the recent past, we will have to confront a range of difficult choices that go beyond our current difficulties in achieving fiscal solvency. Over the next few years, our Government will have to face up to serious tradeoffs in dealing with expenditure and taxation issues. How they deal with them will have fundamental implications for the type of Irish economy and society that will emerge.

If I had to offer one over-riding lesson to be learned from our recent economic history, it would be that Irish economic policy should be formulated on the basis of an expectation of relatively low sustainable growth rates, and that it is far safer to have a pessimistic bias than an optimistic one.

If, as is projected by a number of forecasters, un-employment rates reach the high teens by next year, then Ireland will again be starting from a point of having a significantly underemployed population. If our major macroeconomic and financial problems are dealt with successfully in the coming years and the world economy picks up again, then this starting point will allow room for a period of fast growth. It will be essential, however, that this fast growth not be interpreted as a return of the Celtic Tiger. Analysis based on a clear understanding of our demographic profile, labour market structures and productivity performance are unlikely to justify such a conclusion.

Mistakes Made and Remedies Needed

Dermot Gleeson SC
Former Chairman, AIB Bank

Born in Cork and educated in Blackrock College, Dublin. Holds BA and LL.M degrees and qualified as barrister at King's Inns. Called to bar in 1970. Appointed Senior Counsel in 1979. From 1994–1997 was chief legal advisor to Government of Taoiseach John Bruton, serving as Attorney General. In early 1970s was a part time lecturer in Constitutional Law at UCC. Visiting Fellow at School of Law at UCD and member of the Royal Irish Academy. Was Chairman of the Review Body on Higher Remuneration in the Public Sector, Chairman of the Irish Council for Bioethics, and Director of Gate Theatre. In 2000 joined board of Independent News and Media Plc as a non-executive director and in 2003 was appointed Chairman of AIB Bank. In 2007, was appointed Chairman of Governing Body of UCC.

Introduction

The global economy is in the middle of a synchronized contraction that will push global growth into negative territory in 2009 for the first time in decades. At the start of 2008, there were five large international investment ianks, now there are none. The fall of Lehman Brothers on 15 September last, detonated a series of shocks to the global financial system, whose full effects are still not fully understood, but are being felt and experienced in every country on the planet.

In this country, there has been a dramatic contraction in economic activity and employment, a startling deterioration in Government finances, a sharp drop in property prices. It is clear that a lot of things have gone awry. But it is still not even remotely true to say that everything has gone wrong. Some comparisons with the 1980s are in many respects quite far fetched. Government debt as a percentage of GDP was 112 per cent in 1984 and now it heads perhaps towards 50 per cent by the end of 2010. Unemployment in 1984 was 15.4 per cent and it heads now for something close to that, but the number at work in 1984 was

As a former Chairman of AIB the first thing for me to say in plain and unvarnished language is that some serious mistakes were made in Irish banking, and there is no getting away from that.

1,114,000 and in 2007 the figure was almost exactly a million more at 2,117,000. Inflation in 1983 was 10.4 per cent; in August 2008 it was 4.3 per cent and now it looks like minus 5 per cent.

The achievements of the last fifteen years include at least the following: major employment creation even if you exclude construction, significant improvement in infrastructure especially in roads, advances in education including significant advances in third level participation rates, significant real increases in welfare and significant poverty reduction, bigger investment in research and development, and a significant increase in female participation in the workforce.

I am not convinced that we fully understand every aspect of the financial crisis that we have experienced. I think that it is at least possible that some of our systems become too complex to understand. As a former Chairman of AIB the first thing for me to say in plain and unvarnished language is that some serious mistakes were made in Irish banking, and there is no getting away from that. It is perhaps especially galling that Irish banks by and large avoided the mistakes that wrought havoc in the balance sheets of leading US, British and Continental European Banks where Credit Derivatives and Collateralized Debt obligations did the damage.

But we made mistakes of our own, and they became exposed at the same time as international money markets shut up shop last September. Let me look at some international causes and then at some local mistakes in public policy before I return to the mistakes made by the Irish banks. These lists are by no means comprehensive, not ranked in any particular order and subject to my earlier caution against single factor explanations.

> **Really low medium and long-term real interest rates drove rapid credit expansion in certain developed countries like the US, UK and Ireland, specifically for residential mortgages.**

International drivers of crisis

Global imbalances

Notwithstanding my scepticism about a complete under-standing of the current crisis being yet available it is clear that some of the most significant drivers have already been identified by, amongst others, Paul Volcker in the US, the de Larosiere Group in Europe, and Lord Adair Turner in the

United Kingdom. Global imbalances was one. There was the accumulation of large current account surpluses in the last ten years by oil exporting countries, China, Japan and certain emerging developing nations in East Asia. Within the USA, but also more recently, in the UK, Spain and Ireland to name just some, large current account deficits have emerged in the same period. Really low medium and long-term real interest rates drove rapid credit expansion in certain developed countries like the US, UK and Ireland, specifically for residential mortgages. This, combined with other factors, helped fuel the property boom. Critically, that property boom for a time made lower credit standards appear costless.

Mistaken view on risk dispersion gained widespread currency

The accepted theory was that securitized credit intermediation would reduce risks for individual banks and the whole banking system by passing risk through to end investors. Consequently, credit losses would be less likely to produce banking failure.

Risk models failures

The failure of banking risk models was eloquently described by Patrick Honohan in his Michael Littleton Memorial Lecture at the end of 2008. He drew attention to the fact that UBS was awarded the title of 'best risk management house in the world' in 2005 pointing out that the following year manipulation of risky contracts within UBS managed to lose them $44 billion.

Failures in regulation

The accountancy standard setters worldwide changed the accountancy rules, to increase the transparency of accounts and address what were seen as the failures of accountancy standards to cope with the dot-com bubble. Arguably in setting new rules to address the last crisis, they took steps which positively facilitated the next crisis, the banking crisis. New IFRS Accounting rules introduced in 2002 made it much more difficult for banks to provide, in the good years, against losses in the bad; this probably increased transparency a little but at the expense of making banks much more vulnerable to a cyclical downturn. The Spanish

Government finances were not well managed. In the public policy area, public spending expanded much too quickly on the back of tax revenues which were clearly unsustainable in the long term because they were so tied to property.

Public expenditure grew too rapidly. Monopoly power was not challenged.

NAMA has the potential for being a very good solution. NAMA is going to be a very large undertaking. There is no single model which can be taken off a shelf from some other country in Europe or South America or Asia which will solve the Irish problem.

Banking Regulator, alone amongst twenty seven European Banking Regulators, resolutely opposed this change for as long as possible, taking a position which has been fully vindicated by subsequent events.

Closing of money markets last September

This is a story by now well told. When Lehman Brothers fell, trust collapsed, no one knew what other bank might be next, everyone hoarded their liquidity. Between 90 per cent and 95 per cent of the funds that banks lend are borrowed; when the source of funds dried up, banking, here and elsewhere, was thrown into turmoil.

Then there are a whole range of local factors including but not confined to the banks. First, Government finances were not well managed. In the public policy area, public spending expanded much too quickly on the back of tax revenues which were clearly unsustainable in the long term because they were so tied to property. Second, property-related tax incentives played a particular role and there were too many of them. There were a myriad of these schemes in the health, tourism, and infrastructure sectors. Then, there were area-based property tax incentives, for example, for urban renewal, town renewal, rural renewal and seaside resorts. With a few exceptions most of these arrangements have now terminated. Third, public expenditure grew too rapidly. Monopoly power was not challenged. Examples of matters not addressed or not sufficiently addressed include the efficiency of the ESB, the GPs' contract and competition in professional services. The excesses of social partnership played some role in our downfall. So did benchmarking. Fourth, the public played a role as well. Many of us participated in the property bubble which saw a three-fold increase in average property prices from 1994-2006, the largest boom in any advanced economy in recent times, even if it was only to provide some financial assistance for our children trying to get on the property ladder. Many others became amateur landlords in the private rental sector and have suffered accordingly.

And finally there were the banks. Irish banks made mistakes, and some of the mistakes were big ones. I was Chairman of AIB and, as I made clear at our Annual Meeting, loans were made which should not have been made; risk models proved unreliable because they had insufficient risk injected into them. Risk models that provided for a 1 in 20 year downturn which seemed highly improbable in 2005, 2006 and 2007 proved inadequate to the downturn in the second half 2007 and 2008, a one in 50 possibly a one in 100 year event. The impact of a synchronised worldwide contraction was manifestly given insufficient weight. People who had always repaid their loans on time, who had successfully grown their businesses and had become progressively richer over perhaps 30 or 40 years, are now unable to pay their interest.

What needs to be done?

The map of the way out of our current difficulties is by now fairly well known and I have nothing original to add. But the obvious is perhaps worth repeating. As Don Thornhill, Chairman of the NCC said in a presentation given on the 9 December 2008, competitiveness is central. He also observed that 'decline is not inevitable, but neither is success' and that our own choices can importantly determine our future. The key competitiveness challenges he identified are: restoring fiscal sustainability, regaining cost competitiveness, implementing public sector reform and positioning for the upturn. To this list one would now add restoring normal banking both locally and internationally

Let me rapidly make a few suggestions of some things we need to do, in no particular order.

We need to broaden the tax base by cutting out reliefs which are no longer justified; this is very much preferable to raising tax rates. Property taxes need to be less dependant on transactions and a property tax of some sort, needs to replace stamp duty, at least in part. There may be need for more user charges to fund high quality infrastructure in the form of road tolls, water charges and university fees. A carbon tax needs to balance the demands of climate change and competitiveness. In relation to expenditure we need more difficult decisions while maintaining investment in research and infrastructure. The cost of public services needs to be brought into line with costs in the rest of the economy. Excessive regulation and outdated work practices need to be eliminated. We need to reduce the long term inflation expectation back to the Euro zone average and we are well advanced on that

Will Government be able to make and implement the difficult policy choices that must be made in a context where there is a constant clamour for short term solutions and where all politicians are obliged to compete for attention in a noisy market where sound bites prevail above complex or painstaking analysis?

project. We need to stop the deterioration in our energy competitiveness; electricity charges need to fall. We need to promote competition and the competitive agenda. We need to reduce the administrative burden of regulation without compromising the integrity of the system. We need to implement public sector reform with real urgency. On public service reform let me give just one example. The Report of An Bord Snip Nua affords us many others. In education a great deal of money has been spent on reducing class size, without sufficient attention to the fact that there is a weak relationship between pupil teacher ratios and student outcomes. Good teachers determine student outcomes. We need to ensure that the best teachers are rewarded for excellent performances and that school principals are managers of education and not of paperwork.

I do not propose presenting a set of remedies for the global or Irish Banking System, but it is obvious that in banking we need improved prudential supervision. I believe that NAMA has the potential for being a very good solution. NAMA is going to be a very large undertaking. There is no single model, which can be taken off a shelf from some other country in Europe or South America or Asia which will solve the Irish problem. I think that it is possible that it was launched and announced before some critical details had been worked out and indeed that some of the details that were announced may not have been fully thought through but the debate that has ensued since NAMA was announced, and the participation in it by knowledgeable commentators, has served in my view to radically improve the prospects of a workable version coming out of the legislation which is shortly expected.

Conclusion

Notwithstanding these formidable challenges I remain confident about the future. We are in a markedly better condition to deal with our difficulties than we were to face the crisis of the mid-80s. The bottom line in my view is that the real challenge is for the Government and the people. Will Government be able to make and implement the difficult policy choices that must be made in a context where there is a constant clamour for short term solutions and where all politicians are obliged to compete for attention, in a noisy market where sound bites prevail above complex or painstaking analysis? Even more to the point will 'We the people' (to borrow a phrase from the Constitution) accept what needs to be done in order to achieve a sustainable future for our children?

Difference between Ireland and Iceland

Fridrik M. Baldursson
Professor of Economics, Reykjavik University

Has a PhD in statistics and applied probability from Columbia University, New York. Chairman, Board of Directors, Icelandic Marine Research Institute since 2002. Chairman, Finance Minister's committee for reviewing Iceland's system of taxation with emphasis on efficiency and competitiveness (2006–2008). Chairman, Board of Directors, Icelandic Telecommunications Infrastructure Fund (2006–2008). Acting Director of the Icelandic Competition Authority in the division and merger of Burdaras with Landsbanki and Straumur Investment Bank (2005).

> The difference between Ireland and Iceland, so the current joke goes, is one letter and six months. (The Economist, February 5th 2009)

The Economist article quoted above had the heading 'Reykjavik-on-Liffey'. There were other comparisons of this nature made last winter, including 'Reykjavik-on-Thames'. To 'go the way of Iceland' was another way of saying that a nation was headed for national bankruptcy. And it is true that Iceland, if not bankrupt, is in serious trouble.

Ireland is obviously in crisis too and, in some cases, its macroeconomic indicators are even more negative than the Icelandic ones: the OECD predicts gross domestic product (GDP) to fall by 10 per cent in Ireland this year while the corresponding figure for Iceland is 7 per cent; unemployment is predicted at 12 per cent in Ireland, but a 'mere' 8 per cent in Iceland (a historic high for Iceland); fiscal deficit is similar in the two countries at 11 per cent of GDP. The OECD's medium-term scenario for the two countries is rather similar although, remarkably, the one for Iceland is more positive than that for Ireland as regards unemployment and public finances.

How did Iceland come to this situation? The explanation has much in common with the case of Ireland, including a pre-crisis boom, a bubble in property prices, and faulty economic policies. In both countries, as elsewhere, bankers played the Pied Piper's flute.

The situation in Iceland, however, is more serious, fragile and fraught with risks. The banking system in Iceland collapsed almost entirely in early October 2008; all three major banks went into administration. A substantial portion of firms are bankrupt and some households may suffer the same plight. The direct fiscal cost of the crash is huge: the fiscal bill amounts to 90 per cent of GDP; potential costs for Ireland have been predicted to be about 10 per cent of GDP. On top of direct costs of the Icelandic state comes a fiscal deficit that amounts to 11 per cent of GDP this year; luckily the state came into the crisis with low debt, but according to Ministry of Finance estimates, the gross state debt will amount to approximately 125 per cent of GDP at the end of 2009. In addition the state will borrow $5 billion, almost 50 per cent of GDP, from the International Monetary Fund (IMF) and others to strengthen currency reserves. Gross external debt of the country will be 200 per cent of GDP at the end of 2009. There are substantial assets against this debt which bring net figures to considerably lower levels: the Central Bank of Iceland predicts net fiscal debt of 35 per cent and net external debt amounting to 85 per cent of GDP at the end of this year. However, there is much uncertainty around the valuations of assets such calculations are based on and people in Iceland are reluctant to accept them at face value.

The OECD's medium-term scenario for the two countries is rather similar although, remarkably, the one for Iceland is more positive than that for Ireland as regards unemployment and public finances.

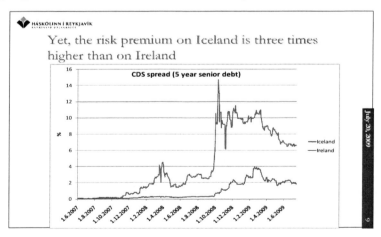

Figure 1

The perception that Iceland is in a much worse situation than Ireland appears to dominate elsewhere. International capital markets place a risk premium on Iceland that is over three times as high as that on Ireland: the cost of insuring Iceland's debt is now over 6 per cent per annum. That premium effectively closes access for Iceland to capital markets. This can have serious second-round consequences, for example, when key enterprises such as the National Power Company – the main supplier of electricity in Iceland – have to refinance their foreign debt.

How did Iceland come to this situation? The explanation has much in common with the case of Ireland, including a pre-crisis boom, a bubble in property prices, and faulty economic policies. In both countries, as elsewhere, bankers played the Pied Piper's flute. However, there are important differences, including aggressive international expansion of Icelandic banks and entrepreneurs which brought the size of the banks to unsustainable levels in terms of the economy and leveraged the country to a high and risky degree. Another important difference is the non-membership of Iceland in EMU; collapse of the nation's currency, the krona, was an important factor in the crash whereas the euro has helped financial stability in Ireland. While Iceland relies on the help of the IMF in its struggle to reopen foreign exchange and regain access to capital markets, Ireland's banks rely on the European Central Bank for liquidity support.[14] More generally, non-membership of the EU may also have been extremely costly for Iceland; actions by the UK in October set off the collapse of Iceland's largest bank, Kaupthing Bank. Perhaps such actions would not have been taken against a fellow EU member country.

Another important difference is the non-membership of Iceland in EMU; the collapse of the nation's currency, the krona, was an important factor in the crash whereas the euro has helped financial stability in Ireland.

Boom 2003-2007

Iceland experienced a big economic boom in the years 2003-2007 with the result that the economy became seriously overheated.

Following are some indicators of the magnitude of the boom 2003-2007:

- Average economic growth was 5.5 per cent per annum.
- Domestic demand growth was 8 per cent per annum.

- Unemployment dropped from 3.5 per cent to 1.5 per cent.
- Inflation increased from 2.5 per cent to 6 per cent.
- The Central Bank's policy interest rate was hiked from 5 percent to 14 per cent.
- Housing doubled in price.
- The stock market quadrupled in price.
- The country's current account went from being balanced in 2002 to a deficit of 25 per cent of GDP in 2006.

There were several important drivers of these developments. Initially big investment projects, for the most part energy related, they were the main underlying factor. They were later replaced by a general boom in construction and consumption. Exports have, however, been an important driver of growth since 2008.

An important underlying driver of the boom was privatization of previously state-owned banks in 1999-2003; most of the banking sector before that time was state owned. The new owners embarked on an aggressive strategy of expansion and lending which had a major impact on credit growth, incomes, and wealth. These factors fed the upswing.

The new owners embarked on an aggressive strategy of expansion and lending which had a major impact on credit growth, incomes, and wealth. These factors fed the upswing. Part energy related, they were the main underlying factor. They were later replaced by a general boom in construction and consumption. Exports have, however, been an important driver of growth since 2008.

Banking crisis

The Icelandic banking crisis may be said to have begun in August 2007 with the onset of the international crisis. In the following months access to market funding became steadily worse due to perceptions internationally of increased risk. All banks were affected to some extent, but Icelandic banks especially so. Market participants seem suddenly to have realized that the banks in Iceland with assets and liabilities worth ten times GDP were too large for the government to back up. Access to market funding became steadily worse as the international crisis progressed and deepened.

The risk premium placed on the Icelandic banks by international markets rose steadily and increased rapidly with the collapse of Bear-Stearns, the US investment bank, in March 2008. Beginning in December 2007 the risk premium on the banks was transmitted to the Icelandic state. This caused a stop in foreign capital inflows into Iceland and the krona subsequently depreciated. The Central bank belatedly tried to get the help of other central banks to increase currency reserves but without much success.

Provided the worst of the crisis would be over within a year, Icelandic banks were generally expected to be able to weather the storm. This was not to be. After the failure of Lehman on 15 September 2008 interbank markets froze and there was a complete evaporation of liquidity. On 26 September 2008 it was made utterly clear that Iceland was on its own and would get no help when the US Federal Reserve agreed on swap lines with all Nordic central banks except that of Iceland. This left Iceland as the only country in Western Europe without such a lifeline in the deepest and most treacherous of waters.

By the end of September 2008 the stage was set for the collapse. Ironically the Central Bank of Iceland – one must hope unwittingly – caused the triggering event. The Central Bank had recently obtained a currency loan from the German Landesbank (not to be confused with the Icelandic Landsbanki). This meant that the country quota for Iceland at Landesbank was exceeded and subsequently a Landesbank loan line to Glitnir Bank was closed.[15] Within days, Glitnir Bank faced a €600 million payment on a loan that it now could not meet. Glitnir asked the Central Bank for an emergency currency loan. The Central Bank, however, decided that in view of further payments due at Glitnir Bank in the near future such a loan would only help the bank for a short time. The risk of lending to Glitnir was deemed too large and the decision was made to nationalize the bank on 29 September 2008.

Rating agencies downgraded Iceland immediately following the nationalization of Glitnir. A currency crisis ensued. The value of the krona collapsed with detrimental consequences for the balance sheets of firms and homes who had borrowed in foreign currency. The devaluation also contributed to the liquidity crisis as the European Central Bank made margin calls on collateralized

On 26 September 2008 it was made utterly clear that Iceland was on its own and would get no help when the US Federal Reserve agreed on swap lines with all Nordic central banks except that of Iceland. This left Iceland as the only country in Western Europe without such a lifeline in the deepest and most treacherous of waters.

If the banks had been allowed to collapse and go into receivership without interference from the government, a complete collapse of the Icelandic economy would have been inevitable. To prevent this, the government – on the basis of the emergency legislation passed in the evening of 6 October 2008 – nationalized the domestic part of the banking sector.

loans made to EMU subsidiaries of Icelandic banks which had placed krona denominated assets as collateral. For this and several other reasons the liquidity position of Icelandic banks collapsed. On Friday 3 October several billion euro were due to be paid by the banks over the next couple of weeks. There was no recourse to credit and no way the Government of Iceland could provide the required funds. In any case, the risk to the people of Iceland of doing so would have been enormous; it would have been a big and risky bet for the government to lend such amounts to failing banks.

Landsbanki became the first bank to collapse in the early morning hours of 7 October. On the following day, Glitner Bank collapsed. An attempt was made to save the Kaupthing Bank, which was thought to have a good chance of survival, when the Government of Iceland granted a loan of €500 million (approximately 5 per cent of GDP). Kaupthing, however, failed on 9 October 2008, after the UK government seized its UK subsidiary.

If the banks had been allowed to collapse and go into receivership without interference from the government, a complete collapse of the Icelandic economy would have been inevitable. To prevent this, the government – on the basis of the emergency legislation passed in the evening of 6 October 2008 – nationalized the domestic part of the banking sector.

Furthermore, each of the collapsed banks was placed under a so-called resolution committee. The new banks took on deposits at domestic branches as well as domestic loans. On 20 July 2009 it was announced that the government would recapitalize the banks as planned. However, the collapsed 'old banks' – now controlled by resolution com-mittees but de facto owned by creditors – would be given options to own two out of the three 'new banks'. Apparently there is an agreement on this with the biggest creditors. However, it remains to be seen whether the creditors use this option.

What now?

The perception internationally seems to be that the state of Iceland nationalized the banks as a whole and took on all the debts of the banks. It is true that the private financial sector in Iceland was essentially bankrupted – although there are small survivors. However, the Icelandic Treasury has not defaulted and does not seem to have any intention of doing so. The state had little gross debt and zero net debt prior to the crisis. However, it will now be highly indebted. There are still few indications that any success has been achieved in establishing confidence by international markets that Iceland is on the road to recovery and that it is safe to lend and invest. This is seen in the high risk-premium placed on Iceland and by the fact that despite the boosting of currency reserves and the imposition of capital controls it has proven very difficult to support the krona.

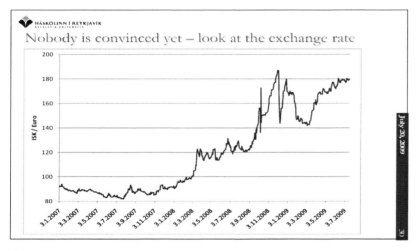

Figure 2

Here, an important difference should be noted between Iceland and Ireland. Ireland, with its EU and EM member ship has benefitted from the stability provided by the euro, whereas Iceland had to turn to the IMF for support, implicitly surrendering some of the sovereign's powers to control its economic policies, Irish banks are now financed to a large degree by the European Central Bank. And even if the depreciation of the krona helps dampen the recession in Iceland through its effect on foreign trade, the krona – having lost all credibility in foreign markets – must be considered a liability in the longer term. Both countries have, of course, learnt at high cost the lesson that monetary policy must be supported by other economic policies.

The IMF and OECD predict a reasonable recovery for Iceland

Here, an important difference should be noted between Iceland and Ireland. Ireland, with its EU and EMU membership has benefitted from the stability provided by the euro, and whereas Iceland had to turn to the IMF for support, implicitly surrendering some of the sovereign's powers to control its economic policies, Irish banks are now financed to a large degree by the European Central Bank.

over the medium term, beginning in late 2010. This is based on the assumption that Iceland sticks to the policies laid out in the IMF programme. However, the overwhelming feeling in the country is that of insecurity and uncertainty. But resignation is not an option – the fundamentals are good – a young and highly educated population, abundant natural resources and excellent infrastructure. Iceland shall find a way out of its troubles. And so shall Ireland.

Chapter 2

THE BANKING CRISIS, REFORM AND REGULATION

THE REST OF THE WORLD KNEW BEFORE WE DID
David Murphy
Business Editor, RTÉ

IRISH BANKING – PROBLEMS AND REFORMS
Alan Dukes
Director, Anglo-Irish Bank and former Leader, Fine Gael

BANKING POLICY DURING AND AFTER THE CRISIS
Patrick Honohan
Professor of Economics, Trinity College Dublin and Governor-Elect, Central Bank of Ireland

FROM INCOMPETENT TO MORALLY SUSPECT TO ILLEGAL
Dan Boyle
Member, Seanad Éireann and Chairman, Green Party

The Rest of the World Knew Before We Did

David Murphy
Business Editor, RTÉ

Has been in the front line of the banking crisis daily. Banksters (Hachette Books), the 2009 book he co-wrote with Martina Devlin, recounts the story of how bankers and property developers engaged in over-borrowing and property speculation that led to an unsustainable property bubble. The 2008 winner of Business Broadcast Journalist of the year, he is a former deputy business editor of The Irish Independent.

The 'we told you so' bandwagon is getting pretty crowded with economists, the IMF and opposition politicians. Some people have engaged in revisionism. John Hurley of the Central Bank said in March of this year that he warned time and again that house prices were rising too fast and too strongly. It is true that the Central Bank did issue that alert. But the bank's main thesis was that Ireland was heading for a soft landing. I am not sure if we have landed yet but it is certainly not soft.

The blame game will roll on. What people say in public and in private are not always the same. Politicians blame banks and regulators. Banks blame regulators. Some people in regulation say there was not the political will to call a halt to the property party. Even some mild measures proposed by the Financial Regulator to slow banks financing the purchase of green field sites were watered down after lobbying from banks. Have I left anyone out? Oh yes, the developers! This time last year, everyone expected the major builders would go bust. Instead it would have been the banks, were it not for the support from the State.

There was one peculiarity about the Irish banking crisis: the rest of the world recognized the scale of the trouble facing the Irish banks before Ireland's authorities. That might sound like a gross generalization. But international investors began to sell off Irish bank shares a full 14 months before the banking guarantee had to be introduced. The share slide in Irish banks began in August 2007. The explanation given

> Politicians blame banks and regulators. Banks blame regulators. Some people in regulation say there was not the political will to end call a halt to the property party.
>
> In September 2007, the Irish banks insisted they were in fine fettle. There were no public sell recommendations by stockbrokers here on bank shares. But in January 2008 the London operation of Swiss investment bank, UBS, told its clients to sell their shares in AIB and Anglo Irish Bank.

by international investors to stockbrokers for selling banks was simple: they were about the the banks' exposure to commercial property. That was a month before Northern Rock collapsed causing the first run on a bank in this part of the world for 160 years.

In September 2007, the Irish banks insisted they were in fine fettle. There were no public sell recommendations by stockbrokers here on banks shares. But in January 2008 the London operation of Swiss investment bank, UBS, told its clients to sell their shares in AIB and Anglo-Irish Bank. UBS analyst, Ross Curran, said there was a danger that commercial property values in Ireland could fall by 30 per cent, which would represent a 'significant risk to earnings' over the next two years for Irish banks. Unfortunately, Irish stockbrokers still believed the story that everything was okay. Some brokers even privately expressed the view that the London-based traders were engaged in 'Paddy bashing'.

Fast forward six months to July 2008 and Richie Boucher, who was at the time Head of Retail Banking at Bank of Ireland, appeared before an Oireachtas committee. He (Richie Boucher) assured politicians in terms that cannot be misconstrued: He said: 'If bad debts and the economy get worse, we believe we are sufficiently capitalized.' Then he added: 'We believe we have enough capital to meet bad debts of a significantly greater magnitude than we believe them to be.' He also said: 'We are very often wrong but we have a strong belief that we have significant and sufficient capital to meet even worse scenarios than we envisage.' He was not the only optimist. Every Irish bank was making similar noises. But what was the market telling us? What were the international investors in shares and bonds telling us? It was the same message they had been sending for 12 months.

Even the Regulator did not seem to be paying attention. The Chief Executive of the Regulator's office, Patrick Neary, made an appearance on Prime Time in September 2008. The interview was an attempt to reassure the public that there was no run on the banks. In it, he fostered the impression that the banking system was in good shape. Eleven days later, the Government was obliged to provide a blanket guarantee for all the banks.

After Mr Neary's interview, Fine Gael's finance spokeman

Richard Bruton said: 'I found it astonishing to hear Patrick Neary say that the risky lending of banks and the property market collapse had nothing to do with the current crisis. ... His insistence that liquidity was the only issue, rather than including bad lending and levels of capitalization, suggests that the Regulator thinks we are largely dealing with a business-as-usual situation.'

People talk a lot about Lehman Brothers, a venerable institution which pre-dated the Irish Famine. It did enormous damage when it folded on 15 September last year. That event loosened a corner stone and the financial edifice was no longer structurally sound. But why? Banks have gone bust before. The simple reason was that everyone who lent it money watched in horror as the value of their bonds turned to zero. That meant that lending to a bank was now a very risky proposition. Two weeks later, the Irish banks were brought to their knees.

In Dublin on the evening of 29 September 2008 shares in Anglo Irish Bank had fallen 46 per cent, Bank of Ireland had 17 per cent lopped off its value, Irish Life and Permanent lost a third of its value and AIB was down 15 per cent. The shares did rally the following morning after the Government announced the guarantee. It did go some way to address the liquidity issue. But the banks were still living in a state of denial about their need for new capital. On 23 October 2008 Eugene Sheehy the chief executive of AIB said we would rather die that raise new capital.

On 20 November 2008 the chief executives and chairpersons of the banks met Finance Minister Brian Lenihan in Farmleigh. By this stage the value of all the Irish financial stocks was just €4 billion compared to €55 billion on 20 May 2007. The market had reached the blindingly obvious conclusion that the banks would need to be recapitalized. But the bankers had not. By this time, across the water the British Government had been seen to act boldly. Gordon Brown had seized the moment. He provided a £37 billion bailout shared by Royal Bank of Scotland (owner of Ulster Bank) and Lloyds TSB, which was taking over Halifax Bank of Scotland. We know what happened here afterwards: a €3.5 billion recapitalization of both AIB and Bank of Ireland, a nationalization of Anglo followed by €3 billion recapitalization with the prospect of a similar figure again.

Nobel Prize winning economist, Paul Krugman, recently wrote

Even the Regulator did not seem to be paying attention. The chief executive of the Regulator's office, Patrick Neary, made an appearance on Prime Time in September 2008.

The interview was an attempt to reassure the public that there was no run on the banks; he fostered the impression that the banking system was in good shape.

a guide to the financial crisis with the uplifting name, *The Return of Depression Economics*. He says carelessness offers a tempting opportunity to unscrupulous businessmen; just open a bank, making sure it has an impressive building and a fancy name. Attract a lot of deposits, by paying good interest if that is allowed, by offering toasters or whatever if it is not. Then lend money out, at high interest rates, to high rolling speculators, preferably friends of yours or maybe even yourself, behind a different corporate front. The depositors will not ask about the quality of your investments since they know that they are protected in any case. And you now have a one way option: if the investments do well you become rich, if they do badly, you can simply walk away and let the Government clean up the mess.

Eleven days later, the Government was obliged to provide a blanket guarantee for all the banks.

So much of what happened in Anglo is not new. It is just new to us. This could explain why people remain bewildered by the speed of the slump and its severity. There are two questions put repeatedly by members of the public. The first; where did all the money go? The second; Will anyone go to jail? The first is easy to answer: it was never there in the first place. The second is tricky: we do not know yet.

But the various tentacles of the Anglo affair under investigation are as follows. First is Anglo's secret loans to directors warehoused by Irish Nationwide, primarily the €106 million lent to Seán Fitzpatrick. These loans are being examined by the Regulator, the Irish Stock Exchange and the Corporate Enforcer, Paul Appleby. Next is the Golden Circle. Those investors were lent money by the bank to buy Anglo shares from Seán Quinn. The potential loss to the bank and, by extension, the tax payer is €300 millon. This is being probed by the Gardaí and Paul Appleby. The investigation will also examine the role of Anglo and advisers who set up the scheme. Next is the back-to-back deposits involving Anglo and Irish Life & Permanent which totalled €8 billion. Those transactions allowed Anglo dupe investors into believing it had more deposits than was actually the case. This has been referred to the Gardaí by the Regulator.

The Institute of Chartered Accountants in Ireland is investigating the role of its members. They are Ernst & Young who audited Anglo, the Bank's former directors Seán

Fitzpatrick, David Drumm and Willie McAteer and Irish Life and Permanent's Peter Fitzpatrick. The most serious aspect of the multiple investigations relates to the Anglo and Irish Life & Permanent deposits and the Golden Circle deal. These scandals may involve potential breaches of market-abuse regulation, which carry penalties of up to €10 million in fines and or ten years in jail.

Anglo was the most risky of the Irish banks. Just to answer the question of how the banking crisis happened take a look at its lending. From 2004 to 2008, lending to customers at Anglo almost tripled from €24 billion to €72 billion. Over the same period, lending at AIB nearly doubled from €67 billion to €129 billion. The scale of this expansion was unnerving – particularly as it coincided with the later years of a boom. Lending in general at all the banks rose dramatically. In total the loans to developers was in excess of €60 billion. We know the National Asset Management Agency (NAMA) is taking the land loans as well as the development loans. By that it means lending for completed developments like shopping centres.

But what exactly is now happening to Anglo? The Government has ruled out an orderly wind down of the bank. There is no published business plan for the bank, no chief executive appointed and potentially half of the banks' loans will go to NAMA. We know the size of the balance sheet is going to be shrunk and the Government is open to offers from those willing to purchase parts of its loan book. So while the Minister for Finance may rule out a wind down – not much will be left over.

What about the other banks? There is going to be vast consolidation. There has to be. And possibly 10,000 job losses in banking over the coming years. Bank of Ireland is confident it will not need more capital and therefore will be 25 per cent owned by the State. But the State could end up owning a majority of AIB, Irish Life and Permanent, EBS and Irish Nationwide could in future merge to become a third force in Irish banking.

The IMF puts the losses at the Irish banks over the coming years at €35 billion. The banks' capital will absorb some of that, but not all, by a long stretch. Taxpayers will foot the bill and will continue to do so for years. Maybe we have learned our lesson – but history repeats itself for those who were not watching the first time.

There are two questions put repeatedly by members of the public. The first: where did all the money go? The second; Will anyone go to jail? The first is easy to answer: it was never there in the first place. The second is tricky: we do not know yet.

Next is the Golden Circle. Those investors were lent money by the bank to buy Anglo shares from Seán Quinn.

The potential loss to the bank and, by extension, the tax payer is €300 millon. This is being probed by the Gardaí and Paul Appleby.

There is a frequently misquoted paragraph from Karl Marx's *Das Kapital*. He says:

> In every stockjobbing (or stockbroking) swindle every one knows that some time or other the crash must come, but everyone hopes that it may fall on the head of his neighbour, after he himself has caught the shower of gold and placed it in safety. Après moi le déluge! is the watchword of every capitalist and of every capitalist nation. Hence Capital is reckless of the health or length of life of the labourer.[16]

That was Marx. But as we know the Marxists never made it to the board rooms of the Irish banks!

Irish Banking – Problems and Reforms

Alan Dukes

Director, Anglo-Irish Bank and former Leader , Fine Gael

Educated at Coláiste Mhuire and UCD. Chief Economist Irish Farmers' Association (1969-1972). Adviser in Cabinet of EU Commissioner, Richard Burke (1977-1980). First elected to Dáil Éireann in 1981 for Kildare constituency. Minister for Agriculture (1981-2), Minister for Finance (1982-86) and Minister for Justice (1986-7). Elected leader of Fine Gael in 1987 to succeed Dr Garret FitzGerald. Minister for Transport, Energy and Communications (1996-7). Former Director General, Institute of European Affairs. Appointed to board of Anglo-Irish Bank as a public interest director by Irish Government in 2008.

The Irish banking problem is a relatively simple one which, in its origins, has only a few features in common with what we have come to regard as the global banking problem. Our problem is almost entirely a direct result of the property sector bust. Basically, all of our banks got too deeply involved in lending for property development and construction. The property sector bust has left them with 'assets' that have massively reduced in value and huge volumes of lending on which very little, if any, return can be expected until the property sector recovers.

Irish banks have not been significantly involved in the kinds of 'toxic' products that have wrought havoc in the US. Our public policy problem lies in the fact that we have to deal with the fall-out of the banking problem at a time when financial markets worldwide are in disarray and the supply of credit is severely constrained.

> **Our problem is almost entirely a direct result of the property sector bust. Basically, all of our banks got too deeply involved in lending for property development and construction.**

Problem

Banks (convenient shorthand for whole financial services sector)

A period of sustained economic growth (sometimes rapid, sometimes modest) through the mid-1980s, the 1990s and the early 2000s (punctuated by occasional mild slowdowns) gave rise to an exuberant attitude to credit creation and demand.

Securitization facilitated further credit expansion and created an atmosphere favourable to further innovation in financial instruments and 'products'. Securitization also increased the 'distance' between financial instruments and the debt events underlying them. In this way, the financial economy became more and more remote from the real economy. Financial instruments have become more and more opaque.

Financial instruments and 'products' were tailored so as to fall outside the scope of regulatory control. This facilitated the movement of assets and liabilities off the balance sheets of banks and financial intermediaries. In turn, this facilitated the avoidance of the need to reinforce the capital base of many market operators. In effect, the whole system became more and more highly geared, even though this high level of gearing was not reflected in balance sheets drawn up in accordance with regulatory rules.

Sustained growth led to property booms in many countries (e.g., the US, Ireland, UK, Spain). The property boom and competition in financing attracted many financial operators, which had not previously been much involved, into the property market (e.g., in the US and in Ireland). The boom also led lenders to increase Loan to Value (LTV) ratios and to engage increasingly in offering sub-prime mortgages. Sub-prime lending was further facilitated by securitization.

The financial services sector shared in the obsession with 'driving shareholder value' which (at least until very recently) has become the mantra of management gurus. This obsession has been a large part of the reason for a strong movement towards concentration and mergers. In Europe, this has led to the emergence of a number of multi-national banking groups. The effects of the obsession with shareholder value have included the adoption in the financial services sector of staff remuneration and bonus policies with a very strong focus on short-term results, frequently based on commission.

The effects of the obsession with shareholder value have included the adoption in the financial services sector of staff remuneration and bonus policies with a very strong focus on short-term results, frequently based on commission.

Regulators

As in most other fields, regulators in the financial sector are much less nimble than market operators. Market operators are adept at exploiting gaps in the regulatory system. In the financial sector, many instruments or 'products' have been designed to fit into the cracks in the regulatory rules.

In some key jurisdictions (notably the US) regulatory authority is dispersed between a multitude of agencies, leading to a lack of coherence and to 'turf wars' between regulatory agencies. There are unresolved arguments as between 'principles-based' regulation and 'rules-based' regulation and between 'light touch' regulation and 'heavy-handed' regulation. While this argument has gone on, the financial services sector has exploited the gaps left by the arguments.

Although they will not admit it, regulators typically suffer to some degree from two constraints. One is rather nationalistic. The UK regulatory authorities, for instance, are concerned to ensure that the City of London does not lose its position of prominence and influence among international financial markets (similar considerations apply in the case of New York). Another constraint is that there is a degree of mutual 'capture' by both regulators and financial operators. From time to time, they arrive at accommodations which dilute the integrity of the regulatory system while impeding the operation of market forces and compromising transparency.

Regulators seem sometimes reluctant to use their powers, particularly if the exercise of particular powers seems to go against the economic or political orthodoxy or fashions of the day. In the US, the UK and Ireland, for example, regulators failed to take action even when it had already become clear that a 'soft landing' after the property boom had become increasingly unlikely. This contrasts with the situation in Spain, where the financial regulatory authorities prevented the banking system becoming involved in the property boom: the effects of the property crash in that country have been dramatic for mortgage lenders, but have left the main banking groups largely unaffected.

There are problems with regulation which seem inherent and unavoidable. The more detailed and prescriptive regulatory rules are the greater is the incentive to find ways around them. The

In the US, the UK and Ireland, for example, regulators failed to take action even when it had already become clear that a 'soft landing' after the property boom had become increasingly unlikely.

income tax avoidance industry (peopled by highly ethical and scrupulously law-abiding operators) is a case in point.

On the other hand, loose general rules always give rise to arguments about interpretation and implementation. On top of all that, financial market operators have, on the whole, successfully lobbied against regulatory strengthening. That is true of the City of London. It is true also of Wall Street. The US regulatory system and the financial authorities in the US Administration include many former senior executives of the 'big beasts' of Wall Street. In both places, there is already abundant evidence of a 'push-back' by the financial services sector against the pressure for a new approach to regulation.

Reforms

In Ireland, we are to have new legislation on financial regulation. Ideally, this should be framed so as to be consistent with action at EU and global level.

Although our fundamental problem is domestic, its resolution is being made exceedingly difficult by the fall-out from the global problem. Global problems require global solutions and we have a very direct interest in the search for global solutions. Ideally, domestic action in individual states should be consistent with a coherent global approach. In Ireland, we are to have new legislation on financial regulation. Ideally, this should be framed so as to be consistent with action at EU and global level. The G20 is making slow progress on drawing up an agreement on coordinated action. I would like to be hopeful of relatively quick and substantive progress. I have not yet got to that point.

The following are the elements of what I consider to be the necessary approach. As I have worked them out over the past year or so, I have discussed them with commentators and some financial sector operators. They are deeply disliked in the financial sector, which makes me think that I am on the right track.

'Too big to fail' is too big. No systemically important bank (in any jurisdiction) should be allowed to get so big that its failure causes irremediable collateral damage to other systemically important banks. Regulatory and competition authorities must ensure that concentrations and mergers do not create new risk situations.

Capital adequacy ratios should be an increasing function of size. Recent experience shows that bigger banks incur higher levels of risk, including the level of risk of collateral damage.

- **Regulators must be given explicit powers to halt excessive concentrations of risk.** Our Central Bank warned repeatedly over a period of at least three years that a 'soft landing' for the property sector was increasingly unlikely. It should have the means to act on such warnings by requiring the necessary restrictions. Current measures of risk concentration are clearly inadequate.
- **Regulatory systems must be made more coherent and unified.** The dispersion of responsibility for financial regulation has facilitated the kinds of conduct which have given rise to the current global and domestic problems.
- **We need new rules for the operation of rating agencies.** Rating agencies currently downgrade market operators and sovereign borrowers which they themselves rated highly before the bust which they, like many others, failed to anticipate. Their credibility is open to serious questioning. In addition, some of them engaged in dealing in 'products' which they rated (favourably and for far too long).
- **We need much stricter and internationally-agreed rules on securitization.** Current practice has allowed debt originators to separate themselves wholly from the debt instruments. This is perhaps the greatest source of moral hazard in financial markets. There is abundant evidence to the effect that many securitized instruments are beyond the understanding not only of purchasers but also of sellers.

Regulatory and competition authorities must ensure that concentrations and mergers do not create new risk situations.

There is abundant evidence to the effect that many securitized instruments are beyond the understanding not only of purchasers but also of sellers.

The accounting rules which allowed wholesale shifting of assets and liabilities off banks' balance sheets must be changed. Regulators have been left in the dark about the true levels and solidity of both assets and liabilities.

'Over the counter' dealings in securitized instruments should be banned. Transparent clearing systems are required and can be put in place without great difficulty.

Banking Policy During and After the Crisis

Patrick Honohan
Professor of Economics, Trinity College Dublin and Governor-
Elect, Central Bank of Ireland

*Has a PhD in Economics and an MSc in Econometrics and
Mathematical Economics from the London School of Economics,
and an MA (Economics) and BA (Mathematics and Economics)
from UCD. Since 2007, has been Professor of International
Financial Economics and Development at TCD. Worked at The
World Bank, Washington DC from 1987 to 1990 and from 1998
to 2007. From 1990-8 he worked at ERSI as Research Professor
and Director of Institute's Banking Research Centre. Was
Economic Advisor to Taoiseach, Dr Garret FitzGerald (1981-2
and 1984-6). From 1976-84 worked at the Central Bank of
Ireland. Also held positions at the International Monetary Fund,
Australian National University, UCD, University of California,
San Diego and the London School of Economics. Member, Royal
Irish Academy.*

At a time of crisis the character and priorities of prudential banking policy move through three distinct – albeit interrelated – phases: containment, resolution and prevention.

Containment

Containment entails preventing or stemming panic and stopping the rot in terms of loss-making activities. Irish containment moved into top gear at the end of September 2008 with the announcement of emergency legislation for an extensive guarantee of the liabilities of the main Irish-controlled retail banks. Triggered by the effective failure of Anglo-Irish bank in very difficult international funding conditions, the guarantee was just one of several dramatic containment steps taken by Governments in Europe and the US during September and October. The first by an OECD country for some time, the blanket guarantee was quickly followed by other countries, albeit the other guarantees were less extensive and in most cases less formal. In contrast, Iceland, whose banks recklessly plunged into

Containment might not have been possible without the help of the European Central Bank, which has now lent Irish banks a staggeringly large sum of money needed to allow them to repay foreign market borrowing they had made over the previous five or six years.

Because of the unprecedented depth of the macro crisis here and abroad, getting a reliable estimate (not only of development property-related loans but also loans secured on residential property, loans to commercial and manufacturing firms, credit cards and so on) seems beyond reach.

into grandiose international adventures, was unable to backstop their failure.

Many people ask me whether a blanket guarantee was really necessary. Although one can quibble with the scope, with the inadequate consultation with partner regulatory authorities elsewhere in Europe, and with the denial of underlying solvency issues at Anglo, there is little doubt that an extensive guarantee of Irish banking liabilities was needed as an immediate containment response, given the situation that had emerged.

Credit Institutions Borrowing from Central Bank
Dec 2006-May 2009

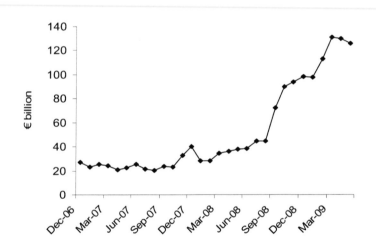

Figure 1

In order to stay in business Anglo needed to find more capital, hence the injection of Government funds.

The scale of the Irish banking crisis, and the fact that it occurred against the backdrop of the parallel but different collapse in international banking confidence, have made containment quite difficult. Indeed, containment might not have been possible without the help of the European Central Bank, which has now lent Irish banks a staggeringly large sum of money needed to allow them to repay foreign market borrowing they had made over the previous five or six years.

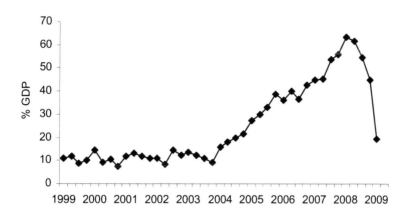

Net international position of Irish credit institutions
1999q1-2009q1

Figure 2

Maintaining confidence is not the only criterion for good containment. Indeed obsessing on this aspect can lead to suboptimal decisions. But confidence aspects are central, not least because of the knock-on effects on government borrowing costs. In the febrile atmosphere of financial markets that has prevailed during the past year, revelation of Irish banking difficulties has had a clear knock-on effect on the cost of Irish Government borrowing.

I have proposed a two-part payment mechanism whereby NAMA would pay the bank for loans of uncertain value only a small part in cash – well below the realistic best estimate of the net amount they will eventually yield – with a sweetener in the form of an equity stake for the bank shareholders in any future recoveries by NAMA.

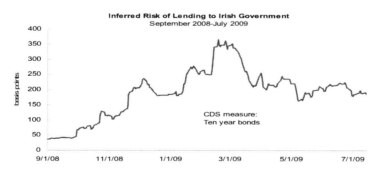

Figure 3: CDS spreads on Irish Government bonds (Sept 2008 to July 2009)

Resolution

Resolution of a banking crisis entails getting the banks back on to a self-sustaining financial basis, and ensuring that lenders are confident that this is so. It also requires ensuring that an effective management team is in place in each bank and that it has the capacity both to deal with inherited problem loans, and to move forward with new lending activities. It is in this context that we should interpret the Government's injection of capital into three of the banks, the departures of some senior staff and directors, and the creation of NAMA. Evidently this whole process is still in its early stages.

Sequencing is an issue here. The textbook says that among the first things to be done in the resolution phase is to decide on the allocation of who should bear the losses. Evidently it is intended by the Irish Government that it will assume whatever of the losses are not taken by the shareholders and other providers of risk capital. But beyond that, it is not yet possible to be precise. In order to get more precision, a good estimate of the prospective losses is needed. Because of the unprecedented depth of the macro crisis here and abroad, getting a reliable estimate (not only of development property-related loans but also loans secured on residential property, loans to commercial and manufacturing firms, credit cards and so on) seems beyond reach.

As losses crystallize and get taken into account in a bank's balance sheet, its cushion of capital (essentially the difference between its assets and its non-risk-bearing liabilities) shrinks. For example, their last balance sheet showed Anglo's capital to have dipped well below regulatory minima, and they had to be given temporary regulatory waivers. In order to stay in business Anglo needed to find more capital, hence the injection of Government funds. Now, any such injection has the incidental side-effect of boosting the likely value of the remaining capital, owed to risk-taking subordinated debt holders, because it makes it less likely that any further losses will be absorbed by them. Buying out those sub-debt holders (whose claims are traded below par because of the sizable risks they bear) helps reduce this unfortunate side-effect.

NAMA

NAMA can be seen as part of the resolution process: an asset purchase scheme that can i) free the banks from being pre-occupied with trying to recover from their largest delinquent borrowers, thereby allowing them to focus on identifying the borrowing needs of healthy customers; and ii) replace problem loans of uncertain value in the banks' portfolio with sound, marketable assets that can be used to mobilize liquid resources for lending.

Other countries have also been moving to set up some kind of asset purchase agency, notably the US and Germany. Neither has managed to get a formula that commands widespread approval among experts. A particular sticking point is pricing. If an asset management company such as NAMA mistakenly pays too much for the loans it buys, this will entail an unwarranted gift to the shareholders and other unguaranteed providers of capital to the banks. The US system is stalled for want of a solution to this problem. The UK has chosen a different route, offering the banks partial (90 per cent) insurance against further loan losses – this too exposes the UK taxpayer if the premium and deductible paid by the banks prove to be too low.

I have proposed a two-part payment mechanism whereby NAMA would pay the bank for loans of uncertain value only a small part in cash – well below the realistic best estimate of the net amount they will eventually yield – with a sweetener in the form of an equity stake for the bank shareholders in any future recoveries by NAMA. This strategy ('NAMA 2.0') ensures that the taxpayer does not pay too much. It still separates the bad loans from the bank, while sharing the pricing risk fairly between taxpayer and shareholder. Unless the loans are valued at unrealistically high prices, the NAMA process will leave the banks with insufficient capital. This is especially true considering the additional loan losses in non-property lending that are inevitable given the depth of the recession and which will have to be provided for.

As is well understood, the Government will therefore have to step in again and inject more capital funds. Thus it will end up owning a large fraction of the shares unless it can find new providers of capital (which should not be impossible since the

As we begin to see in very recent court proceedings, there are going to be huge complications in achieving effective corporate workouts ... there are multiple bank claimants. This is true with or without NAMA.

If bank insiders and shareholders are seen as getting off too lightly, this will surely worsen recklessness next time around – moral hazard as it is known.

new investors would be buying a cleaned-up concern). Some have jumped the gun by calling for an outright nationalization come what may. I do not see this as a goal in itself. My reading of the international evidence is that any protracted period of outright government ownership is more likely to have adverse consequences on economic recovery. Therefore, I prefer to see the government's ownership share as something that falls out of the loan valuation calculations and the success or otherwise in finding (presumably abroad) other potential capital providers, public or private.

As we begin to see in very recent court proceedings, there are going to be huge complications in achieving effective corporate workouts, where, as is going to be the case for most of the big cases, there are multiple bank claimants. This is true with or without NAMA. The whole area of workouts and recovery is not my area of comparative advantage, so I will not dwell on it. Let me just mention one reminder: seizing collaterals, and liquidating them, are two different things. While it may very well be true that this is not the best moment to be liquidating development land and half-completed buildings, that is not in itself an argument for forbearance in dealing with a delinquent borrower.

To avoid disappointment, it is worth stressing that restoring the flow of credit is not simply a question of pouring money in one end and expecting it to come out in the form of loans on the other. Injections of capital are mainly about rebuilding the cushion of capital that protects the depositors and other creditors against future risks. That helps the bank raise additional loanable funds, and helps reduce management's levels of anxiety and fear, thereby restoring some of their willingness to make new loans. But they will still not want to lend to poor prospects. And, given that it is going to be largely Government money that is at risk, the general public should not want them to be lending to poor prospects. A bank loan given to a loss-making firm without much hope of survival by a largely state-owned bank is in essence a budgetary grant.

Prevention

As the resolution comes to completion, regulatory emphasis will shift to preventing the next crisis. Of course, the way in which the crisis is resolved will help set the scene here. If bank insiders and shareholders are seen as getting off too lightly, this will surely worsen recklessness next time around – moral hazard as it is known. In addition, though, there is much international discussion these days of ideas for better prudential regulation that would help prevent the next crisis.

Most of these reforms centre around improving the alignment of banker incentives with social welfare, and improving transparency so that regulators and other market participants can help forestall problems. More equity capital – i.e., a higher proportion of banks' lending and activities to be funded by shareholders – is a goal on which there is wide agreement. The structure of individual banker remuneration is also rightly under the microscope. Mechanical rules limiting rapid balance sheet growth and other ratios could also help. Other types of regulation, especially those relating to fancy derivatives (should be traded through organized exchanges and not over-the counter), rating agencies (downgrade reliance on them) and loan sales (obligation for originator to retain some of the risk), are all moves in the right direction, though they do not really speak to the problems we have had in Ireland.

Instead, the goal of better 'macro-prudential' regulation should strike a chord for us. It was not just that one bank that went bad (although one bank's egregiously rapid growth certainly accelerated the infection of others). The error of judgement that led into an unprecedented property bubble reflects a system wide failure to appreciate the scale of the risk being assumed. Technical discussion of mathematical risk models is irrelevant here. Instead, what is needed is improved organizational and decision making skills by the regulator, including a way of taking into account the warnings of dissident sceptics whose views tend at present to be dismissed as cranky. Here, institutionalizing an outside view – provided for example by international sharing of supervisory staff – would in my view be one valuable element.

> **It was not just that one bank that went bad (although one bank's egregiously rapid growth certainly accelerated the infection of others). The error of judgement that led to the banks lending so much with so little solid security into an unprecedented property bubble reflects a system wide failure to appreciate the scale of the risk being assumed.**

Protecting consumer and economy

I do not want to close without mentioning consumer protection. The worst aspects of this, such as out-of-control loan originators pushing unaffordable sub-prime mortgages, seem not to have been as widespread an issue in Ireland as in the UK or of course in the US. But, more generally, the future banking landscape in Ireland needs not only to be safe and sound, but inclusive and low cost. There had been the beginnings of work on this aspect in recent years, not only by Combat Poverty, but also by the Financial Regulator, whose public information function had indeed come to be seen as somewhat gold-plated. If we end up with a smaller handful of main players, this must not be allowed to result in monopoly pricing and neglect of small and vulnerable customers. In this regard, the apparent *de facto* retreat of several of the foreign banks is a regrettable development which I hope will only be transitory.

An effective financial system has been shown in numerous academic studies to have the potential to accelerate long-term growth. Even before the crash, Ireland's banking system had not displayed conspicuous effectiveness of this type. As we move through the steps of containment and resolution towards rebuilding a safe and sound system, let us try to ensure that it makes a better national contribution in the future.

From Incompetent to Morally Suspect to Illegal

Dan Boyle

Member, Seanad Éireann and Chairman, Green Party

Nominated by An Taoiseach to Seanad Éireann in August 2007. Subsequently appointed Deputy Leader of Seanad. Elected to Chair of Green Party in October 2007. First Green Party councillor elected to Cork City Council (1991). Member of Cork City Council (1991-2002). In 2002, elected to Dáil Éireann for Cork South Central. In 2007 General Election narrowly failed to retain seat. Was Green Party Whip in Dáil and is Party's spokesperson on Finance and on Social and Family Affairs and member of influential Public Accounts Committee. Sits on boards of Firkin Crane Centre, Wandesford Quay Artist Studios, Lavit Gallery and Corcadorca Theatre Company. Former Community Youth Worker and also worked in the areas of disability rights and the arts.

Among the many changes in economic, social and political life that have occurred in Ireland over the past thirty years, bankers have seemed more immune in protecting their place within the establishment's pecking order. Some of the lapses that have taken place have been glossed over or have been easily explained. The ICI debacle of the 1980s was thought to be more about individual competencies rather than any type of collective responsibility. The DIRT scandal of the 1990s was certainly an act of mass collusion within the banking sector, but it was a conspiracy shared with a large number of Irish citizens, and so blame was diffuse.

Under similar circumstances, the current crisis in financial services could have been attributed to international factors, but the folly exposed has been too deep, the greed engendered too incredible for citizens to continue to accept. The questions that now remain are: what is the price tag that the taxpayer is expected to pick up? How were things ever allowed to get this far? And when will those who have individually contributed to this state of affairs take responsibility and be held accountable?

We live in a small country. Many people know many other people. There has been an historical cultural reluctance to

The questions that now remain are: what is the price tag that the taxpayer is expected to pick up? How were things ever allowed to get this far? And when will those who have individually contributed to this state of affairs take responsibility and be held accountable?

The then government, represented through its Minister for Finance, Charlie McCreevy, felt that a new Irish Financial Services Regulatory Authority would bring a new bolder approach to regulation. It is hard to imagine that argument now and keep a straight face.

challenge in this country. In this context an effective system of regulation would always prove less effective than in a more standards-based country. Add to this conceit the impression that banking has been seen as an honour based profession where standards would be set but rarely would be measured, then little surprise that the seeds of not knowing and not acting were allowed to spread so wildly.

Even in the simpler times of the past, when a traditional Central Bank was responsible for money supply and for interest rates, the conservative nature of Irish banking meant that reserves and lending ratios were easily adhered to. Later, as gentlemen's agreement regulation gave away to large scale deregulation, and Irish banks engaged in expansion policies in foreign markets, new questions arose, many of which remain unanswered. What was to be regulated, how, by whom and where allowed huge gaps to be opened that were ruthlessly exploited. The near absence of any effective type of international financial regulation, even in transnational regions such as among Eurozone countries, created a charter for those more concerned with quick profit return than maintaining proper standards of financial regulation.

The turn of the millennium saw a flurry of activity in changing national financial regulatory systems. In Ireland this process was informed by the commissioning of the McDowell Report. It was an irony that subsequently Michael McDowell was to become a member of the cabinet that selectively acted on the recommendations of his group's report. The legislation which followed this report recast the role of the Central Bank and brought into being the Irish Financial Services Regulatory Authority. As opposition finance spokesperson in the Dáil who spoke on the legislation at that time, it would have been hard not to have been aware of the turf war that informed those bills. Then was the time to re-imagine the Central Bank – having entered the Euro currency, intrinsic functions of the Central Bank were at a stroke removed. The then government, represented through its Minister for Finance, Charlie McCreevy, felt that a new Irish Financial Services Regulatory Authority would bring a new bolder approach to regulation. It is hard to imagine that argument now and keep a straight face.

A secondary debate was on the role of consumer protection in the then to be established IFSRA. It was important that this be included. It is important that it be included in any new system of financial regulation to be established now. Consumer protection is the canary in the coalmine approach towards financial regulation. Abuse of consumer rights can very often be indicative of lax financial standards within an institution. An argument has been advanced that the need to concentrate on consumer protection has been at the expense of the prudential role of the regulatory authority. I find this a hollow argument, a convenient excuse for the failure to meet the prudential function. These are coexistent, parallel functions. One does not exist at the expense of the other.

The legislation that established IFSRA was not deficient in the powers that were available to the new agency. The greatest failings of the inability to regulate in recent years has not been because of a lack of resources, or a negligence in legislation. It has been the decisions not to activate many of the powers available to the regulatory authority. Of course there have been other factors. Because of the incestuous nature of recruitment in financial services the same pool of likely employees has existed from which the financial institutions and the regulatory authorities have dipped into. Higher wages in the private sector deprive state bodies from recruiting all but the most highly motivated of people. **The high turnover of staff within IFSRA would indicate a high level of transfer from IFSRA to financial institutions. A practice that could be seen as buying off expertise from IFSRA.**

There was a mirror practice that IFSRA sought to encourage through the offering of work experience to employees from financial institutions. It happened on a far smaller scale, and does not seem to have delivered on its intention of increasing expertise within financial institutions of the importance of regulation. I feel that it is important that in any new system of financial regulation that cooling-off periods be provided for, to discourage the active recruitment of regulatory authority personnel with a set time period of leaving employment with a regulator.

It could be that, just as it has been applied to the debate on the deterioration in public finances, the science of hindsight can be a great thing. Prior to the collapse in major international banks, there seemed to be little discussion that Irish banks were

The litany of bad practice we have since learned about, pertaining to activities within the banking sector, has varied from the incompetent to the morally suspect to the illegal.

It has been the failure of culture and the deficit that exists in terms of political accounta-bility that has been responsible for the near absence of financial regulation in this country.

benefitting from the existence of lax regulation, or that IFSRA was failing in its responsibilities. However, as an opposition finance spokesperson, my colleagues Eamon Ryan – the then Green Party spokesperson on Enterprise and employment – and our former party leader Trevor Sargent, and I would together have had a series of meetings with banking leaders that revealed to us the sense of hubris that surrounded the Irish banking industry.

The litany of bad practice we have since learned about, pertaining to activities within the banking sector, has varied from the incompetent to the morally suspect to the illegal. It has indicated a system of regulation that not only failed to act on its responsibilities but often chose not to act on those responsibilities at all. This is the essence of where we stand with lack of any effective regulation of the Irish financial services sector. It has not been the lack of resources. It has not been the lack of appropriate legislation, although the lack of clarity of the relationship between the Central Bank and IFSRA and the lack of balance between the prudential duty and consumer protection role hasn't helped. It has been the failure of culture and the deficit that exists in terms of political accountability that has been responsible for the near absence of financial regulation in this country.

Whether it has been the over-emphasis on property-based loans with the widespread use of personal guarantees, the scale of directors' loans, the avoidance of annual reporting procedures, the use of clients to buy stocks to artificially bolster share prices – we have all become familiar, over familiar, with the Byzantine world of Irish banking. The twin peaks of incompetence and illegality have been scaled with a frightening regularity. There is a public hunger that prosecutions should be made, and I hope they will be, but this will be more difficult to achieve because of the failure of financial regulation that has occurred.

It could be that many of the more shocking revelations have yet to be heard. Anecdotal evidence exists that some lenders linked lending to becoming involved directly in development projects, either individually or though a company structure. It seems clear that our major banks were not involved in this activity, but the extent to which it existed at all must be exposed, and the NAMA mechanism must not be used to allow any individual or financial institution escape responsibility for such activity.

Added to this is the convention that the elected political system should not criticize the appointed political system. I was surprised when ahead of any of opposition spokespersons on finance, I first called for the resignation of the Chief Executive of IFSRA. It could be that the culture where resignation is not expected and is not encouraged in elected political office, means that a type of political *omerta* extends to others in the public service. This is a culture that has to change if confidence is ever to be gained in financial regulation in this country. That has not been helped by the delay in removing the IFSRA Chief Executive, or the over- generous package offered on resignation, that seemed to indicate that no personal responsibility existed.

This is what we are leaving behind. New legislation and the new structures that result from it are where future financial regulation will lie in this country. The government has announced it intends to establish a new Central Banking Commission. This repairs in the first instance the rift caused by the 2002/2003 legislation. The new structure is meant to be more diffuse. **Having a number of commissioners should bring particular expertise to specialized areas of financial regulation. It is imperative, though, that at least one of these commissioners should not be an Irish national, and should be versed in international financial systems.**

Some recent legislation on corporate governance and director responsibility improves matters but does not go far enough. This legislation needs to be changed further. There are still too many grey areas that need to be cleared, such as the financial and business relationships with family members, and the permitted level and extent of cross board memberships.

A new financial regulatory system requires not only a new system but also a willingness to absorb best international practice. The recent visit to Ireland by Mr Bo Lundgren, a member of the Swedish cabinet at the time of their banking crisis of the early 1990s, was revelatory. His comments on his visit showed how banking crisis can be dealt with and in the short term, but it also showed how a better functioning regulatory system can identify problems earlier and provide the inform-

Our best learning should be from Canada, which stands alone in not having had a banking crisis, due largely to having a system of regulation that is more interventionist and more stringent in the standards applied to its banks.

ation to help bring about recovery.

Our best learning should be from Canada, which stands alone in not having had a banking crisis, due largely to having a system of regulation that is more interventionist and more stringent in the standards applied to its banks.

We can learn from international practices, but we must also work to ensure that international structures of regulation are put in place. This is especially important in the Eurozone area as a country we should be influencing the development of these new necessary structures.

The era of light-touch regulation was meant to unleash a period of self regulation within the industry itself. We have since learned a valuable lesson: that many within the financial services sector cannot be trusted to engage with ethical norms of behaviour. However, some self regulation is needed. In a post Lehmann Brothers world we cannot return to the level of salary payments and bonuses that were made. More openness and transparency is especially needed now with regard to how banks and other financial companies conduct their business. Diversity in investment and to some extent a return to the cautious optimism that had previously characterized banking is what is needed.

Chapter 3

CLIMBING OUT OF RECESSION – THE OPTIONS?

THE PLAN FOR RECOVERY
Brian Lenihan TD
Minister for Finance

RESTORING TRUST IS CRUCIAL
George Lee TD
Fine Gael Deputy and former Economics Editor, RTÉ

BUILDING A NEW REPUBLIC
Eamon Gilmore TD
Leader, Labour Party

THE STEPS TO ECONOMIC RECOVERY
Peter Bacon
Economic Consultant

The Plan for Recovery

Brian Lenihan TD
Minister for Finance

Born in Dublin and educated at Belvedere College, TCD, University of Cambridge and King's Inns. A former barrister, was first elected to Dáil Éireann in 1996 to succeed his father, Brian, in constituency of Dublin West. Appointed Minister for State in 2002 with responsibility for children in the Depts. of Health and Children and Justice, Equality and Law Reform. Appointed Minister for Justice, Equality and Law Reform in June 2007 following the General Election and Minister for Finance in 2008.

Causes of the crisis

If you look at what international commentators are saying, many are suggesting that the Celtic Tiger model has failed; the model is no longer sustainable in the Ireland of today. But in fact if you look at what happened in the 1990s, we saw huge export-led growth right up to the year 2000. That was the era that saw an alignment of our living standards with those of other European countries. Those exports are still there and still being made.

Our problems emerged due to overdependence on house building. New house building as a share of national wealth grew dramatically. Up to 2002, growth met capacity but after 2002 growth in house supply led to a radical deterioration. That over-dependence on construction was caused by a number of factors. Naturally and understandably the Opposition will hold the Government to account for that. But I did not see the Opposition parties at the time hold the Government to account for this at all. Hindsight is a wonderful thing. It is clear that the Government should have taken far more steps to correct that housing bubble. But no alternative was propounded on the other side of the benches in Leinster House.

Our problems emerged due to overdependence on house building. New house building as a share of national wealth grew dramatically. Up to 2002, growth met capacity but after 2002 growth in house supply led to a radical deterioration.

If you have phenomenal growth year on year it is very difficult to prick that bubble, to get a soft landing or persuade people that competitive-ness should transcend all other con-siderations.

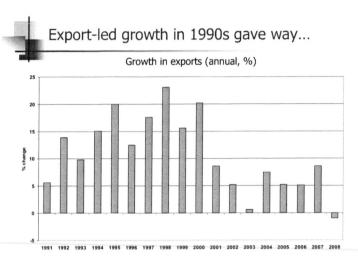

Figure 1

We have to face facts, we all got something out of the Celtic Tiger, or at least the vast majority got something out of the Celtic Tiger. It was not something for bankers and developers.

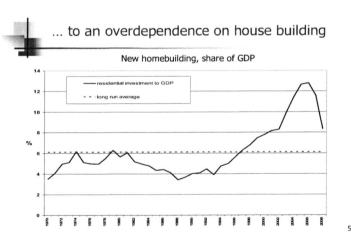

Figure 2

It is very clear that the fundamental problem we have been facing since the turn of the millennium, is a loss in competitiveness. Some of that can be accounted for by the fact that we are in a strong exchange rate area. But it is also due to excessive costs of labour, of public services and of sheltered sectors overcharging for goods and services. I am not certain that anybody in public life, Government or Opposition, could have dealt with that competitiveness issue. Because we all know the sheer scale of the growth we saw in Ireland from the mid-90s on.

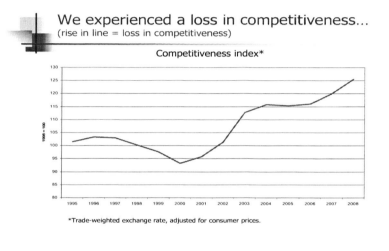

We experienced a loss in competitiveness...
(rise in line = loss in competitiveness)

Competitiveness index*

*Trade-weighted exchange rate, adjusted for consumer prices.

6

Figure 3

If you have phenomenal growth year on year it is very difficult to prick that bubble, to get a soft landing or persuade people that competitiveness should transcend all other considerations. We have to create the Ireland of our dreams in terms of public services, health, education and welfare but this all has to be paid for and it can only be paid for through the strength of the productive economy. That productive economy can only flourish if it is competitive in the wider world. We cannot expect the rest of the world to owe us a living. That is what independence meant in the 1920s as much as it means now.

During the years from 2003 to 2007, there were substantial benefits from what the Government did. There were social welfare increases of 7 to 10 per cent every year. There was huge spending

In the end, when it comes to day-to-day expenditure, a state is like a household, it has to live within its means. We have lived within our means for two decades but we are not living within our means at present. Addressing that is a fundamental issue which any Irish Government has to face.

What are the options? There is only one possible path to recovery and there are three elements to it. One is to have sustainable public finances, the second is to regain our competitiveness, boost our employment and create real jobs and the third is to repair our banking system.

on education. Spending per student rose by more than one-third at primary and secondary levels. Spending on health increased by 80 per cent. The numbers employed in the health sector rose by 15 per cent. Public sector wages rose 6 per cent every year. Capital expenditure of €31 billion took place during the boom years. We all know what was done, what is going on and still to be completed in terms of national motorway networks. Income tax cuts of €3.5 billion were made and a Pension Reserve Fund of €21 billion was built up.

We have to face facts, we all got something out of the Celtic Tiger, or at least the vast majority got something out of the Celtic Tiger. It was not something for bankers and developers. It led to social welfare increases, public services and increased living standards for many citizens. That is something very welcome and something we all struggled for and wanted. Yes, the economy has been very badly affected, not just by domestic factors but by the worst global recession since the Great Depression. There is no point in being insular in our attitudes. If there is an imbalance in the public finances and we had gone a little bit too far after two decades of unrivalled prosperity in terms of our public services that can be corrected. But all this correction has to take place not in a uniquely national context but in an international context where many other countries are experiencing the exact same problems as ourselves. Ireland is not unique and when we study what has happened in other countries we learn from them. We do not, as Seán Lemass always said, feel sorry for ourselves all the time. We look at what we can do for ourselves when we are faced with a crisis which is not just a local crisis but an international crisis.

Look at the position in the United Kingdom with a more than 4 per cent decline in national wealth this year. Look at the position in the United States where this is approaching a 2.5 per cent decline. Look at the position among our partners in the Euro area where the decline is almost 5 per cent. The idea that our problems are unique is a fallacy.

Remedies

What are the options? There is only one possible path to recovery and there are three elements to it. One is to have sustainable public finances, the second is to regain our competitiveness, boost our employment and create real jobs and the third is to repair our banking system. These remedies are complementary. If Ireland wants to pay its way in the world and get on as a country, then all these elements must be addressed.

Sustainable public finances

There is no point when discussing the public finances in suggesting that this has all been caused by bankers. If we had no banking problem, if we had no developer problem, we would still have a public finance problem. From 2000 to 2007, there was a broad match between revenue and spending. But since then there has been a marked deterioration. On the revenue side, there has been a deterioration because of the big decline in discretionary taxes and receipts from stamp duty, capital gains and other forms of tax. We harvested those taxes in the good times but they are not available to us now. Big amounts of them are not going to become available in the future because asset values have declined and hence capital gains tax receipts are not going to increase.

I have made it very clear that I do not intend to increase the burden of taxation to any great extent in the next Budget. It is not open to us to do it. Our income tax levels were increased in the September Budget last year and in the Supplementary Budget in April. That had to be done because of the scale of the decline in our income tax receipts. We had the lowest income tax in the world apart from two countries. But there is a limit to the extent to which you can increase income tax. There is a very definite limit because Ireland will not attract investment or any kind of economic development if we raise income tax to unsustainable levels.

We increased our expenditures to a level where there is now a €20 billion gap between spending and revenue. Some of that gap relates to investment expenditure which is very important such as investment in roads, infrastructure, science and technology. We can justify asking our children to pay interest on that borrowing. We cannot justify asking our children to pay the cost of our own salaries as public servants or the cost of welfare.

So there has been a 7 per cent improvement in our unit labour competitiveness in the last year. That is a tremendous tribute to Irish workers, public servants and those in the private sector who have made huge adjustments.

There is no doubt that the banks were utterly delinquent in borrowing vast sums overseas.

Bank deposits were guaranteed by the Government last September because we believed the only option was to give a very clear message to the outside world that Ireland was not going to follow the path of Iceland.

It is not as if a stimulus and the injection of more cash is suddenly going to create loads more jobs. Were that the case, I would have recourse to it immediately.

We have to face that issue. And it is not an issue that can be postponed forever. Because we are doing it now and the interest payments mount up. In the end, when it comes to day-to-day expenditure, a state is like a household, it has to live within its means. We have lived within our means for two decades but we are not living within our means at present. Addressing that is a fundamental issue which any Irish Government has to face. Last year, when we saw for the first time the radical drop in tax revenues, we immediately moved to take action. In July 2008 we contained expenditure by €1 billion. In the October Budget, we carried expenditure containment further. Remember that expenditure was growing at 8 per cent. We drew that back to less than nought per cent for all of the Government Departments except Health, Education and Social Welfare. We raised taxes in that Budget. In February, because the position had deteriorated further, we were obliged to look for further savings of €2 billion and included in that the pay reduction for the public sector through the pension levy. Then in April 2009 the Supplementary Budget saw further expenditure reductions and revenue increases. All that has added up to a 5 per cent adjustment in our national wealth this year. Suppose we had not done that, what would have happened? Our borrowing requirement would have gone to over 15 per cent of our annual wealth. There is no country in Europe at the 10.75 per cent level which we will be at this year. It was essential that this corrective action take place. It is not something that Europe forced upon us. We knew that this would not be popular but we knew that this was required to keep this country on the road.

We have set out a multi-year fiscal consolidation programme leading to an adjustment of €4 billion in 2010 and 2011. The European Commission has endorsed these actions. We have not just set out that plan for the benefit of the European Commission in Brussels. We have set it out because it will build up confidence in Ireland overseas. This will allow us to borrow the money we need to keep building roads, schools, piers and industries. We need to do this also so we can continue to pay public servants and welfare payments some of which have to be funded by borrowing.

An argument made repeatedly is that we should engage in a stimulus. The point to make is that we are borrowing 10.75 per cent of our annual national wealth and that is a big stimulus in itself. Additional borrowing will push up the costs of servicing our debt and a stimulus leaks out of a small open economy through higher imports. It is not as if a stimulus and the injection of more cash is suddenly going to create many more jobs. Were that the case, I would have recourse to it immediately. The stimulus might well lead to an increased purchase of imported goods, increased foreign holidays and further deterioration in the State's overall position.

Regaining competitiveness and boosting employment

The public finances are important, but not the only problem we face. We have to boost employment and create jobs. In recent years, we have been very successful in building up real jobs through export-driven industries. But our pay rates are well above all of the European averages. When I was appointed Minister for Finance we had the highest unit labour cost of any country in the Euro zone, way out of line with every other country. In the last year, we have seen rapid adjustments in our unit labour costs. The European Commission projects that Ireland will see this year an average 4 per cent reduction in unit labour costs; the EU average is a 3 per cent increase. So there has been a 7 per cent improvement in our unit labour competitiveness in the last year. That is a tremendous tribute to Irish workers, public servants and those in the private sector who have made huge adjustments. We all know what adjustments in the private sector have involved: people taking huge wage cuts to avoid unemployment, in some cases as high as 30 and 40 per cent. We also know that there are those who have taken more modest decreases or have taken pay freezes, giving up bonuses, overtime and the like. We also know that in the private sector there are still some sheltered sectors that have had pay increases so there has been a very wide divergence in private sector pay rates, between plus 3 and minus 30 or 40 per cent. We know in the public sector the pension levy averages out at a minus 6.8 per cent reduction in public salaries, higher for those at the top and lower for those at the bottom.

The European Central Bank is willing to honour that paper, giving the banks cash for that paper. In return, the banks can focus on lending to small and medium-sized enterprises and households while NAMA works out the distressed loans over time.

That is how you regain competitiveness in unit labour and terms. It is something we have to do, and something no other European country is doing

Repairing the banking system

There is no doubt that the banks were utterly delinquent in borrowing vast sums overseas. The banks became increasingly stressed as the world banking system became stressed. Governments throughout the world have not had to face a banking crisis on this scale since 1929. Most of us heard about what happened in 1929 from our parents and grandparents. The Stock Exchange collapsed in New York in the famous Great Crash of 1929. In those days we did not have the type of technology we have now and it took a long time for signals of that stock crash to transmit themselves through different economic markets. In the United States, many banks had loaned money to Stock Exchange speculators much as they loaned money in Ireland to building speculators. The Stock Exchange speculators went bust very quickly. But the United States banking system tottered on until early 1930. Depositors then began to form queues at banks to demand their money back and the banking system went into collapse. Credit did not just dry up in the economy, it collapsed completely. The United States found itself by 1933 with 33 per cent unemployment. So when you let banks collapse it is not a cost free decision. If you decide to let a bank go to the wall, there are very big consequences. President Obama has spoken very well about this, pointing out that there is the natural and understandable wish to let those who loan the money to the banks suffer. But if you do let them suffer, the consequences spread the arc of suffering to a very wide degree. Because when a bank collapses, all its depositors and all those who the bank owes money to, lose their deposits. That means small businesses, cooperatives and individuals. It is right across the board. Bank deposits were guaranteed by the Government last September because we believed the only option was to give a very clear message to the outside world that Ireland was not going to follow the path of Iceland. Ireland's credit was such that we would stand

There is no doubt that the banks were utterly delinquent in borrowing vast sums overseas.

behind those who had deposits in the banks, who had loaned to the banks and insure that the banks did not collapse. And we succeeded in that.

We felt that it was important for the larger banks that everyone dealing with them understood that these banks were creditworthy and we stood behind them. We believed in the case of Anglo-Irish Bank that the country could not stand the strain of an €80 billion default. That is half our national wealth. Were we to go down that road, we would have a collapsed economy as well as a collapsed banking system. So there is no point pretending that these are easy decisions. It is very easy to be populist about them and say the wrong track was taken. We had to do it; we have to protect the reputation of this country because the Government is borrowing money to fund the country. The Government would not be able to borrow a cent if we permitted the banks to go into default. That is the reality of the fiscal position. Any high school economic analyst will tell you that.

What we had to do, having given the guarantee, was to reform the Irish banks, to remove the personnel at board and executive level who caused these problems. That cannot be done overnight. In addition, the State has had to invest in the banking system and get a definite rate of return as we have done. We had to nationalize Anglo-Irish Bank because it was such a mess. We had to take a 25 per cent share in Bank of Ireland and Allied Irish Bank. We are getting an 8 per cent return on the €7 billion we invested in the latter banks. That stake has gone up in value since I purchased it last February and will go straight into our National Pension Fund. We get something in return for the rescue we were obliged to carry out. I recall when Fine Gael was in Government in 1984, Allied Irish Bank was bailed out and not a penny came back to the tax-payer. That will not happen on my watch.

In every step I have taken in relation to the banking system I have made sure that the tax-payer gets a definite return; that as well as socializing losses we socialize gains. We do not have a choice about this and it is not unique. What we have done in Ireland is being done by the British Government, by the authorities in the United States and the recommended course of action of the G-7. We cannot have a repeat of 1929. We cannot have a position where we decide that the whole motor of the economy should seize up; we should simply close down banks and

Bank deposits were guaranteed by the Government last September because we believed the only option was to give a very clear message to the outside world that Ireland was not going to follow the path of Iceland.

If you do not clean up balance sheets and reassure the world that the banks are fit to lend to, you have continued uncertainty about the operation of these institutions. So we will issue paper to the banks under NAMA.

allow mass unemployment and a total cessation of economic activity take place. Of course, we have to ensure that banks never behave like this again, that the tax-payer and the public who invested in and rescued them are rewarded. We have to replace the irresponsible bonus-driven culture of reckless lending with a culture which encourages lending to people who create jobs in the economy, householders who want to make improvements to their houses and green changes that have to take place throughout our economy.

Banks cannot lend unless they attract funds. That is the core problem. If you do not give a guarantee that funds are safe you are not going to have any funds. If you do not clean up balance sheets and reassure the world that the banks are fit to lend to, you have continued uncertainty about the operation of these institutions. So we will issue paper to the banks under NAMA. The European Central Bank is willing to honour that paper, giving the banks cash for that paper. In return, the banks can focus on lending to small and medium-sized enterprises and households while NAMA works out the distressed loans over time.

NAMA will buy the loans at a discount. We have made it clear in the case of the two larger banks that if their losses are of a scale which requires fresh capital, we will invest that capital and minimize the risk to the taxpayer, and insure that the taxpayer benefits from the upswing. Borrowers, those to whom the banks extended money, will remain fully liable for the full value of their loans. This is not a bailout for borrowers or developers as has been constantly misrepresented. NAMA will have to pay its own way. The interest received on the performing loans which are working out will roughly match the interest paid on the bonds and the proceeds on the loan repayments and the property sales will pay off the bonds in full. If there is any further shortfall at the end of ten years we can levy the banks.

Hope for the future

There are real signs of hope. Our exports have proven resilient and they will drive growth and jobs as competitiveness improves. Our exports have seen a decline of 3 per cent but this is in contrast with much larger declines in other countries. Our exports have remained remarkably robust. Our pharmaceuticals, chemicals, ICT and other industries are still exporting vigorously and there is big demand for their products. Of course agriculture is going through a very difficult patch and tourism has seen a decline in numbers. But a mere 3 per cent decline in exports suggests that there is an underlying strength in the Irish economy, a labour force which is hard-working prepared to take the pain. This is a labour force which is also one of the best educated in Europe; after Sweden it has the highest proportion of third level graduates.

Our external position is also moving into balance. Ireland from 2004 on began to have a big balance of payments deficit; we owed the world far more than the world owed us. This year the deficit has contracted to less than 1 per cent caused by the strength of our exports and of course by the weakness of consumer demand. But next year the forecast is that we are going to have a balance of payments surplus. That is not what is happening in Iceland or Hungary or any of those countries that got into difficulties in Europe. This surplus is there because of the underlying strength in the Irish economy.

We cannot postpone the adjustment indefinitely but if we make the adjustment, have better public services and make them more efficient, improve our competitiveness and take the necessary adjustment now we will bequeath something very good to those who come after us. We did it before in 1987 after years of dithering. I grew to manhood in the late 70s and early 80s and I remember how successive governments of my own Party under Mr Haughey and of Fine Gael under Dr FitzGerald dithered and dithered, refusing to make decisions, pandering to vested interests. Then Ray McSharry and others in 1987 took steps that put this country on a road to recovery. That is what is needed now, not dithering, posturing and postponement, but facing up to the issues.

We were founded as an impoverished State in 1922 when the

I grew to manhood in the late 70s and early 80s and I remember how successive governments of my own Party under Mr Haughey and of Fine Gael under Dr FitzGerald dithered and dithered, refusing to make decisions, pandering to vested interests. Then Ray McSharry and others in 1987 took steps that put this country on a road to recovery.

We will have that recovery. Let us make that bit of an extra effort now, doing it not just for our own sake but for the sake of our kids who want to live in an Ireland that is not Argentina, defaulting on its debts, or Uruguay pretending that it can have public services it cannot afford. Let us be a responsible country.

British cleared everything bar the typewriters out of the country. We built a successful State and I give all credit to the Cumann na nGaedhael element who founded the State to do that. In the 1930s, we had to face a crisis under de Valera, MacEntee and Lemass when we had an economic war. We fought through them. In the 1950s we had an intellectual, cultural and economic stagnation and Seán Lemass led us out of it. We can bring ourselves out of this as well. This is not a case of us going back to the 80s, 70s and beyond, but is a case of us facing up to the reality which Colm McCarthy has pointed out, which the World Bank has pointed out, which the European authorities have pointed out, which every economic commentator has pointed out, that we have gone that bit beyond what we can afford for ourselves.

We have the capacity to do that unlike a lot of bigger countries. IMF economists came here in May and they interrogated me at length. They said our policies are right, what is needed now for recovery is 'determined execution' of NAMA and the Government's budget plans. We will have that recovery. Let us make that bit of an extra effort now, doing it not just for our own sake but for the sake of our kids who want to live in an Ireland that is not Argentina, defaulting on its debts, or Uruguay pretending that it can have public services it cannot afford. Let us be a responsible country. That is, the country our forefathers fought for, a country that takes responsibility for itself in the best sense of that word, a sinn féin country, a country that believes not just in ourselves alone, but ourselves with others, working together, building up a community, building up public services we want but recognizing where we are in the world and what we can afford.

Restoring Trust is Crucial

George Lee TD

Fine Gael Deputy and former Economics Editor, RTÉ

Born in Dublin and educated at UCD (BA in Economics) and London School of Economics (MSc). Prior to move to broadcasting, was Senior Economist at Riada Stockbrokers, Treasury Economist with FTI and an Economist with the Central Bank. Joined RTÉ in 1992 and appointed Economics Editor in 1996. Won Journalist of the Year award in 1998 for reporting on tax evasion and overcharging in National Irish Bank. Elected to Dáil Éireann in 2009 By-Election for Dublin South constituency.

Ireland is in the grip of one of the biggest economic and social challenges any country has faced in modern history. In its latest economic commentary, the International Monetary Fund described what we are going through as the deepest slump in economic activity any country has experienced since at least the Second World War. More recently, the Economic and Social Research Institute estimated that GNP per capita here will have declined by 16.5 per cent by 2010.

At the start of 2007, just before the last General election, the Department of Finance estimated that by this year, 2009, the exchequer would collect just over €56 billion in taxes on economic activity of all sorts. That is a very big sum, and it was on the basis of that €56 billion sum – and the official forecast that there would be even more money available in 2010 and 2011 – that all political parties drew up their election manifestos and packed them with lavish promises for the electorate in 2007.

What a disaster all that has turned out to be. Were it not for massive tax hikes in the two budgets since last October the actual amount of tax collected in 2009 would be less than €31 billion – that is 45 per cent short of the €56 billion we were led to believe would be available just two years ago. The result of course is a requirement for the Government to borrow over €20 billion to run the economy this year.

Official figures demonstrate just how badly our taxation system is structured. The Government budgeted in April this year

What a disaster all that has turned out to be. Were it not for massive tax hikes in the two budgets since last October the actual amount of tax collected in 2009 would be less than €31 billion - that is 45 per cent short of the €56 billion we were led to believe would be available just two years ago.

It is a mistake to proceed to correct the sudden and catastrophic imbalances that have opened up in our public finances at the pace that is now being planned.

Unless the global economy experiences the fastest revival since Lazarus got up out of his bed and walked then the burden of fiscal adjustment the Government is planning to place on the Irish public may be too great.

for economic activity to contract by 7.75 per cent in 2009. To deal with the effect of that, they raised taxes by €3.75 billion between the October and April budgets. If they had not done so, the overall tax revenue forecast for 2009 would be as low as €30.6 billion, down from €42 billion in 2008. That is a fall of 27 per cent in taxes paid as a direct result of a 7.75 per cent slump in economic activity.

What we are going through now is not a normal recession. Our banking system has collapsed, our prosperity has been decimated, our unemployment rate has soared and living standards are plummeting. There is nothing but fear and retrenchment among business and workers alike, and precious little hope is being offered by those in charge. The fact that the Government feels it has no choice but to cut public spending so drastically and raise taxes so spectacularly at this, the worst possible moment, is evidence of its massive failure. Fiscal retrenchment on the scale being considered will make matters far worse, not better, at this point in time.

It is a mistake to proceed to correct the sudden and catastrophic imbalances that have opened up in our public finances at the pace that is now being planned. The Government's objective is to bring our general Government deficit back down to 3 per cent of GDP by 2013. This has been forced upon us by the rules of Europe's Stability and Growth pact – the rules of fiscal management that came as part and parcel of membership of the Euro. Under normal circumstances these are good rules, designed to underpin the integrity of the single currency. However these are not normal circumstances.

The blow to the Irish economy has been far too severe. In the late 1980s and throughout the 1990s, Ireland made great efforts to qualify for full membership of Europe's fledgling economic and monetary union. There were fears that in such a union, economic activity and wealth would migrate to the centre, and that peripheral countries like Ireland might do poorly. Regional transfer policies including structural and cohesion funds were central to addressing those fears and to ensuring a more level playing field. It was never Europe's intention to allow Ireland to wither in a monetary union or to turn into what, in 1988, former Central Bank Governor

Maurice Doyle labelled the 'Appalachia' of Europe'.

The best cure for the fiscal nightmare that we are in is the resumption of robust economic growth. Such economic growth means more activity; more activity means more revenue for the government and some light at the end of the tunnel. The problem is of course, that we cannot tell when global economic growth will resume, or how strong it might be, or how the type of international economy that emerges might suit Ireland. The international environment is outside of our control. In the meantime, the Government's strategy is to do all in its power to prepare for it by slimming down the public sector, raising taxes on all and sundry, and ploughing billions of euro into our broken banking system. There are a lot of risks in all of that. Surely it is expecting too much of heavily indebted, heavily taxed, insecure, fearful domestic taxpayers to fund all of this out of declining wages and fewer jobs. Unless the global economy experiences the fastest revival since Lazarus got up out of his bed and walked then the burden of fiscal adjustment the Government is planning to place on the Irish public may be too great. Surely a stronger case could be made at European level for greater recognition of the real difficulties we are in and of the fact that the cure as proposed by conventional economics runs a very significant risk of making our problems substantially worse. What is so sacred anyway about having a General Government deficit of 3 per cent of GDP by 2013, especially if achieving that target runs the risk of turning an economic recession into a depression?

It is true that one of the lessons of the 1980s was that running large fiscal deficits and losing control of our public finances ruined the economy. And it is true that a cheaper public sector will reduce the burden on the productive sector of our economy; that it can contribute to lower taxes than we otherwise might have; and that all these things can help improve competitiveness. But timing is important. If we try to do it all too aggressively, and the global economy takes longer to recover than we expect, then the social and political cost could be extremely high. In that regard trying to adjust our public finances too aggressively without at the same time finding new ways to promote economic growth could prove to be disastrous.

But the need for a correction in our public finances is not the only area in which we risk paying an extremely high price for

Why would any region in a big economic and monetary union feel it is imperative to save every single bank in its region and to pile the cost of those bailouts onto the backs of ordinary taxpayers? It defies logic. Banks go bust elsewhere quite regularly, even in the United States.

irresponsibility. Our rush to bail out banks and save each and every one of them at great expense to ordinary taxpayers is extremely risky. Ireland is now a regional economy in a much larger economic and monetary union. We no longer have our own money, or our own exchange rate, or our own interest rate. In addition, our own Central Bank has no real independent control over banking regulation or monetary policy – that is all coming from Frankfurt. We have entered a new monetary world. We have been there for all of the past decade. Yet the Government's mindset in relation to our banks appears to be stuck in the last century.

Why? At the height of their mad lending spree the Irish banks were borrowing the equivalent of 45 per cent of GDP on international money markets, and lending it on to property developers and investors and others here. Any banks could have done that – they would not have had to be Irish owned.

Why would any region in a big economic and monetary union feel it is imperative to save every single bank in its region and to pile the cost of those bailouts on to the backs of ordinary taxpayers? It defies logic. Banks go bust elsewhere quite regularly, even in the United States. Why does our Government think all Irish banks must be saved irrespective of the cost? The Taoiseach has been recently quoted as saying he would be there with a cheque book to save any Irish bank. That's barmy! Why? At the height of their mad lending spree the Irish banks were borrowing the equivalent of 45 per cent of GDP on international money markets, and lending it on to property developers and investors and others here. Any banks could have done that – they would not have had to be Irish owned.

Irish taxpayers are now far too exposed to the losses in relation to the banking system.

Last September, the Government gave the most generous guarantee that any government has ever given to a banking sector in the face of a crisis. It promised that Irish taxpayers would refund all deposits in Irish banks if those deposits were lost due to a bank failure. It also promised that ordinary taxpayers would pick up the bill for any defaults on any money loaned to an Irish bank by any other banks or investors including bond holders. The guarantee was to last for two years until 2010. At the time this guarantee was portrayed by the Government as essential in order to ensure a supply of liquidity to the Irish banking system. It was all done behind closed doors and the advice given, as well as the debates that took place, were secret.

The guarantee that was given is too generous. No other country anywhere gave as much. Irish taxpayers are now far too exposed to the losses in relation to the banking system. In the meantime seven billion euro of public money have been invested into the banking system with precious little in terms of new lending into the economy to show for it. There is a widespread view among the public that when it comes to banking we are paying too much for too little – and this is before we learn how much the proposed national asset management agency will pay our damaged banks for their distressed loans.

There is no sane reason why Irish taxpayers should continue protecting investors who bought bonds issued by Irish banks. Those investors are private risk takers and they should be made live with the consequence of the risks they have taken. The protection given by the guarantee to bond investors in Irish banks should be removed next September when the first two-year term for that guarantee is up. This should not preclude the Government from renewing the guarantee for normal wholesale borrowing by Irish banks. It would, however, help send a message to the international financial markets that the Irish government is reducing its debt exposure in a rational way and is not lumbering ordinary taxpayers with debts obligations they should have no liability for.

Ireland has lived though an era of enormous irresponsibility. We had irresponsibility in the way the Government managed the economy; irresponsibility in banking; irresponsibility by developers and associated professions; we had irresponsibility in the personal sector as evidenced by the enormous debts people took on; irresponsibility in so many others sectors too. The result of all that irresponsibility now is that trust has been shattered. The restoration of trust is essential to the restoration of our prosperity. There can be no greater demonstration of the massive economic cost of the breakdown of trust than what happened to all those who invested in the stock market. When the banks no longer trusted each other, they stopped lending, stock markets and economies collapsed, and prosperity has been destroyed.

It seems unlikely that our economy can be restored to full health without a restoration of trust. This represents an enormous challenge because trust once it has been broken is extremely difficult to restore. What Ireland needs is a new era of responsibility; an era where Government takes responsibility

The protection given by the guarantee to bond investors in Irish banks should be removed next September when the first two-year term for that guarantee is up.

Ireland has lived though an era of enormous irresponsibility.

We need a new an era where political leaders take responsibility for the mistakes they have made.

and stands up for ordinary people in the face of powerful vested interests; an era where banks are held to account for the massive public rescue effort they have been gifted with and are forced to play a far more active part in the restoration of credit flows throughout the economy; an era where the fiscal burden of adjustment placed on ordinary people takes into account the responsibility to ensure that those very people are not broken by the weight of that burden and an unacceptable pace of adjustment. We need a new era where political leaders take responsibility for the mistakes they have made. They need to recognize that when they fail to live up to their responsibilities then the trust of the people is lost. Without that trust the Government cannot lead.

Building a New Republic

Eamon Gilmore TD
Leader, Labour Party

Born in Galway and educated at Garbally College, Ballinasloe and NUIG (BA). Former trade union official, former President of USI 1976-8. First elected to Dáil Éireann for Dún Laoghaire in 1989. One of the six Worker Party deputies in the 26th Dáil who formed a new party, Democratic Left. Minister of State at the Dept. of the Marine (1994-7). Was Labour Spokesperson on Communications and Natural Resources (2002-2004) and Spokesperson on Environment and Local Government from 2004 until his uncontested election to leadership of Labour Party in September 2007.

Now, more than ever, we need a sense of direction, a sense of what we are trying to achieve, of what we are about. It would be easy to be downcast at the scale of our problems. The economy is in deep trouble, and there are multiple crises to be addressed. But we have been in trouble before. We have had crises before, and we have dealt with them. More than that, we have shown before that, as a people, we can emerge from a crisis and build something new and better.

We are, if we choose to be, at a major turning point in the history of our country. Over the coming years, we will be celebrating a number of centenaries that mark the beginning of independent Ireland-the Lockout, the Rising, the First Dáil. These were all events that took place as Ireland struggled to gain political independence. In the forty years that followed, the first phase of the history of our state was devoted to consolidating that independence. It was a vital phase in our history, with many accomplishments, but it ended in crisis. A profound crisis – one which tested our people to the limit. T.K. Whitaker has described that moment in history in the following terms:

> the years 1955-56 had plumbed the depths of hopelessness. One of the recurring series of balance-of-payments crises was overcome, but only at the cost of stagnation, high unemployment and emigration. The mood of despondency was palpable. Something had to be done or the achievement of national independence would prove to have been a futility.

Now again, we must launch a new stage in our history. Call it what you will: a new stage, a third act, a paradigm shift, the Fair Society, or an expression that I find increasingly appealing, The New Republic.

And yet, from that moment of despair was built a national revival. It began with the document Economic Development and the First Economic Programme, which started to open up the economy. But opening up the economy was only a prelude to broader change – to the opening up of society. Over the decades that followed, Ireland changed – or rather was changed – radically: free education, membership of the European Union, the expansion of third level education, the liberal agenda. The achievement of political freedom was followed by the achievement of personal freedom.

It did not happen on its own. It happened because people made it happen. People who were mortally sick of watching their brothers and uncles carry cardboard suitcases onto the boat to England, to work in labouring jobs and live in doss houses. People who had had enough of an over-bearing Church and an over-bearing society, and were prepared to demand change. People saw that there was no contradiction between being fully Irish and being fully engaged with the wider world.

Now again, we are at a moment of crisis. Now again, we must launch a new stage in our history. Call it what you will: a new stage, a third act, a paradigm shift, the Fair Society, or an expression that I find increasingly appealing, The New Republic.

We have an economic crisis, but it is part of a political and social crisis. The model that drove us since the late 1950s has been under pressure for some years. We built a strong open, exporting economy, but it was hi-jacked by property developers and speculators. We embraced the European Union, but we failed to convince our people of the merits of that membership. We opened up society, and gave people greater freedom, but we have seen a coarsening of society in the wave of crime and death driven by drug crime.

Too often, our people were treated as economic units, not as members of a society subjected to poor planning, high house prices, inadequate services, and now left with the bill. Our economic model was simply not environmentally or socially sustainable. Of our present housing stock, approximately one third was added in the past 10 years, yet the environmental standards to which they were built were shamefully inadequate.

We built a strong open, exporting economy, but it was hi-jacked by property developers and speculators.

Despite the rising tide, Ireland has remained one of the most unequal societies in the developed world. In the prosperous times, social welfare rates increased, but the opportunity to reform the social welfare system – to make a trampoline out of a safety net – was passed up. We did not grapple with our social problems with any degree of determination or vigour.

We suffered too from a lack of confidence and ambition. In 2006, at the height of the boom, it was deemed acceptable for Government to set a target that illiteracy would be lowered to 15 per cent by 2016. In other words, it was acceptable that one in six children in disadvantaged schools would have reading problems.

The great opportunities to reform public services were missed. In 2001, Labour proposed universal health insurance as the means to develop a better and fairer health service. Since then, health spending has increased by €10 billion, the policy of building super-private clinics has utterly failed and we are left with the bureaucratic monster that is the HSE. So, the task that confronts us now is a great one. But the scale of our ambition must also be great; to avoid another lost decade, by making the right decisions on the economy. But at the same time, we must launch a new phase in our history to build a New Republic marked by both responsibility and expectation. That is, where the opportunities available to our citizens are matched by their sense of responsibility to the State and to each other; a place where Government is exercised, not on behalf of a privileged few, but on behalf of the many; where personal freedom is buttressed by social solidarity.

The first three building blocks of that New Republic are a return to full employment, a health service that is both excellent and equitable, and an outstanding system of free education. We must finish the educational revolution. We must establish, and vindicate, as an indisputable element of citizenship, the right to read.

The New Republic must be based on building a sustainable and enduring progress which meets our global obligations on aid and carbon reduction which marks Ireland out, not as the Klondike of Europe, but as the clean man of Europe. That progress will not just be measured in material terms. The yardstick by which we measure the quality of our children's lives

We did not grapple with our social problems with any degree of determination or vigour.

The first three building blocks of that New Republic are a return to full employment, a health service that is both excellent and equitable, and an outstanding system of free education.

cannot be the designer brand on the back of their jeans. We will measure our legacy to them in the quality of their lives, the texture of their civilization, their sense of duty to each other and their contribution to the world.

To achieve this, we will need to pursue an agenda of reform led by reform of Government itself. We cannot pretend that the difficulties we face are solely the result of the global financial turmoil, or of the irresponsible actions of a few. We are where we are because there have been profound failures of governance. This is the second time in a generation that Ireland has been brought to the brink of bankruptcy. Once, between 1977 and 1981, when a reckless and divided Fianna Fáil abandoned all restraint, and created a national debt that took a decade to resolve. Now again, after twelve years when an export boom was allowed to be turned into a property bubble, and the exchequer was once again turned into an electoral war-chest, we have an even worse crisis.

> **This is the second time in a generation that Ireland has been brought to the brink of bankruptcy. Once, between 1977 and 1981, when a reckless and divided Fianna Fáil abandoned all restraint, and created a national debt that took a decade to resolve.**

But of course, we must begin by confronting the immediate economic crisis. This crisis has three dimensions – the banking sector, the public deficit, and the crisis in the real economy – the loss of jobs and businesses. These three dimensions are inter-linked. Each affects the others, and each must be dealt with in parallel.

My chief criticism of the Government has been its almost exclusive concentration on the banks and the public finances, and the relatively limited attention that has been given to the real economy. That is a mistake. Every worker who loses his or her job costs the exchequer at least €20,000 in taxes foregone and social welfare benefits paid. Every person who loses his or her job is potentially another mortgage in arrears and another strain on the banking sector.

So, we must have a strategy to deal with the crisis in the real economy, as well as the problems in the banking sector. I want to see more done to support enterprise. I want to see a meaningful scheme emerging from the social partnership talks that would help to protect existing jobs. I want to see support being provided where employers create new jobs. Labour has proposed a time-limited PRSI exemption where a firm creates a new job that is filled by someone on the live register.

I have also been arguing for a new approach to public

investment. With the fall in economic output, we must reassess our infrastructural requirements. Yet, we also know that there are very many infrastructural projects that could be carried out, which would yield a positive long-term return to our economy. There are hundreds of schools with poor quality buildings. There are urban regeneration projects that are ready to go, but unfunded.

We need a new assessment of the size of the capital spending envelope over the coming years and how it should be allocated. And we should be prepared to front-load that allocation. There is an opportunity to make those investments now, when there is spare capacity in the building sector, and tender prices are at an historic low.

To drive this process, Labour has been calling for a new National Development Plan to be drawn up. We believe there is potential for some of it to be funded through National Recovery Bonds which could potentially allow the Government to raise funds on more favourable terms than are available through money markets. We have proposed a State Investment Bank that would play a key role in financing investment by the State, semi-state and private sectors.

For more than a year now, Labour has been arguing for a determined effort to be made in providing new opportunities for people who have lost their jobs. It is simply not economically, socially or morally sustainable for the state to sit back and ignore half a million people on the live register. There are a variety of needs, and there must be a variety of responses. We know, for example, that construction employment will not return to former levels, so there are construction workers who need new skills and training to find work in other sectors. We need work experience programmes for them.

There can be no doubt that dealing with the banking crisis is absolutely essential. Where I differ from the Government is on the best means of doing it. I opposed the blanket guarantee, because it was too far-reaching, and because it handed over too much power to the banks. Now, we see the natural consequence of that decision, in NAMA. I do not say that NAMA will not work – eventually. But it will only work after the state has taken on an unacceptably high burden of risk. The approach Labour has favoured, of temporary nationalization, allows the bad loans to be

It is simply not economically, socially or morally sustainable for the state to sit back and ignore half a million people on the live register.

dealt with, but at a lower risk to the state.

We know that there is a need for public sector reform. But what we need is surgery, not butchery. If we try to roll back the clock by five or six years to undo the recent expenditure growth, then we will fail. What we need is to look forward five or six years, and, through fundamental reform, build a leaner, more effective public service. The cuts agenda must not stand in the way of more fundamental reform. We will not re-build the health service unless we fundamentally change it, through universal health insurance. We will not reform local Government though arbitrary cuts, but by reform which sets out a clear division of responsibilities between local, regional and national level.

We are living through dark and difficult times. We are being confronted by failures of the past. We are living though a period which is visiting pain on those who deserve no share of it. We have difficult days ahead. And yet, there is still potential. There is still the opportunity to build a New Republic.

The Steps to Economic Recovery

Peter Bacon
Economic Consultant, Peter Bacon and Associates.

Grew up in Drumcondra and attended Coláiste Mhuire, Parnell Square. Has PhD in Economics from TCD. Entered Dept. of Finance in 1975 and later moved to OECD, Paris. Worked in ESRI and World Bank before joining Goodbody Stockbrokers as chief economist and later as managing director. Was economic adviser in the Department of Finance when Bertie Ahern was Minister. Over past decade, has done consultancy on wide range of interests, including marine sector, M1 interchanges at Drogheda and influential analysis of property market.

Public Finance Constraint

There is widespread consensus around the need to achieve stability in the public finances and that escalating annual borrowing requirements are not sustainable. However, there is rather less agreement as to how stability should be secured or the pace of adjustment needed.

For most years over the past decade, Ireland's public finance imbalance recorded a surplus. This was equivalent to almost 5 per cent of GDP in 2000. However, from 2006, when the surplus was about 3 per cent, a sharp turnabout occurred. A deficit of 7 per cent of GDP emerged by 2008 and further deterioration to about 12 per cent is in prospect for 2009.

A consequence of the comparative experience outlined above was that Ireland's level of gross public indebtedness as a proportion of GDP declined. This trend is being reversed since last year, with the sharp deterioration in the public finances and a return to substantial annual deficits from 2008 and prospectively.

Ireland's growth experience for most of the decade to date was a multiple of that being recorded in both the Euro Area and the UK, and the contraction since 2007 has also been much sharper than in these other economies.

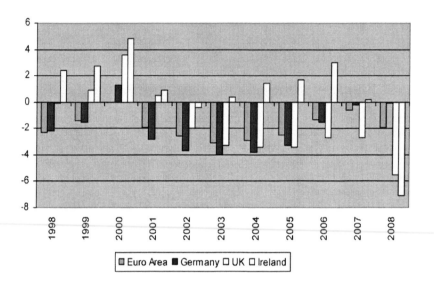

Figure 1

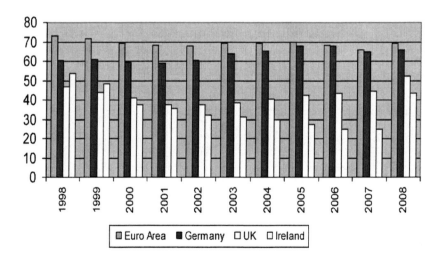

Figure 2

However, in addition to a sharp turnabout in the *rate* of economic growth there has also been a marked change in its *composition*. Thus, in the five years 1998-2003, the average annual contribution of net exports to GDP growth was over 27 per cent, compared with 13 per cent per annum in the five years to 2008. Economic growth became increasingly reliant on expanding domestic demand (much of which was property related), was dependent on rapid expansion of household debt and to a smaller extent on net exports. Property related revenues (stamp duties, VAT and capital gains taxes) remained particularly buoyant. However, a major error was to regard these as durable and a basis for expanding public expenditure.

Achieving credible control over the turnabout in the public finances outlined above at a time of weak economic activity both at home and internationally, as well as a deteriorating situation as regards competitiveness, represents a formidable challenge. In addition, capital markets became alarmed by the potential exchequer implications of the contingent liability entailed by the guarantee (€440 billion) of deposits of certain credit institutions, which became necessary in September 2008, in light of deposit outflows at that time. Of course, the resolution of banks' capital adequacy and cleaning-up of banks' bad lending through NAMA will have further substantial implications for public indebtedness into the medium term.

Property related revenues (stamp duties, VAT and capital gains taxes) remained particularly buoyant. However, a major error was to regard these as durable and a basis for expanding public expenditure.

Deteriorating Competitiveness Position: Negative Impact on Potential Growth

Numerous indicators point to a deterioration in competitiveness from about 2002. For example the IMF has noted that the share of Irish exports, in total imports of the UK, the Euro Area, European non-Euro Zone and US peaked around 2002 and has since declined. In addition, Ireland's share of global FDI has fallen more sharply than the Euro Area as a whole. These trends have emerged as Ireland's price levels rose rapidly to stabilize at the highest in the Euro Area and as unit labour costs rose.

This brings us to the nub of the policy dilemma. Without gains in competitiveness, potential output growth is likely to remain weak. This will complicate the task of public finance adjustment, which in turn will hamper the restoration of competitiveness and so on. Such a vicious circle is likely to have a detrimental impact on confidence and credibility of the policy response with attendant risks that the economy could be left in a sluggish state of maladjustment into the medium term.

Therefore, it is vital that measures to adjust the public finances have a positive effect on competitiveness and are simultaneously accompanied by initiatives which lead directly to improvements. If they are not, securing stability in the public finances may prove as illusive as restoring the economy to a positive growth path.

Achieving Sustainable Fiscal Balance

Credible Target

A credible fiscal target articulated over a clearly defined time horizon is a first necessary step in the adjustment process. A key issue is to separate 'structural' from 'cyclical' influences behind the current deterioration in the public finance imbalance. For example, a recent IMF Report estimated a structural deficit of 6-8 per cent of GDP.[17] The implication is that almost all Ireland's deficit is structural and bubble related which, if true, is quite depressing.

Realistic Time Horizon

Evidently, the elimination of a structural deficit of 6-8 per cent of GDP represents an enormous policy challenge, which will entail significant disruption and upheaval, bearing in mind that to achieve this outcome *ex post* will entail even greater *ex ante* contraction, allowing for the short-term deflationary impact on aggregate demand. Considering these factors it seems unrealistic to expect that the scale of this adjustment could be achieved in anything shorter than a 3-5 year time horizon, with the upper end of this more likely in the event there is failure to stimulate growth through competitiveness and/or productivity gains.

Balance between Revenue and Spending

Another critical issue is how the burden of adjustment should be borne as between revenue generating and expenditure reduction measures. The share of taxes (excluding social security) in Ireland relative to GDP has fallen by 3.5 per cent

Therefore, it is vital that measures to adjust the public finances have a positive effect on competitiveness and are simultaneously accompanied by initiatives which lead directly to improvements. If they are not, securing stability in the public finances may prove as elusive as restoring the economy to a positive growth path.

between 2000 and 2008 and stands 2.3 per cent below those in the Euro Area. This probably indicates the extent to which upward adjustments in taxes can be used, bearing in mind there is scope to broaden the tax base in Ireland but also that a significant policy position to date has been to use a relatively attractive tax regime as an inducement to FDI. Therefore, the bulk of the adjustment needs to fall to reductions in expenditure, about 2 per cent per annum, sustained over three years or more. Easily stated, but the implications in terms of delivery of public services to end users could be self defeating in the absence of genuine reform of the public service. The increase in social benefits followed by compensation of employees and capital investment have been the main categories which account for increased public spending between 2000 and 2008 and increasing public indebtedness.

Having regard to the importance of reversing the trend in competitiveness and securing productivity gains in restarting the economy and facilitating adjustment of the fiscal imbalance, it will be necessary to maintain a programme of capital investment. That is not to say public investment should be a 'sacred cow'. Nor, however, should it become a focus of reduction or deferral because such decisions are more politically expedient. Rigorous pursuit of effectiveness, contribution to productivity and competitiveness and value for money should be the criteria, which determine the capital programme.

The brunt of adjustment will need to fall on pay, numbers employed and the organization and delivery of what are considered to be essential and necessary public services. There is abundant anecdotal evidence of downward adjustment in private sector pay, in the face of the requirements for economic survival of firms and businesses which are under threat. The same kind of drastic steps need to be made in the public sector as regards pay rates and numbers too will need to fall. A nominal pay cut of 10-15 per cent is the order of magnitude by which pay costs need to fall, if they are to mirror what appears to be happening currently in sectors which are exposed to competition. However, simply cutting pay, numbers and programmes across the board in incremental fashion will not deliver the kind of results which are needed and the risks of disruption and policy reversals will undo much of the potential for durable progress. Genuine public

For example, a recent IMF Report estimated a structural deficit of 6-8 per cent of GDP. The implication is that almost all Ireland's deficit is structural and bubble related which, if true, is quite depressing.

Genuine public service reform and new initiatives in public service management, however prosaic, tedious and boring these issues may seem, are probably vitally necessary.

service reform and new initiatives in public service management, however prosaic, tedious and boring these issues may seem, are probably vitally necessary.

Delivering Public Sector Reform

A nominal pay cut of 10-15 per cent is the order of magnitude by which pay costs need to fall, if they are to mirror what appears to be happening currently in sectors which are exposed to competition.

The Annual Competitiveness Report 2008 of the National Competitiveness Council notes that a well managed, innovative and efficient public administration system is essential to driving Ireland's economic recovery.[18] The public sector is not homogenous in terms of its objectives, structures, desired outcomes and service delivery. Reform measures need to be carefully considered in light of the specific roles and outcomes required from individual public sector organizations. The statement from Government on transforming the public services which aims to improve performance, create flexibility in the deployment of people and assets, and identify a precise agenda for transformation in specific sectors needs to be given an effective implementation platform. New governance structures need to be considered as the activities of a wide range of Government departments and agencies impact on the success of enterprises. Ireland needs to have structures and processes that ensure that these departments act in mutually complementary and supportive ways. Achieving an integrated public service, capable of maximizing value for the taxpayers' money, will require targeted actions in a number of areas.

Reversing Competitiveness Losses

The message is simple. The cost of doing business in Ireland is too high. The remedy is to bring this back into line.

Economic indicators of competitiveness show losses of up to 25 per cent since 2002. The effects have become manifest in a very palpable and practical way by droves of retail shoppers travelling to Northern Ireland to meet their retail needs. Most recently a study by the Competition Authority has confirmed a price differential between groceries in Northern Ireland and the Republic of Ireland of 21 per cent.[19] The message is simple. The cost of doing business in Ireland is too high. The remedy is to bring this back into line.

Promoting a Smart Economy: Step in Right Direction

An Taoiseach, Brian Cowen TD, recently announced the appointment of an Innovation Taskforce to advise the Government in making the Smart Economy a reality. The Smart Economy combines the successful elements of the enterprise economy and the innovation or 'ideas' economy while promoting a high-quality environment, improving energy security and promoting social cohesion. A key feature in building the innovation component of the economy is the utilization of human capital – the knowledge, skills and creativity of people – and its ability and effectiveness in translating ideas into valuable processes, products and services. The Smart Economy has, at its core, an exemplary research, innovation and commercialization ecosystem. This will be the successful formula for the next phase of the development of the Irish economy and delivering quality and well-paid jobs.

Conclusion

To some degree what may appear strange is that the policy prescriptions are clear:

- Fix broken banks
- Achieve a sustainable position in the public finances
- Reverse competitiveness losses
- Have a clear vision of the kind of economy needed to foster future growth and employment.

It would be difficult, I suspect, to find strong resistance or widespread disagreement that these are not requirements for a resumption of growth. However, there would be great difficulty I believe in gaining consensus around *how* these requirements should be met. I wonder why that is so? One thought is that economic success in Ireland has been thought of and judged by an ability to *spend* rather than an ability to *create*. The boom in residential property development and prices and on conspicuous consumption goods from new and bigger cars are one dimension of this, but only one. Another is the fact that much of this consumption was financed by credit creation, secured against rising asset prices rather than sustainable income growth based on selling goods and services in competitive markets. Government's success too has been judged in terms of spending: witness the growth in social benefits expenditure, pay and numbers employed in government sectors against what has been

A key feature in building the innovation component of the economy is the utilization of human capital – the knowledge, skills and creativity of people – and its ability and effectiveness in translating ideas into valuable processes, products and services.

In effect, government for most of this decade became just as caught up as households with spending on the back of asset price inflation, without due regard for the sustainability of the basis for that spending.

happening to taxes. In effect, government for most of this decade became just as caught up as households with spending on the back of asset price inflation, without due regard for the sustainability of the basis for that spending. There was a sense of hubris. But the miracle has turned to nightmare and the question is *how* can the needed changes, around which there is broad consensus, be achieved? A successful approach requires a new mindset to change – public sector reform, for example, is about change and creativity. A culture which measures success by reference to attributes such as the ability to manage change and harness creativity, rather than an ability to spend, would have the capacity to piece together the jigsaw of initiatives required to put the economy back on a path of sustainable growth into the medium and longer term.

Chapter 4

HOW TO CREATE THE SMART ECONOMY

RIGHT LEADERSHIP AND PEOPLE MAKING HARD DECISIONS
Jim O'Hara
Chief Executive, Intel (Ireland)

SMART ECONOMY IS ABOUT SMART INTEGRATION
Michael Fitzgerald
Managing Director, Abtran Ltd

REPOSITIONING IRELAND'S ECONOMY
Mary Coughlan TD
Tánaiste and Minister for Enterprise, Trade & Employment

Right Leadership and People Making Hard Decisions

Jim O'Hara
Chief Executive, Intel (Ireland)

Born in Dublin, worked for Digital Equipment Corporation for seventeen years, including five years in the US before joining Intel in 1991 as part of the Fab 10 start-up team. Became plant manager for Fab 10 in 1996 and subsequently managed both Fab 10 and Fab 14, now known as Ireland Fab Operations. Took over role of General Manager, Intel Ireland in 2002 and is responsible for Intel's operations in Ireland which employs directly and indirectly 5,500 people. A member of the governing board of IBEC. In 2006, was conferred with an honorary degree of Doctor of Science by NUI Maynooth.

I would like to give my perspective on what we can do to provide ourselves the best chance of creating a Smart Economy, a digital island here in Ireland. These are my personal opinions and observations, and are informed by my career working in US multinational companies and as the Head of Intel in Ireland. This year marks the 20th anniversary of Intel's manufacturing presence in Ireland. Over that time Intel Ireland's site strategy has been to build technical and management capability to flawlessly start-up and ramp successive generations of new process technologies and then leverage that capability and our existing infrastructure to develop new competencies and increase our research mandate. We have observed that R&D cannot thrive in a vacuum isolated from advanced manufacturing. We need a base of manufacturing industry interacting closely with the academic system to create future sustainable growth based on innovation, practical application and collaboration.

So starting from that premise, I would first like to ground us on what is a Smart Economy and in reality how this could work in an Irish context. In many ways the term smart or knowledge society is more appropriate as it captures the more inclusive needs of the whole population. We can train a certain proportion

In many ways the term smart or knowledge society is more appropriate as it captures the more inclusive needs of the whole population.

of our society to be true knowledge workers but fundamentally if we are to operate as a knowledge society then we must also build on the competencies currently existing in the large majority of the workers of this country and find new applications for these skills and build from the foundation of the past. Therefore the focus must be on four key strategic areas:

We have to have the best teachers teaching in the subjects vital to the country's economic interests. From my perspective these are the STEM subjects: Science, Technology, Engineering and Maths.

1. Education: We must cultivate an educated and skilled workforce with expertise in Science, Technology, Engineering and Maths (STEM).

2. Research and Development Systems: We must create a healthy, efficient network of universities, research centres and companies (MNC and SME) operating in an efficient R&D and innovation system that prioritizes resources to allow us to build local IP, exploit our natural advantages and exploit and adapt global knowledge, to create wealth and employment.

3. Digital Infrastructure: We must build a dynamic digital infrastructure to facilitate the effective communication, dissemination and processing of information throughout the whole country.

4. Pro-business Government Policies: The 3 basic components above must be underpinned by a stable, transparent, pro-business environment that enables the free flow of knowledge, supports investment in ICT and encourages entrepreneurship.

So let me take this as a basic model and build a simple plan for how we might implement that in Ireland.

1. Education

In order to build a truly world class Smart Economy, it is self evident that we must have a world class, digitally connected education system and a coherent strategy that maps across all four levels of education and beyond into lifelong learning. The core ingredients necessary are well trained teachers, using the right digital tools and physical facilities, and supported by a clear Government strategy.

Teachers

We have to have the best teachers teaching in the subjects vital to the country's economic interests. From my perspective these are the STEM subjects: Science, Technology, Engineering and Maths. These subjects will be the fundamental building blocks for this country in the digital economy of the 21st century. Teachers need appropriate tools and training in order to be able to lead and mentor students and effectively transfer their knowledge.

Tools

Our students should have access to the best computing power that we can provide, connected to ubiquitous broadband in the classroom and beyond so the learning experience can continue after school, with the best facilities that we can afford. Education systems around the world are beginning to invest in 1:1 eLearning environments. These are learning environments in which children can develop the 21st century knowledge and skills they need to succeed in today's global economy – including media literacy, critical thinking, abstract problem solving, collaboration, global awareness, and civic literacy.

I support the current Government strategy of strong investment in 4th level education and hope that this will continue.

Incentivizing Students

The government can communicate what exciting future career opportunities are open to a young student who chooses to study science, technology and engineering base subjects and provide incentives, for example, using the points system, for them to take these subjects to Leaving Cert level, or making it financially attractive for students to chose 3rd level STEM related courses. Business also has a clear role to play by working to create a vision for the young people of tomorrow, that has them aspiring to careers in technology and advanced manufacturing, as well as R&D. I support the current Government strategy of strong investment in 4th level education and hope that this will continue.

Lifelong Learning

The common wisdom is that the children of today will have 4 or 5 different careers in their working life. As such we cannot educate them simply for a particular job – we must teach them to constantly re-educate themselves for life. We need to build an entrepreneurial culture, and prepare children to own their personal employability. We must promote a vision that people will create their own employment to service global needs rather than prepare them for jobs today which are geography specific and which may not be around tomorrow.

We must promote a vision that people will create their own employment to service global needs rather than prepare them for jobs today which are geography specific and which may not be around tomorrow.

2. Research and Development Systems

The next area I wish to address is our national system of research and development. In this country we are well on our way to developing a solid network of Universities, Research Centres, Businesses and Government working together. The next step should be to build a collaborative efficient national system that shares information and resources, prioritizes goals and 'weeds and feeds' research projects to divert resources to those projects that have the best chances of solving real problems and generating real IP and ultimately employment.

The Network

The existing closely integrated network between academia, industry and government makes this country an attractive location for R&D. There is a flexibility here and a willingness to work together to get things done. A simple analysis of the Irish eco-system would suggest that Government develops the overall vision for the R&D system. It provides funding, integration mechanisms such as the Competence Centre programmes and develops the support infrastructure.

Build on Strengths

It is crucial for the Government to continue to strongly support and develop the existing installed base of advanced manufacturing in this country and to continue to build appropriate and sustainable R&D opportunities around the successful industry and academia cluster strategy. It makes most sense to build from strengths that we already have in this country. Fundamentally, we should only be planning to enter a space if we feel we have some chance of making a breakthrough, creating some new knowledge that leverages strengths that we already have and that we can defend in the future.

Streamlining Systems

I believe that we need to streamline the systems and align our efforts closely to our clear, visible national strategy with a definite understanding by all players of what we are trying to achieve. Our connected vision for this country should have quantifiable expectations of its R&D system and look for measureable, tangible outputs. Given the diverse players in any R&D system, with their different roles, it is essential that all understand the core objective and expectations of them, or efforts can seem fragmented. There are a large number of institutions, departments and funding agencies with overlapping roles in the Irish R&D system. This creates an unnecessarily high research output to researcher overhead ratio.

Weed and Feed

We must reinforce a culture of either culling or promoting initiatives based on their contribution to the overall objective. Historically, the Government has invested heavily in a wide variety of programmes, with control of funding dispersed across many agencies. However, in the current climate of limited resources, hard-nosed evaluation and affordability exercises have to be undertaken and resources diverted to prioritized, strategic programmes. The focus should be on how to get more research from the same budget and achieve greater commercialization of that research.

Monitor and Measure

There are also improvements we can make in our monitoring and measurement systems. Focus on output variables (e.g., patent, spin-offs) rather than input variables (e.g., R&D spend as a per cent of GDP) would be more appropriate. Similarly, progress on research projects tends to be evaluated through an annual peer review with a high emphasis on publications as the measure of output. There should be a more regular monitoring drumbeat. The evaluation should be continuous and drive mid-course re-alignment with overall national goals – thereby

Fundamentally, we should only be planning to enter a space if we feel we have some chance of making a breakthrough, creating some new knowledge that leverages strengths that we already have and that we can defend in the future.

There are a large number of institutions, departments and funding agencies with overlapping roles in the Irish R&D system. This creates an unnecessarily high research output to researcher overhead ratio.

including industry interaction and commercialization as pertinent activities.

Collaborative Models

For our research network to perform optimally, we need the overlay of effective collaboration models so that these groups can work effectively together. Genuinely collaborative models cannot be dominated by any one network member. Otherwise the opportunity for synergies is lost. There may be a need for more industry-led research agendas. In general, whatever model is chosen, it is crucial that the programme has the right leadership and the right people making the hard decisions.

3. Digital Infrastructure

In order to aspire to a Smart Economy or smart society we must fully develop our national digital network to facilitate the effective communication, dissemination and processing of information throughout the whole country. I am a strong supporter of the Digital 21 initiative that looks to prioritize the completion of our digital infrastructure in the way that the physical road infrastructure has been developed over the last decade. The digital economy underpins our whole economy and its competitiveness. As a small geographically disconnected island, being seamlessly digitally connected to our trading partners around the world is key to our national prosperity.

4. Pro-Business Government Policy Environment

The 3 basic components of Education, R&D and Digital Infrastructure must be underpinned by a stable, transparent, pro-business environment that encourages entrepreneurship, enterprise and inward investment in this country.

Financials

In general, we should seek to have a flexible government

The focus should be on how to get more research from the same budget and achieve greater commercialization of that research.

In order to aspire to a Smart Economy or smart society we must fully develop our national digital network to facilitate the effective communication, dissemination and processing of information throughout the whole country.

environment that is small, nimble, and operates with only light touch interventions in the market. Our incentive system in this country is world class and has had far reaching consequences for our development as an economy. But we must not get complacent – if we do not remain innovative in our incentive 213 systems we will be overtaken by our international competitors for Foreign Direct Investment. At a minimum we must retain the low corporation tax band while avoiding any tax gimmicks that invite scrutiny.

Enterprise

I believe that future prosperity must be built on both MNCs and SMEs. Multinational FDI has been and will continue to be a mainstay of our industrial base. However, in addition we need, as a country, to do everything in our power to create more entrepreneurs and to help them to be successful – these are the country's future SMEs. We must as a nation imbue our young people with the vision, ambition and confidence to create start-ups and believe that they can grow all the way to be the so-called Irish Nokia or Google. We must help give them access to funds, access to markets, and access to experience of multinationals who know the system internationally. I fundamentally believe that Ireland has the ability, using these small indigenous firms, to recreate itself.

Heart of the EU

For many reasons, Ireland must remain strongly integrated with our European partners. When MNCs initially chose Ireland as an investment destination Ireland was at the heart of the EU and the EU has developed into one of the largest consumer markets in the world. US multinationals want certainty when they are considering big investments and it becomes a very uncertain environment when they are confused about Ireland's position in Europe. We must recognize that our membership of the EU is crucial to our future aspirations to create a knowledge and we should remain at the heart of the European Union's Lisbon Strategy to become the 'most dynamic competitive knowledge based economy in the world'.

At a minimum we must retain the low corporation tax band while avoiding any tax gimmicks that invite scrutiny.

We must as a nation imbue our young people with the vision, ambition and confidence to create start-ups and believe that they can grow all the way to be the so-called Irish Nokia or Google.

Conclusion

Today we are facing significant challenges in the global economic environment. However, it is important to recognize that we have weathered cyclical slowdowns before and we will do so again. In these highly competitive and rapidly changing global markets, success is hard earned, and founding future sustainable growth on education, investment in our digital infrastructure and an efficiently functioning R&D network is the way forward for Ireland. There is no reason why we cannot return to our previous growth levels and build on the achievements of the past. Our small size and flexibility as a nation can be our greatest strength. Remember, it's not the big that eat the small, it's the fast that eat the slow.

Smart Economy is About Smart Integration

Michael Fitzgerald
Managing Director, Abtran Ltd

Originally from Barraduff, Co. Kerry, moved to Cork when young. Chartered accountant, worked for Smithkline Beecham for less than a year before going into business for himself. Established Abtran, a business process outsourcing company, in 1997. Other shareholders include brothers Ger and Pat and client services director Pat Ryan. Abtran has more than 25 clients, including ESB, Hibernian Aviva, Sustainable Energy Ireland, the National Consumer Agency, local authorities, Government Departments and broadcaster Sky. Company plans to create at least 250 high-value jobs through €6 million investment in new learning and innovation centre to bring total employment to 850.

As you all know, innovation is 99 per cent perspiration and only 1 per cent inspiration. So I should be ok! So what is my big idea? I thought about our need to focus and play to our strengths. The opportunities in bio-medical and life sciences, green energy, technology, tourism, food and the smart delivery of services. I thought about our pool of experienced and talented, confident people as our key strength. We need to pursue many, if not all, of these opportunities.

I realize that the big idea may be quite a simple one – a small, simple idea capable of developing the Smart Economy. The Smart Economy cannot be developed in isolation, a silo – over here, away from the whole economy. The Smart Economy is the whole economy. We need to recognize the real interdependencies that exist already. Our public services are dependent on our banking system. Our health services are dependent on our enterprise and business sectors creating value. Our enterprises are dependent on our education system. All are interdependent.

We are dependent but not integrated and until we are, we will not create a Smart Economy. We need smart integration to have a truly Smart Economy and a sustainable solution to

We need to recognize the real interdependencies that exist already. Our public services are dependent on our banking system. Our health services are dependent on our enterprise and business sectors creating value. Our enterprises are dependent on our education system. All are interdependent.

the current challenges. We surely recognize that we are dependent on our fellow Europeans and American cousins to sustain and enrich our economy. And they are dependent on us. We need to check-in on these dependencies when making choices – will these enhance smart integration? The Lisbon Treaty is a case in point – we need to ensure that we are integrated in a smart way with Europe and look to play our part in the creation of competitive advantages for Europe. If we wish to create a Smart Economy then the answer is obvious.

So to the big idea: we are all inter-dependent but we need smart integration. If we are to succeed we need to align around a vision for Ireland and look for opportunities to integrate the public and private sectors, universities and enterprise, state agencies and citizens. The Smart Economy is about smart integration creating a whole economy that is greater than the sum of its parts.

I had better very briefly tell you who we are. Abtran was founded 12 years ago with 6 people and currently employs over 800, with 250 of these graduate jobs created since 2007. Abtran works across the economy with large corporations such as SKY and Hibernia Aviva Health, semi-state organizations such as the ESB and An Post as well as local and central government. It may surprise you to know that everyone here, at some point, in the last few months will have been in contact with Abtran. We partner with both public and private sector clients with a wide reach across all our daily lives from the processing of insurance claims to handling license fees. So when you query an ESB bill you probably are talking to one of our staff, whether you have paid your e-toll or not, we will be dealing with you.

So what of our learning can we bring to the creation of a Smart Economy? Our business is about creating long-term sustainable partnerships. Abtran's success is based on creating a win-win – recognizing that our success is based on our clients being able to achieve a competitive advantage. Their success is our success and their growth is our growth. Let us be clear about this. This is not easy and is not for everyone. Win-win requires a commitment and honesty from

Win-win requires a commitment and honesty from both sides. We invest significant resources in understanding the culture and aligning with the vision of our clients.

both sides. We invest significant resources in understanding the culture and aligning with the vision of our clients.

Alignment is never easy but when you get the Alignment Effect, the advantages achieved make it unstoppable. We first need to share a clearly understood strategy – what will success look like? We then align our resources behind that strategy – optimizing strengths on both sides. And we execute it through a process of smart integration – ultimately it is about our people and the way they integrate in a smart way with our clients' organizations.

If there is one thing that can be learned from Abtran it is the lesson of smart integration and we believe that this approach can be applied to create a Smart Economy. This alignment and smart integration enables us deliver economies of scale, to leverage our experience and expertise, to be innovative in our approach to problem solving, to reduce costs, increase value and get more for less.

We need to measure the contribution made to creating a sustainable Smart Economy. Their success needs to be integrated with growing the economy.

Earlier this year Abtran launched our Learning and Innovation Centre. This Centre represents collaboration between our public and private sector clients, government, universities and Enterprise Ireland. This provides an environment to pilot new ways of doing business and delivering services. The insights gained can build future solutions. Enterprise Ireland deserves major credit for making this possible. This Centre is an opportunity to pilot new initiatives in a low risk environment. We are not afraid of failure but the key for us is to fail fast and learn from those mistakes. The key focus is to create better solutions and new ways of doing business.

This approach to trying new ways of doing things on a pilot basis has been endorsed in the Bord Snip Nua Report and can also be a catalyst for smart collaboration and integration between universities, government, as well as the public and private sector. This model – as it is developed and refined through a process of trial and error – can be developed to provide a model for smart integration across the economy. Costs can be cut while value is being created if the opportunities available are seen and turned to action.

We could not see the valuable resource, UCC, on our door step for 11 years. We in Abtran are dependent on UCC for graduates for our work-force but we never thought of developing strategic links with them until now, creating a competitive advantage for our partners, by accessing their expertise and talent. But this new smart integration only works both ways. We also bring commercialization and talent to the university. Win-win plus our clients win. As I said the alignment effect is unstoppable. We are taking cost out while creating multiple competitive advantages. Measurement – and smart measurement – means that we need to measure the right thing. For example, the success of a university should no longer be based on measuring the line of PhDs being produced. We need to measure the contribution made to creating a sustainable Smart Economy. Their success needs to be integrated with growing the economy. This smart integration can deliver improved public services at lower cost.

For example, the success of a university should no longer be based on measuring the line of PhDs being produced.

I can also point to Enterprise Ireland's sponsoring of the Learning for Growth Programme in Stanford University, for 27 Irish CEOs. I am proud to be part of the programme. The development of links between universities and business is another example of the type of smart integration that is possible. This integration has the ultimate objective of creating Irish companies that can scale to over €1 billion in revenue annually.

Ireland's new, smarter economy can be rebuilt on the basis of smart integration. We now need a smart plan that outlines our strategy for integration between all our stakeholders – private and public, nationally and internationally. It is now time for the creation of An Bord Smart. If Colm McCarthy is not too exhausted, he should be immediately appointed to set-up and chair the new Bord. The cuts are coming. To create the economy for the future we need to cut smart. We need to cut forward as well as cut back. Newspaper editorials tell us we have no choice. We need to take our medicine. But it is how and when the medicine is administered that will make the difference.

And we can create new opportunities. As a nation we are smart, with a new hunger, so we will create opportunities, if Government sets up the conditions to win. We will fix it if the conditions are in place. An Bord Smart will set the strategy for smart integration that will deliver a sustainable, scaleable, Smart Economy. Cuts alone will only deliver short-term gains – not sustainable growth. Outsourcing for cost alone – trust me, from my experience – will not work. It is not just about the cuts that represent 7 per cent of government spending. Even if we get these cuts of €5 billion we are not focusing enough on optimizing the €50 billion we will be spending and asking if this is in line with smart integration.

However, the best laid strategies will fail in the present culture where we have the public sector on one side and the private sector – represented by IBEC and other interest groups – on the other side. There is a frightening lack of collaboration. There is a risk at present that the publication of An Bord Snip Nua's report will fuel the existing culture of win-lose.

We need to remember – as we all know from experience ourselves – that an OK strategy well executed will succeed where an excellent strategy, poorly executed, will fail. Success is all about execution. The How? In the words of Professor Charles O'Reilly *'culture eats strategy for breakfast'*. We need to recognize this and look to change the rules of engagement if we are to successfully change to a winning culture.

We need to ensure that the vested interests are integrated and that all parties can see what is in it for them – how they can win. We now need An Bord Smart to recognize the inter-dependencies that exist across the economy and create a vision for the future based on smart integration. Smart integration can create more value and build a whole economy – an economy that is greater than the sum of its parts. In the words of Ghandi:

> The difference between what we do and what we are capable of doing would solve the problems of the world.

Repositioning Ireland's Economy

Mary Coughlan TD
Tánaiste and Minister for Enterprise, Trade & Employment

Educated at the Ursuline Convent, Sligo and UCD. Former social worker. First elected to Dáil for Donegal South-West in 1987 on death of her father Cathal. Her uncle, Clement, represented the constituency (1980-3). Minister for State at the Dept. of Arts, Heritage, Gaeltacht and the Islands (2001-2). Served as Minster for Social and Family Affairs and Minister for Agriculture and Food before present appointment in 2008. On Donegal County Council (1986-2001) and North-West Heath Board (1987-2001). Elected Hon. Sec. of Fianna Fáil in 1995. Has been member of the British/Irish Parliamentary Body.

Introduction

Be in no doubt, however, that addressing Ireland's cost competitiveness is of fundamental importance to recovering long term sustainable growth and is a foundation stone for the building of a Smart Economy.

What a year it has been since last we gathered in Glenties. The dramatic change in the tone of our debate this week is heightened by a perception of ourselves that has altered significantly. We have been reminded that Ireland is a small vessel on the economic tides. This reality has been brought home to individuals and families across the country through jobs lost, income reduced or tiger-era certainty dashed. It is a difficult time for many. If we really want to realize the Smart Economy, we must work to overcome these hurdles. Only then will we have a solid foundation for investing in the knowledge, skills and creativity of people who will create the valuable processes, products and services of tomorrow.

Competitiveness

With this in mind, I therefore want to say a few words about one of those hurdles that falls firmly within my own remit – competitiveness. Much of my own work over the past year centred on the drive to restore our competitive position. In certain ways it is the most difficult of the three hurdles to overcome and on which to achieve quick results. It requires a myriad of actions across government and across both the public and private sectors. Be in no doubt, however, that addressing Ireland's cost competitiveness is of fundamental importance to recovering long term sustainable growth and is a foundation stone for the building of a Smart Economy.

Inflation

First, the decline in Irish inflation reached minus 5.4 per cent in the year to June 2009. It is the sharpest fall since the early 1930s. Inflation fell significantly across most goods and services groups in 2009. Input costs for manufacturing and services have witnessed several months of consecutive decline. The OECD has predicted mild deflation in Ireland for the next two years. This will maintain the current downward pressure on wages and prices. While the eurozone is also experiencing deflation, estimated to be the lowest for the region since 1953, the IMF belives that Irish prices should continue to decline at a pace greater than the rest of the eurozone. This in itself will help improve our competitiveness.

Labour Costs

Second, the Government has stepped in to exert downward pressures on prices and costs. Although it has been a painful adjustment, the reduction in unit labour costs, delivered through public pay reform, will strengthen our longer-term position. For most exporting companies, labour costs account for more than half their input costs. Significantly, the EU estimates that Irish unit labour costs will fall by 4 per cent this year, compared with a 3 per cent increase in the EU on average. This translates into a significant cost advantage for those Irish firms competing in the export market.

Although it has been a painful adjustment, the reduction in unit labour costs, delivered through public pay reform, will strengthen our longer-term position.

Competition Recommendations

Third, the Government has committed to implement the recommendations of the Competition Authority and tackle excessive costs in the non-traded sectors where they can best contribute to overall competitiveness. The IMF acknowledged the importance of Irish labour market flexibility in helping our competitiveness adjustment. It also suggested that competition policy should be used to support the process of price and wage adjustments.

Competition policy in a small open economy is relevant for all sectors of the economy but particularly the services and non-traded sector, since the non-traded sector is a key determinant of Ireland's cost competitiveness. The Competition Authority has tended to focus its efforts, especially its advocacy efforts, on thenon-traded sectors of the economy. The Authority has issued a number of reports in the past few years on non-traded sectors, including the areas of banking, utilities and professional services, such as engineers, architects, the legal profession, dentists and others. Implementation of the Authority's recommendations is essential to remove competitiveness bottlenecks in the economy and to deliver better value and more innovation in those sectors.

Controlled Costs and Energy

Fourth, we are working to control costs in administered sectors of the economy, such as local authority charges, as well as easing the administrative burden that regulations can create. I have now met several times with the county managers about actions local authorities can take to ease cost pressures on businesses. This is difficult at a time when local authority budgets are already under pressure, but the level at which local authority charges are set have a very real impact on the ability of local businesses to compete.

Energy costs represent one of the key issues where costs need to be managed. The recent trend of energy prices has been downward, with a 10 per cent drop in electricity prices for residents and small and medium enterprises from 1 May, while gas prices have reduced by an average of 12 per cent. These reductions will result in a further easing of cost pressures for businesses. The result has been that, according to the latest published Eurostat comparisons, smaller SMEs are paying 1 per cent below the average EU-27 price. Approximately 60 per cent of the ESB's SME customers are in this category.

Sheltered Sectors

It is my view that we must never again allow costs to drift out of line with those of our competitors. We have learned a harsh lesson, but as a Government we have acted with resolve and will continue to take the necessary actions to restore our external competitiveness. There is more work to be done. There are certain sectors where competition and the chill winds of economic reality have yet to reach. Certain professions have yet to play their part and have yet to tell us how they will reduce their fees and charges. There is no place in Ireland where the majority have to make painful choices for this level of economic conceit.

Skills and People

But Ireland's competitive position is not all about costs. Productivity and the skills base of our people are key advantages. Last week I was again reminded of Ireland's key competitive advantages. Grant Thornton ranked Ireland first out of thirty-six developed economies for access to skilled labour. Our focus on high skills, high educational attainment right through to fourth level is as relevant and necessary today as the investment in education which we made since the 1960s. It is also at the core of the Smart Economy concept. People, their ideas and the environment we put in place to support them, as they work to transform those ideas into commercial successes, is simply what the Smart Economy is about.

Investment To-Date

The truth is that we were already well on the path towards creating a Smart Economy in Ireland. Or perhaps it may be better said that we had many different paths underway but all heading in that direction. While recent events have brought adversity, they have also brought opportunity. The need by Government to robustly address the economic challenge and set out clearly the medium term vision meant that from last summer we were working on, specifically, what that vision should be. That process culminated in the articulation of the Smart Economy, a vision that brings together in a new and more radically focused way the work underway in the enterprise economy, in our research institutions, and in the innovation or ideas space, together with work starting on the drive for commercialization of our research

There are certain sectors where competition and the chill winds of economic reality have yet to reach. Certain professions have yet to play their part and have yet to tell us how they will reduce their fees and charges. There is no place in Ireland where the majority have to make painful choices for this level of economic conceit.

and development spending outcomes, and in fledgling areas such as the green-tech and energy sectors.

Pervasive Innovation

While all of these initiatives remain essential, the Smart Economy logic urges us to go further. It firmly embraces the concept of innovation, not just in the science and enterprise research that we support, but in the way we approach problems and challenges across all sectors of our economy. Our ability to innovate and to develop new processes, products and services must become pervasive across all of our academic endeavours. The convergence of ideas from across disciplines must combine with the application of new technologies to deliver products and services that people both need and want.

Our ability to innovate and to develop new processes, products and services must become pervasive across all of our academic endeavours.

Funding for Research

To deliver on the potential of the Smart Economy, and establish Ireland as an innovation and commercialization hub in Europe, the Government must send a clear signal to all stakeholders, and to those looking in from outside, that this is the direction we are taking. It is therefore time, I believe, that we consider whether Government funding for all research activities should be viewed through the same innovation prism. The delivery of all fourth level research funding through one body charged with an innovation-grounded mandate is something we must therefore consider. Given the resource challenges we face, and the level of funding we continue to ring-fence for research at the expense of other areas of public spending, research can no longer be for its own sake. It must produce real results in terms of generating new ideas, solving old problems, creating new intellectual property, spinning-off new businesses and ultimately, delivering new jobs. There must be a greater return on the taxpayers' investment. A move of all relevant funding streams to one body so charged would, I believe, send out a clear signal that Ireland has taken a key strategic decision that research, development and innovation are going to drive, not only our path to recovery, but the economic progress of our people in the years ahead.

Commercialization

The biggest challenge remains commercialization and the spin out of new businesses from our campuses. While it is a well-worn cliché, it is a fact that today's innovative ideas and fledgling businesses are the global corporations of the future. In my role as Minister for Enterprise, Trade and Employment, I want to take every possible step to foster a healthy entrepreneurial and commercialization culture, among both the on- and off-campus innovators across this island. It is why I established an Enterprise Feedback Group, whose terms of reference include an overview of the commercialization of public investment in research and development. It is one of the reasons I continue to prioritize supports such as the Commercialization Fund, the Innovation Voucher Scheme and the Innovation Growth Fund. Incentivizing a nexus between research, innovation, the market and consumers' needs and wants is key to the development of strong and successful future enterprises.

Scale and Growth

Venture capital to drive growth and scale will also have an increasing role to play. We have seen progress in this regard over the past year, with several new funds up and running. Start up businesses in the Smart Economy will need access to more venture capital however and that is why the Government has made provision in the Smart Economy framework for up to €500 million to be provided through 'Innovation Fund Ireland' to support early stage research and development intensive small and medium enterprises.

FDI

Foreign direct investment will continue to play a central role in the development of the Irish economy, and is critical to the establishment of a Smart Economy. Ireland continues to be one of the most attractive locations for global companies investing in Europe. The quality of such investments is also of the highest standard, reflecting the remarkable evolution of the business ecosystem in Ireland as international competition and Irish economic conditions have developed. Investments in the past

Given the resource challenges we face, and the level of funding we continue to ring-fence for research at the expense of other areas of public spending, research can no longer be for its own sake.

year, such as those by Intel, Cook Medical, Cisco, Boston Scientific and Hewlett Packard are clear evidence of this evolution. Just as implementing the correct combination of policies drove the development of the IFSC, Ireland is now also fast becoming an international hub for a new generation of ICT companies involved in cutting edge software development, the provision of on-line services and e-commerce.

Ireland continues to be one of the most attractive locations for global companies investing in Europe.

Conclusion

Ninety-two years ago, almost to the day, the New York Times published a striking tribute to the genius of Patrick MacGill. Introducing its readers to MacGill's prose, the paper said of his works *Children of the Dead End* and *The Rat Pit* that they were unlike other vivid pictures of deprivation, because 'they had in them the lights as well as the shadows of life'. Ireland today is far from the Ireland of MacGill's childhood, yet as we face up to challenging times, it is important that we look for the 'lights' among the economic 'shadows' cast around us. The opportunity to reset Ireland's competitive position and to reposition Ireland's economy as a Smart Economy are two of those 'lights' and have the potential to illuminate the future trajectory of this small but vibrant island nation.

Chapter 5

NEED FOR A NATIONAL STRATEGY AND VISION

A NEW POLITICS FOR A NEW SOCIETY
Enda Kenny TD
Leader, Fine Gael

TIME RIPE FOR RADICAL INDUSTRIAL POLICY
Martin Murphy
Chief Executive, Hewlett Packard (Ireland)

TOWARDS A SECOND REPUBLIC
Michael O'Sullivan
Head of Research, Credit Suisse Bank

A New Politics for a New Society

Enda Kenny TD
Leader, Fine Gael

Born in Castlebar, Co. Mayo and educated at St. Gerald's School, Castlebar, St. Patrick's Teachers' Training College, Drumcondra and NUIG. A former national school teacher, first elected to Dáil Éireann in 1975 following death of his father Henry, who represented Mayo constituency for 21 years. Also elected in 1975 to Mayo County Council. Fine Gael Spokesperson on Youth Affairs and Sport (1977-80) and on the Gaeltacht (1982 and 1987-8). Fine Gael Chief Whip (1992-4). Spokesperson on Regional Development (1994) and on Arts, Heritage, Gaeltacht and the Islands (1997-2002). Minister for State at the Depts. of Education and Labour (1986-7) and Minister for Trade and Tourism (1994-7). Following resignation of Micheal Noonan in wake of 2002 General Election, elected Leader of Fine Gael and led Party in 2007 General Election winning back 20 seats.

This year we celebrate the 60th anniversary of John A. Costello declaring Ireland a Republic, one of the signal moments in Fine Gael's history. Sixty years on, we need to rediscover and reinvigorate that Republic. We need once again to place the 'Res Publicae', that is the things of the people, at the heart of Government.

For the last decade our country was run for the benefit of the few rather than the many.

No one can deny the real achievements of the Celtic Tiger. We became a richer, more self-confident, more diverse Nation. But in building that Tiger, we neglected our Republic and in the process we also sidelined many of our fundamental values. We stopped viewing ourselves as citizens. We became consumers instead. The institutions we had come to rely upon, such as the church, the banks and the legal system, quite often betrayed us and betrayed themselves. Politics failed to fill the void. Instead, we created a huge gap between the government and the governed, between those on the inside and those on the outside.

Abduction of Republic by vested interests.

A recent newspaper headline put it perfectly. In Ireland we

have *an elite governing for a clique.* If the man and woman in the street are cynical about politics and politicians, they have every right to be. For the last decade our country was run for the benefit of the few rather than the many.

The Fianna Fáil Party of today has lost its sense of direction and the political system of today has lost its sense of legitimacy. Our system has failed completely to live up to the vision of its founders.

From the moment of its birth 90 years ago, the First Dáil was forced to work without resources or power, the focus of constant harassment and raids. But the very fact of its existence sent a clear message to all. In the new Irish State, Parliament would be supreme. But in Ireland today, power has been sucked away from the Oireachtas to the Government. Recently, we have seen two very clear examples of how Executive power is being abused.

The Government curtailed scrutiny of important legislation by guillotining 18 separate bills. Then it completely by-passed the Oireachtas by publishing the McCarthy Report and the report on the Leas Cross Nursing Home after the Dáil had gone into recess. If it weren't all so serious, it would be absolutely farcical. This in the face of Government TDs on local radio stations all over the country saying that the Dáil should sit for the month of July and then voting for its closure.

Unfortunately, there seems to be a view in Ireland that political reform has nothing to do with the real economy. This view is completely false.

The Fianna Fáil Party of today has lost its sense of direction and the political system of today has lost its sense of legitimacy. Our system has failed completely to live up to the vision of its founders.

Our political system and its weakness fatally undermined our economy

The IMF tells us that our recession is the worst of all the advanced economies and that we face a 'Lost Decade' of low growth, high unemployment and social misery. But why did this happen?

Why were the bankers and the developers not dealt with before it was too late? Was it not the result of a political culture that liked to cosy up to the rich and powerful, as exemplified by the Galway tent? Why have we tolerated weak competition and high costs in key sectors of our economy? During her speech this week at MacGill, the Tánaiste talked about reducing professional fees. I agree, but why was this not done before?

Could it be because some vested interests seem to have a veto in social partnership? Why do we have a budgetary system in place that is unfit to run a corner-shop, let alone a nation of 4 million people? Has it anything to with the replacement of accountability in the public service by a new cosy relationship between Ministers, senior Civil Servants, Trade Unions, Government agencies and regulators? My answer to all these questions is yes, yes and yes. That is why your money was wasted on useless voting machines and on unworkable systems like the PPARs debacle, to name just two examples.

And then we have the horrors of the Ryan report. Horrors that our political system either ignored or, to our eternal shame, facilitated. How, I ask you, could any self-respecting political system allow the systematic abuse of our children to go on for decades? The fundamental truth is this. Our political system is broken. Our political culture is discredited. We cannot fix our economy or create a just society unless and until we also fix our politics. And that politics has to see that, irrespective of position or circumstance, those who are guilty of criminal activities face the rigours of the law and are seen to pay the price for their wrongdoings.

For the public, political reform tends to mean reducing the number of TDs and their pay. They are rightly outraged at politicians asking for sacrifices, while exempting themselves from major cuts. It is for this reason that I favour a reduction in the number of TDs. Depending on the results of the next census in 2011 the number of TDs could be reduced, without requiring a constitutional amendment. However, reducing the number of elected representatives will not, by itself, do anything for political reform. It will make the current system less expensive, but it will not make it more effective. To do that, we need to go much further down the road of change. In 2000, Fine Gael published a document called the Democratic Revolution. It was a clarion call for radical change in our politics. Needless to say, the Fianna Fáil Government of the day completely ignored it.

Our starting point is simple. The huge centralization of power

The fundamental truth is this. Our political system is broken. Our political culture is discredited. We cannot fix our economy or create a just society unless and until we also fix our politics.

Depending on the results of the next census in 2011 the number of TDs could be reduced, without requiring a constitutional amendment.

The public service in my view will always respond to decisive leadership where clear objectives are held and where cause and motivation are evident.

in Ireland is totally incompatible with a healthy Republic and actively encourages inefficiency. Under the New Politics, we will redistribute power from the Executive to the Oireachtas, from Central to Local Government and from the bureaucracy to the Citizens of our Republic. Fine Gael believes that the State has a vital role to play in Ireland's recovery and does not agree with those who seek to demonize or scapegoat the public service. This Government has sidelined and ignored the potential and the contribution of our public servants. Every time there was a problem, they turned to some consultant or other who produced a long and expensive report for which *you* paid. Too often, these reports were ignored or soon became irrelevant. It was waste on an epic scale and nobody took responsibility. The public service in my view will always respond to decisive leadership where clear objectives are held and where cause and motivation are evident. But if we are to do more with less, we have to create a Smart State that spends our money wisely and prioritizes delivery over bureaucracy.

Under the New Politics, Fine Gael will dismantle the command and control model in the public sector, and give responsibility to those who know best: the people on the front-line. Our recent FairCare health proposals are already based on this approach, which we will roll out across the public sector. The need for fundamental reform has been amply demonstrated by the McCarthy report. It is an absolutely damning indictment of the way that Government has been run for the last decade.

Fine Gael accepts that some very hard decisions on the public sector will have to be taken. We accept, for instance, that public sector numbers will have to come down. But we are deeply concerned at the idea of social welfare cuts when so many other areas of public expenditure remain untouched and unreformed. Investment in job creation and job protection is the answer to rising unemployment, but this is unachievable right now because of the paralysis in a government that remains transfixed at the continuing bank crisis.

While the McCarthy Report is a very valuable contribution to the national debate, I think we also need to be very careful about assuming that it is the only way forward. The Report suggests cuts in our public sector but leaves the basic system intact. It is a big picture observation from an outsider's perspective when what we need is a more fundamental review. The McCarthy Report, or some variant of it, will prove useless if it is not accompanied by a jobs stimulus package. Fine Gael's NewERA plan will create 100,000 jobs by investing €11 billion in areas such as broadband and energy independence. It has been designed so that the debt will not be on the balance sheet of the State.

As leader of Fine Gael, I do not underestimate the scale of the challenges now facing Ireland. I know that families, communities and small businesses throughout the country are struggling to survive every day. But I also know that the Irish people have shown in the past that they can do great things when given a clear vision and a reason to hope. To realize this vision and hope, Ireland's place at the heart of an effective and democratic European Union must be restored and strengthened. That is why a Yes vote to the Lisbon Treaty is essential for this country's future.

When John F. Kennedy announced in 1961 that the United States would put a man on the moon within a decade, many people laughed at the idea. 40 years ago, Neil Armstrong took his first steps on the moon. Anything is possible if we have the courage to believe and the courage to lead.

So what is my vision for Ireland? I want a country with full employment and stable public finances. We did it once before. We can certainly do it again. I want an Ireland where we can export electricity and create tens of thousands of jobs in a low carbon, clean tech economy. Fine Gael's New Era points the way forward. I want a health service where the two-tier system is abolished, where health is treated in a radically different way, with the patient's interests as its prime focus. Fine Gael's Faircare plan will make this happen. I want an education system that meets the requirements of the future where our young can develop and be equipped to meet and win the challenges of the new industries of the 21st century. I want a New Politics that will work for all of the people, and create a vigorous public sector where the people on the front line are in charge, where they are accountable in their responsibilities and not dictated to by centralized departments. I want our country to continue to be an information society as we

But if we are to do more with less, we have to create a Smart State that spends our money wisely and prioritizes delivery over bureaucracy.

The McCarthy Report, or some variant of it, will prove useless if it is not accompanied by a jobs stimulus package.

Fine Gael's New Era points the way forward. I want a health service where the two-tier system is abolished, where health is treated in a radically different way, with the patient's interests as its prime focus.

have been for 2,000 years since we first sent missionaries and teachers abroad to educate and inform other peoples. I want to see our young people able to ride the waves of change moving across the global ocean, to master these changes and direct them Ireland's way for our people's benefit.

I want our country to be up there with the very best, to be smart, nimble, flexible, able to adapt and change according to circumstance. That potential is there but it has to be given the opportunity to flourish. That cannot happen under a government removed from reality and exhausted by its inability to cope with the consequences of its own mismanagement. Most of all, I want to live in a country which is a Republic in reality, not just in name but where the young and vulnerable are protected; where the aged and venerable are respected and where able bodies and agile minds can continue to develop our nation's potential.

These goals are all achievable. But they will require the kind of sustained effort and imagination that allowed the Americans to put a man on the moon. They require our maximum effort to achieve our clear objectives. Fine Gael's New Era points the way forward. I want a health service where the two-tier system is abolished, where health is treated in a radically different way, with the patient's interests as its prime focus. A Republic of which we can all be proud. I am filled with optimism and hope that given the chance, I can meet that challenge and with a new energetic team, lead in charting a course towards creating that reality.

Time Ripe for Radical Industrial Policy

Martin Murphy
Chief Executive, Hewlett Packard (Ireland)

Holds both a bachelors degree in engineering and mathematics and a masters degree in electronic engineering from TCD. In 2000, was appointed Managing Director of Hewlett Packard Ireland, having previously held roles in the company in the consulting and sales divisions. Spearheaded various global acquisitions locally, including acquisition of Mercury Interactive Corporation and Snapfish. He also has managed the acquisitions of Synstar and Schlumberger Business Continuity Services. Serves on board of Dublin Chamber of Commerce and the Irish Management Institute.

In plain language, 'where do we go from here?' From the outset there are a couple of things we need to be clear on. First, Ireland is always going to be export driven; we are too small to be anything else. The dynamism of the global market drove the success of Ireland's industrial model and our economic growth from the mid-1990s. It will drive it again but it will only do so if our national strategy and vision capitalize on both new, as well as traditional, global opportunities for enterprise, expertise and international trade.

Second, the good news is: the great global recession will end. That is the only certainty. It may not end this year, or next, or even for a further two or three years. But it will end. And when it does, the world will have changed. Those famous green shoots that politicians, macroeconomists and financial analysts scurry around looking for in the undergrowth may be found in quite different places to where economic convention dictates they should appear.

Third, we know the key elements of our national survival strategy – fixing the banks, fixing the public finances and fixing our economic competitiveness problem. This is not easy and definitely is not painless. **In a little less than eighteen months we have gone from full employment to 12 per cent unemployment and rising.**

Apart from the impact of the reduction in world trade on our exports – and we need to bear in mind that Irish exports generally have been holding up remarkably well throughout this crisis vis-à-vis other EU countries – rapidly rising unemployment, and even more rapidly shrinking wealth, are inevitable consequences of the continuing crisis in the three public policy priorities I have listed. Understandably, there has not been much room to focus on industrial policy in view of the gravity of our other problems. But our vision of the industrial policy that will shape a new prosperous Ireland for the 21st century is just as great a priority as anything else. **As part of any long term strategy, of a new way forward for Ireland, of a vision for a prosperous future for all our citizens, the choices we make now on industrial policy and building enterprises for the future are essential to the mix.**

Ireland's future wealth rests on becoming an export-driven centre for the global economy. What we have to do is to integrate a new enterprise culture into our national strategy for recovery and put the elements in place now that will make it work. The short term solutions and the longer term game plan for our economy must be welded together in one piece. Unless we locate our vision for wealth creation and job creation within our national strategy for survival we risk leaving our future to chance.

I have heard it said that since we now have an emerging large pool of unemployed labour, perhaps we should simply continue with the strategy of attracting FDI to Ireland to mop it up. There is nothing wrong with that, if there was enough mobile investment doing the rounds looking for an Ireland with access to a European market where the same conditions applied as at the beginning of the 1990s. But there is not and there never will be, ever again. We need to be far more ambitious in our thinking, in our approach, in our vision of what we can create for Ireland in the 21st century. Because we are a small open economy, on the periphery of Europe, excellence has to be our trade mark – both to attract further investment to this country and crucially to build an indigenous internationally trading enterprise culture of our own.

Across a range of economic high value added trading activities, Ireland already has a proven strength and an international track record of achievement – from agri-business and food to the creative arts to pharmachem to information technology. We must build on what we have already to generate new export oriented companies that will create wealth, and create jobs, for Ireland. The capacity for innovation is not restricted to the IT sector. Innovation is a business and opportunities for enterprise arise across a broad range of disciplines and not just limited to science and technology. We need to widen the net for innovation investment.

We need to go further still. We must look to the relatively new, as well. The world is moving away from fossil fuels dependence for energy, so there are new areas for Ireland to explore and exploit in support industries for new energy technologies. There are other new opportunities that will open up in industries of the future, obvious examples being enterprises based on biotech and nano-technologies. What we have to do is create a new 'Brand Ireland'; an Ireland where enterprise culture is dedicated to exploiting unmet global needs across a wide range of economic activities and committed to meeting those needs.

What we are looking to achieve is an Ireland whose wealth creating enterprises are built around:

- high value added exports in goods and services that create wealth and jobs
- an education system that fosters ICT literacy at all levels, particularly primary and secondary education
- an industrial support infrastructure that fits; in particular, a next generation network that will provide a competitive advantage to our internationally trading businesses
- an uncompromising commitment to maintaining national economic competitiveness

Because we are a small open economy, on the periphery of Europe, excellence has to be our trade mark – both to attract further investment to this country and crucially to build an indigenous internationally trading enterprise culture of our own.

On the latter point, our national debate on restoring competitiveness to the Irish economy is, in the immediate sense, rightly concentrated on cutting costs. Prices and the social and economic costs of living and working in Ireland must be reduced from the astronomical levels they rose to during the boom years, levels that are no longer sustainable. No sane individual would argue with that premise.

But we cannot settle for being stuck in the middle of the pile on some international competitiveness index. If Ireland is to succeed, we are going to have to be ultra competitive. I would argue that competitiveness is not going to be achieved just by cutting the general costs of doing business in Ireland, important though that is. Nor will it be achieved by providing more cost effective services simply through wage cuts or headcount reductions. In my own industry, for example, the starting premise is that cutting costs does not mean cutting services. The objective is to deliver a better service at a lower cost through innovation. The aim is to think smart, work smart and buy smart. Whatever reform package is set in place for the better delivery of public services, it has to be hoped that the smarter use of smart technology will be an intrinsic part of it.

Looking briefly to the kind of world in which our enterprise culture must thrive and survive, if I had stood here ten years ago and said, by the middle of the next decade

- young people will not watch television anymore but instead they will pick and choose the programmes they want to watch on their PCs, as recommended by their cyber peers; of course
- we will take our holiday snaps on digital cameras, store them on memory chips, print them at home – to a much better standard and quality, by the way, than the old ritual of taking them to be developed

you would have dismissed me as a fantasist. But it happened. The information revolution of the late twentieth century has forever changed the way we live, communicate and influence one another. It has changed the marketplace for the goods and services we produce. It will keep changing.

If we look at the power and influence of social networks on the choices and decisions that individual people make about what they believe, about what they want and, crucially, about what they will buy, this is not some sort of contemporary fad. It will accelerate in the years ahead. In the broadest sense this means that power in society is shifting away from centralized control; the sort of control traditionally dominated by elites of

... cutting costs does not mean cutting services. The objective is to deliver a better service at a lower cost through innovation. The aim is to think smart, work smart and buy smart. Whatever reform package is set in place for the better delivery of public services, it has to be hoped that the smarter use of smart technology will be an intrinsic part of it.

politics, or industry, or intellectuals, or specialists. From the more narrow perspective of an industrialist, what we are observing is the creation of a new global business model, in which individual choices demand customized product solutions.

Traditional marketing, advertising and sales as we know them are largely redundant. The traditional media model is already redundant. Even the old way of conducting politics is undergoing its own revolution. When it comes to wealth creation and the future, it is not just local manufacturing companies, or globalized industries, that have to change their attitude to business, the market and the consumer. Small open economies like ours must adjust their attitudes too, especially when picking winners to unpick and make good on the global opportunities on offer.

However 'sexy' a project may appear to be, if it does not pass muster according to very strict economic evaluation criteria, then it should be met with a very firm 'no' in terms of any state support on offer. Above all, our new enterprise sector must be competitive in the global marketplace. To achieve this new enterprise culture and create the business and industries that will thrive in it, we are going to have to invest in it. The objective is to confer a competitive advantage on our new globally trading enterprises across every sector of economic activity.

That may mean winding down investment over here – and investing over there. It does not mean shutting investment down. It certainly means bringing a support framework together – the best that Enterprise Ireland and related agencies have to offer – into a purpose built 'strike force' of 'enterprise builders'. It is about fostering a dynamic enterprise culture that is alert to changing market needs and trends and an education system that fosters IT literacy across the entire population.

Thus, the Ireland that will emerge from this Great Recession is not the Ireland of the 1950s, or the 1930s, or even the 1980s, or anything remotely approximating the past. The progress we have made in many areas over the past fifteen years is testament to our capabilities and we have come a long way. What I argue for is a new enterprise culture, focused on exports of goods and services to the global economy, as a vital part of any national strategy for getting Ireland back on track. We will need to define it – that is the easy part – and refine it, as we go along, which is always going to be more difficult since it requires flexibility, some fairly ruth-

Traditional marketing, advertising and sales as we know them are largely redundant. The traditional media model is already redundant.

Above all, our new enterprise sector must be competitive in the global marketplace.

The criteria for selecting winners and deselecting losers must be sustainability of any enterprise and its long term growth prospects.

less selections and decision making and more than a little belief in ourselves.

It is a radical vision for Ireland. Making it work will be a complex task that touches on many sensitive areas of public policy, infrastructure support and public services, in which many other vested interests have a stake. The criteria for selecting winners and deselecting losers must be sustainability of any enterprise and its long term growth prospects. That way, we create wealth to create jobs and build a future for all our citizens in a thriving economy and country. That is what our vision must be about because that is the only way forward for us.

Towards a Second Republic

Michael O'Sullivan
Head of Research, Credit Suisse Bank

Educated at UCC and Balliol College Oxford where he obtained MPhil and DPhil degrees as a Rhodes Scholar. Has taught finance and economics at Oxford and Princeton Universities. Formerly, worked as a strategist for Goldman Sachs International, UBS Warburg and State Street Global Markets. Appears regularly on CNN, CNBC and Bloomberg TV and the BBC World Service Radio. Author of the 2006 book, Ireland and the Global Question (Cork University Press in Europe and Syracuse University Press in US), which examines the economic, social and foreign policy aspects of how Ireland has become one of the world's most globalised countries.

Introduction

Karl Marx once wrote of Ireland that 'society is undergoing a revolution ... which takes no more notice of the human existences it breaks down than an earthquake regards the houses it subverts'.[20] He wrote this over one hundred and fifty years ago, when life in Ireland was very different to now, but it could just as well describe political, economic and social life in Ireland today. Marx is an appropriate figurehead here because so many of the tensions he had described – between state and economy, or government and market – are reappearing in vivid form as the global credit crisis develops. Ireland, having been the poster child for globalization, is now perhaps the leading example of a 21st century casino economy (as Keynes may have put it). Moreover, the revolutionary spirit and strategic thinking of the likes of Marx are badly needed in Ireland today because in the context of the shock, confusion and economic pain being wrought by the credit crisis, Ireland's future as a developed economy and developing society will rest heavily on the quality and execution of a national strategy and vision.

> **Ireland's future as a developed economy and developing society will rest heavily on the quality and execution of a national strategy and vision.**

This paper argues for the importance of a strategic or more visionary approach to policy making in Ireland and proposes a return to core republican principles in order to build a 'Second Republic'.

The National Question

Until the current wave of globalization came upon Ireland the dominant framework in public life has been what is referred to as the National Question, the pursuit of sovereignty and independence from Britain. While the National Question is not yet fully resolved it no longer captures and describes the multiple changes occurring in Irish society, politics and economics. Globalization is presenting the Irish state with a new defining question, the Global Question.

What did we do right?

Looking back on the past twenty or so years we can divide the Irish 'miracle' into two broad parts, the first wave based on investment in Ireland by foreign multinationals and increasingly stable investment climate, and the second the flourishing of the domestic economy as aided and abetted by low real interest rates.

The latter part is easier to understand, and it has largely respected the patterns of previous asset price bubbles. The first part is more difficult to analyse as it is hard to spot a single factor that ignited Ireland's economy after so many years of slumber. A salad of economic factors, both domestic and international, seems to have combined to drive the turnaround in Ireland's economy. At this stage a consensus has emerged that identifies the main domestic factors in this mix as Ireland's education system, credit growth, the role of the IDA, Ireland's membership of the EU and its flexible labour market.

What is interesting from the point of view of those who look to Ireland as an economic model is that most of these factors were in place during some of the bleakest years for the Irish economy, as well as the best. To a large degree they were catalyzed by outside factors, principally by a falling cost of capital, the trend toward the opening up of international markets and trade, diminished geopolitical risk and the advent of new technologies – all of the ingredients of what are now taken to drive economic globalization.

Looking back on the past twenty or so years we can divide the Irish 'miracle' into two broad parts, the first wave based on investment in Ireland by foreign multinationals and increasingly stable investment climate, and the second the flourishing of the domestic economy as aided and abetted by low real interest rates.

World Post the Credit Crisis

With its very stable political climate, business friendly economy, general respect for 'intangibles' like the rule of law and education, Ireland had fitted well into a globalizing world where, though this is now a well-worn catch phrase we hear of the 'death of geography', and 'softer' rather than hard forms of power (i.e., military strength) are more influential.

Ireland's intangible infrastructure (i.e., educated workforce, low taxes and uncomplicated approach to doing business) rather than its physical infrastructure is what appears to have attracted a large number of (largely American) multinationals. In this respect, advocates of low and simplified taxation systems who point to Ireland in support of their case, miss the bigger more complicated picture. As a number of Eastern European countries have found, low taxes themselves are not the sole means of attracting foreign direct investment. They need to be coupled with a variety of other factors, such as the rule of law. Furthermore, this view is also embedded in the Lisbon Agenda which underlined the EU's goal to become

> the most competitive and dynamic knowledge based economy in the world, capable of sustainable economic growth with more and better jobs and greater social cohesion.

The important point here is that in the aftermath of the credit crisis, high leverage and de-regulation will most likely be replaced by more regulation and lower leverage. **This means that the Irish economy will have to move away from a bubble or casino type economic model toward one where companies make and sell things, and importantly, innovate.** In short, Ireland and its policy makers will have to revisit the notion of intangible infrastructure and importantly, the role of institutions in guiding and executing strategy.

It is ironic that at a time when the lazy cliché of the 'Celtic Tiger' has become a model for so many other countries (China, Chile and Bulgaria, amongst others, sent their wise men and women to Ireland to study its economy), Ireland itself is badly in need of a lodestone to guide both its economy and society.

In this respect there are three challenges. First, to rescue Ireland from its bad banks, 'property entrepreneurs' and politicians while managing the deflation of its bubble economy.

Over the course of the credit crisis, the litany of policy failures in Ireland is in contrast to the more successful strategic thinking adopted by other small countries like Chile and Switzerland.

The bursting of its economic bubble and the lacklustre political response to it underline the need for a large scale reassessment and renewal of political values and structures.

Second, to lay the ground for a meaningful and durable economic recovery. Third, to profoundly reform the existing institutions of the state while building new ones that equip Ireland to act independently in a globalized world.

Rescue, recovery and reform

Allowing the Irish economy to adjust and de-leverage from its bubble in an orderly manner is going to be hard. Entrenched levels of denial need to be broken – denial that there was a bubble in the first place – denial that high levels of growth will not quickly reoccur. As the history of bubbles past shows, the breaking of denial usually comes when markets inflict overwhelming pain on policy makers and consumers. In the Irish context, it is unfortunate though likely that expectations will be only be 'normalized' once a very sizeable correction in the housing market is behind us, and once indicators like bankruptcies and unemployment have risen to levels probably not seen since the 1980s (or worse).

Policy makers do not yet appear to be attuned to a post-bubble Ireland. The majority of policy actions to date – such as the banning of short selling, the issuing of guarantees to all of the Irish banks, the nationalization of Anglo-Irish bank and the planned establishment of the National Asset Management Agency (NAMA) have been reactive, myopic and have more generally displayed an air of overconfidence that each bold action had saved the day, and a blustering assurance that the worst was over and the recovery is in sight. Over the course of the credit crisis, the litany of policy failures in Ireland is in contrast to the more successful strategic thinking adopted by other small countries like Chile and Switzerland.

Reform – The Second Republic

Major economic crises often provide the context and motivation for fundamental philosophical and institutional changes in policy making – from Meiji Japan in the 1860s to the Thatcher era in 1980s Britain. In a similar respect, Ireland needs radical institutional reform now. The bursting of its economic bubble and the lacklustre political response to it underline the need for a large scale reassessment and renewal of political values and structures.

It may not be too much to say that Irish society and public life have lost touch with the values of those who established the Republic. Ireland's economic depression is exposing further the hubris of the recent past, and the many social, political and economic problems that have gone unattended in the past ten years. This, together with the lack of a convincing strategic response to the crisis suggests that a renewal of our republic is needed. In short, we need to start thinking about what a second republic might look like.

Some of the reasons why our republic needs to regenerate are that many long-standing institutions are malfunctioning, various pillars of excellence are crumbling and the values of Irish society have become less republican in the traditional sense. From an institutional point of view, the failure of the Irish banks and of the institutions and mechanisms that were supposed to oversee them is the one that stands out. A deeper failure is the lack of serious strategic thinking on the part of the political and policymaking classes, not just in the past six months but in an habitual way. By and large the skills and incentives of our political class draw them toward small, local issues and leave them unprepared for 'bigger picture' ones. The political havoc sown by the smaller political parties during the EU Treaty debate was a warning signal of where the abilities and motivation of the mainstream political class lay.

There is also a sense that the moral paradigm shift that took place in Irish politics from the 1970s onwards has now caught up with us. Moral courage, accountability and leadership are in short supply. At the same time, many of the institutional successes that drove our economic success are themselves beginning to falter. For example, education is widely accepted to be one of the bedrocks of Ireland's economic success, though in recent years the state has invested less in it relatively speaking. Educational standards, especially in maths and science, are unremarkable by comparison to most other European and many Asian countries.

From a purist, traditional republican point of view (as opposed to the dissident variety) Irish society has ducked and dived away from the values of equality, fraternity and liberty over the past twenty years. The cohesion of a previously fraternal society is breaking down as trust in institutions withers, and as levels of

A deeper failure is the lack of serious strategic thinking on the part of the political and policymaking classes, not just in the past six months but in an habitual way.

Moral courage, accountability and leadership are in short supply.

crime and anti-social behaviour rise. Despite the wealth created by Ireland's economic boom, its distribution has changed little in thirty years. Serious inequalities remain and on many socio-economic measures Ireland is more comparable to some of the poorer Mediterranean states than the 'model' Nordic countries.

If we really do want to live in a republic, how do we get back on track? A good starting point is the definition of a republic by the (Irish) philosopher Philip Pettit as simply 'a state where citizens are free from domination' by which he means 'not being subject to the arbitrary sway of another or being subject to the potentially capricious will or the potentially idiosyncratic judgement of another.'[21]

This definition is particularly relevant to the notion of the Global Question, and more so in the context of today's credit crisis as it points toward a type of republic that is able to shield its citizens from powerful external forces such as financial markets or even global organized crime, or potentially where the state acts to check the forces that might lead its citizens to be dominated by speculation and rising expectations of wealth as has happened in Ireland in the recent past.

Here are a few proposals: a smaller Dáil that focuses on 'big picture' national and international issues; a Presidency with more power and resources is also necessary; elevation of local politics to the provincial from county level, and attract better qualified and more accountable local politicians.

We must also institute an unambiguous legal framework to oversee political corruption, and to govern the interaction between commerce and the state. Upgrading the technical skills of politicians and policy makers is also very important. Both groups need a deeper grounding in technical areas like economics, sciences, and management, for example. Something along the lines of a 'Grande Ecole' is an option here, together with cooperation with international universities and institutions like the OECD.

Many policy issues in Ireland have been treated with a far greater dose of pragmatism than careful strategic thought. Ireland is at a crucial juncture with regard to the next stage of its economic development, its place in the world, the well being of public life and the structure of its society.

Sidebar:

Educational standards, especially in maths and science, are unremarkable by comparison to most other European and many Asian countries.

Upgrading the technical skills of politicians and policy makers is also very important. Both groups need a deeper grounding in technical areas like economics, sciences, and management, for example.

Colm McCarthy

Annette Hughes

David Begg

Brendan Tuohy

Peter McLoone

Danny McCoy

Dr Don Thornhill

Prof. John Hegarty

Brian Hayes TD

Margaret Sweeney

Jeremy Gilbert

Pádraig McManus

Simon Coveney TD

Paul Dowling

Dara Calleary TD

Martina Anderson MLA

Dr Joe Mulholland, Noel Dorr, Mícheál
Martin TD, Patricia McKenna, Angela
Kerins and Ruairí Quinn TD

Martin Territt

David O'Sullivan

Angela Kerins

Pádraig MacLochlainn

Mícheal Martin TD

Lucinda Creighton TD

Patricia McKenna

Chapter 6

REFORM AND COMPETITIVENESS

TWO OPTIONS - RAISE TAXES OR CUT SPENDING
Colm McCarthy
School of Economics, UCD and Chairman, 'An Bord Snip Nua'

URGENT NEED TO RESTORE COMPETITIVENESS
Annette Hughes
Director, DKM and Member, National Competitiveness Council (NCC)

COMPETITIVENESS IS A MEANINGLESS CONCEPT
David Begg
General Secretary, Irish Congress of Trade Unions

RESULTS ARE NEEDED NOW - NOT MORE REPORTS
Brendan Tuohy
Former Secretary-General, Dept. of Communications, Marine & Natural Resources

UNIONS MUST HAVE KEY ROLE IN TRANSFORMATION
Peter McLoone
General Secretary, IMPACT Trade Union

GENUINE WORKPLACE CHANGE A WIN-WIN OPTION FOR ALL
Danny McCoy
Director-General, Irish Business and Employers' Confederation (IBEC)

Two Options – Raise Taxes or Cut Spending

Colm McCarthy

School of Economics, UCD and Chairman, 'An Bord Snip Nua'

Born in Dublin. Founding partner of economic consultancy group Davy, Kelleher McCarthy (DKM). Previously worked at Economic and Social Research Institute (ESRI) and Central Bank. Served on boards of the ESB and Bord Gáis Éireann (BGÉ). Has undertaken assignments for the EU Commission and the World Bank and published extensively in Irish and international journals on applied economics.

The usual reaction to shock or grief comes in five stages: denial, anger, depression, bargaining and acceptance. I feel the phase of denial is over. People realize we are in a much greater mess than the 1980s and it is time to push ahead with a solution to it. I will not bore you into anger, or acceptance, by rattling through the 300 pages of the report released recently. It has been covered extensively by the newspapers and people are familiar by now with the main thrust of the proposals we have made.

I thought it would be useful to give an updated background to the kind of situation we are in. People realize, I think, that we are really in a much greater mess than we were in in the 1980s and that it is time to push ahead with finding a solution to it. I want to talk particularly about fiscal consolidation.

There are four priorities in macro-policy that we need to address. First is the restoration of fiscal balance. We are currently borrowing about €400 million per week. We face a penalty interest rate on what we borrow and this for nearly a year now. We must address this problem and that is mainly what I am going to talk about. Secondly, I am going to say a few things about the banking crisis. We cannot have an economic recovery without a functioning banking system to suit our needs. Thirdly, we must restore the competitiveness of the economy which has weakened in recent years. Fourthly, and this is not widely understood, there is the problem of our national balance sheet. There is a notion of a national balance sheet – all the assets and liabilities of all the households and firms and government here in Ireland. The national balance sheet has got out of kilter. It is too big and we

> **People realize, I think, that we are really in a much greater mess than we were in in the 1980s and that it is time to push ahead with finding a solution to it.**

> **We are currently borrowing about €400 million per week. We face a penalty interest rate on what we borrow and this for nearly a year now.**

have ended up with too many assets, or things we thought were assets, and heaps of debt. Unlike the 1980s, these debts have not been caused by government spending but have been contracted through the banking system and we now have a balance sheet that, frankly, is totally unbalanced. More alarmingly still, the difference between assets and liabilities is a lot worse than we thought. We need to de-leverage the national balance sheet – that is make our liabilities smaller. That process is now under way.

The private sector of the economy owes almost €400 billion to the banking system. This is one of the highest ratios to GNP in the world. I might add that about €130 billion in liquidity has already been provided to our financial system by the European Central Bank. Had the ECB not provided that liquidity we would have already hit the buffers. The de-leveraging that has to happen requires an increase in private saving and that is under way. There has been a huge increase in the savings rate recently. There is also a need for asset disposal nationally to reduce debt. The State is also funding a book of assets. That is one of the things mentioned in An Bord Snip Nua Report. The State needs to de-leverage too and dispose of assets it does not need.

The private sector of the economy owes almost €400 billion to the banking system. This is one of the highest ratios to GNP in the world. I might add that about €130 billion in liquidity has already been provided to our financial system by the European Central Bank.

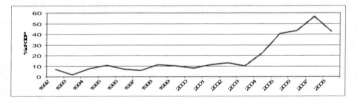

De-Leveraging under way.....

- Net Foreign Liabilities of Banking System

Figure 1

This figure illustrates the nature of the de-leveraging which is necessary. It shows that net foreign liabilities trundled along fairly evenly until we come to 2003/2004. Then they took off and increased really dramatically. This has turned now and part of the de-leveraging is already under way.

Further background to the nature of the financial crisis: the ratio of personal debt repayments has more or less doubled from 2000 to 2008. In 2000 personal debt repayments stood at a little over 10 per cent. By 2008 the personal sector was devoting 24 per cent of their income to servicing their debts. This obviously had a lot to do with the huge borrowing for housing and so on.

People speak as though Ireland had a fantastically performing economy up until about a year ago and suddenly the Celtic Tiger died and we discovered we were poor. That is not how it happened. The really rapid growth period was from about 1995 to about 2002. There was a very sharp fall in the rate of growth between the periods 1995-2002 and 2002-2008. There has been very strong growth in public spending, faster than was prudent, but in addition a great deal of government revenue was coming in from taxes on property. There was a real boom in tax revenue until 2006. Since then Government revenue from taxes has fallen over a cliff. While we do not have the exact figures it looks as if these taxes will be shy in 2009 by at least €6 billion as against what was happening before. It has contributed to the serious public finances crisis. There was an excessive reliance on some tax sources which turned out to be transitory.

People speak as though Ireland had a fantastically performing economy up until about a year ago and suddenly the Celtic Tiger died and we discovered we were poor. That is not how it happened.

The Budget Gap.....

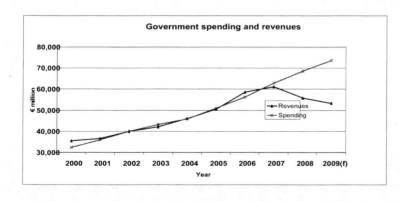

Figure 2

This shows the Government Budget gap. The two lines at first track one another. In other words we have more or less zero deficit until 2006-7. Then one can see the two lines begin to diverge and the spending line has kept rising and continues to rise into 2009. You can see the collapse of revenue. The gap that has opened up is €20 billion a year or €400 million a week and that is what we are now borrowing. So this shows the continuing rise in Government spending coinciding with the collapse in Government revenue. That is the Irish fiscal crisis in a nutshell.

The Government budget deficit this year will be a little under 11 per cent of GDP after four sets of policy changes since July last year. The Government had a cuts package in July, brought the Budget forward to October, more cuts in January and a mini-budget in April. That is four partial budgets in 12 months and a lot of painful measures included. After that we are going to borrow nearly 11 per cent of GDP which is quite unsustainable. Without further measures the deficit would exceed 10 per cent for several years to come.

Our debt, while not as high as it was in the 1980s when we had to make a big fiscal adjustment, is rising very quickly and does not include the bank rescue costs. We are going to face an Exchequer bill for the bank rescue costs and we do not know how big it is. The International Monetary Fund estimates that this could be €34 or €35 billion. One Dublin stockbroker reckons it might be only €20 billion. I do not know what it is going to be. Of its nature, no one knows.

The bank rescue costs could add two years borrowing at the recent high rates, as if we did not have enough headaches. That leaves the Government with very difficult choices. These choices ultimately boil down to two – raise taxes or cut spending.

Real Exchequer spending rose nearly 6 per cent in 2008. It is rising even faster in 2009. People find that hard to believe. Significant tax increases have already been imposed. If you have not inspected your payslip carefully recently, you should do so soon. But the Government has said it is anxious to avoid further heavy tax increases.

Gross current spending, that is spending on health, welfare, education and so forth, as a percentage of GNP had fallen a bit in the 2006 Celtic Tiger years, partly because of growth in GNP. Then it remained a bit flat for a few years. It

> **The gap that has opened up is €20 billion a year or €400 million a week and that is what we are now borrowing. So this shows the continuing rise in Government spending coinciding with the collapse in Government revenue. That is the Irish fiscal crisis in a nutshell.**

> **These choices ultimately boil down to two – raise taxes or cut spending.**

has risen dramatically since 2006. This year it has increased again because, unfortunately there are more and more people on the Live Register and also because there have been continuing increases in voted spending under various headings. The debt service has also begun to rise. This will remind people of the 1980s when the debt burden made things so difficult. We had borrowed a lot of money and interest rates were high. The debt service fell quite dramatically five or six years ago. Even three years ago it was quite small. However, it is ominous that it has begun to creep up again in the last while total Government spending as a percentage of GNP is now back to where it was in 1987. If anybody has you persuaded that we do not have a high Government spending relative to income, they are wrong. The combination of increases in spending in recent years and the squeeze on GNP means the percentage of GNP devoted to public spending is as high as it was back in 1987.

Real Growth, Total Exchequer Spending

Year	Spend % Chg	CPI %	% Real Growth
2000	10.4	5.6	4.8
2001	16.1	4.9	11.2
2002	11.0	4.6	6.4
2003	7.7	3.6	4.1
2004	6.2	2.1	4.1
2005	11.1	2.5	8.6
2006	10.6	3.9	6.7
2007	11.8	4.9	6.9
2008e	9.8	4.1	5.7
2009f	6.9	-3.8	10.8

Figure 3

These figures show what has happened to all Exchequer spending, inflation as measured by the Consumer Price Index and the difference between the two. There was a real increase in total spending of 11.2 per cent in 2001 but in all the other years along the way it was also high. Last year, in 2008, there was an estimated real increase in spending ahead of inflation of 5.7 per cent. This year, and of course one can only make a stab at it because the year is only half over, spending will be up 6.9 per cent but the price level is probably going to be down 3.8 per cent. That gives an even bigger growth in spending this year.

Budget Balance in the 1980s, % GNP

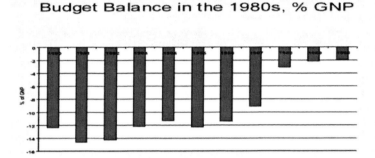

Figure 4

To go back to what happened in the 1980s, the Budget deficit got stuck in a groove of 10 or 12 per cent and we did not get out of that groove for seven or eight years. We ended up with a huge debt burden. Eventually at the end of the 1980s we took a lot of action and we also got lucky. Tax revenues began to recover and we eventually got out of it. I included this figure to remind ourselves that the last time we were in a public finance crisis; it took us a long time to get out of it.

CPI Inflation

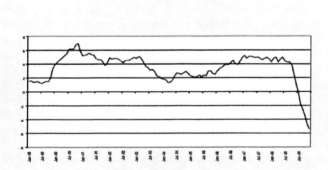

Figure 5

I want to finish by saying a few general things about the An Bord Snip Nua Proposals. The proposals need to be seen firstly as a set of options for the Government. That is all they are. But they must be seen against a background of borrowing of €400 million a week. We are already paying a penalty interest rate. The borrowing markets are terribly difficult, the most difficult since the 1960s. Inflation has turned negative. That has to have consequences for how much we spend.

So to conclude, the sovereign debt markets are the most difficult I can remember. Any notion people have that the international bond markets have settled down and the worst is over and that we have turned the corner, is baloney. I think these markets are going to remain iffy for at least another few years. So it seems to me that we must contain borrowing in 2009 and try to reduce the borrowing requirement as a percentage of GDP decisively in 2010. That means cuts in current and capital spending and may also mean further tax measures and it means we must look at all spending.

The responses to our report have included accusations that we targeted certain areas and I am counting the areas. As far as I can make out, spokespersons for every single Government Department have stated that they were targeted and they are right. We looked at everything, with no red lines, no area of current expenditure exempt. A similar exercise, in which I am not involved, is under way in the Department of Finance on the capital budget. That is the situation we are in and the option is to deal with it or leave it to someone else to deal with if we fail.

A similar exercise, in which I am not involved, is under way in the Department of Finance on the capital budget. That is the situation we are in and the option is to deal with it or leave it to someone else to deal with if we fail.

Urgent Need to Restore Competitiveness

Annette Hughes

Director, DKM and member, National Competitive Council (NCC)

Joined DKM in 1993, having previously worked for John Laing plc, BP Ireland and lectured in economics at University of Limerick. Graduate of UCC. Expert on Irish construction and housing industries as well as on energy, with particular focus on their interactions with demographics and regional development.

Ireland's economic fortunes have changed dramatically

The changed economic realities which have transpired for the Irish economy, both globally and domestically, have placed the economy in an extremely weak position. The reasons are well known. Economic growth since 2000 was based on a credit induced bubble which was not sustainable. As a result we are left with a legacy of unprecedented private sector debt, which has been financing Government expenditure in recent years. The necessary deleveraging of this debt (by private households and businesses as well as banks) is unavoidable, which further complicates the recovery.

The deterioration in economic conditions at home during 2008 plus the severe contraction in the investment side of the economy and weak consumer sentiment levels will give rise to a further sharp contraction in economic activity this year and next. Difficulties in the banking sector mean less scope for consumer and businesses to secure credit to finance spending. The weakening Exchequer position has generated significant budgetary pressures for Government, while further job losses and fiscal retrenchment continue to dampen economic activity.

Following the publication of the report of An Bord Snip Nua, we can expect further cuts in Government expenditure in the 2010 and subsequent budgets. Thus it seems that most risks are on the downside. As a result, forecasts for the Irish economy have been revised substantially downwards with the IMF, the OECD and the European Commission now suggesting that the Irish economy will have contracted, in GDP terms, by a cumulative 14 per cent over the period 2008-2010. As recently as last October the consensus forecast for 2009 was only around +2 per cent.[22] The past really is a different country!

Need a credible medium-term budgetary programme

The very weak position of the Irish economy has been receiving much attention over the past twelve months. Recently, that attention has been dominated by the banking crisis and the measures to restore a properly functioning banking and credit system, most notably about NAMA. The focus now, following the McCarthy report, is correctly on setting out a credible medium-term budgetary programme that will ensure a sustainable return to economic stability by 2013. At the core of that plan must be measures to not just restore but to improve the long-term competitiveness of the Irish economy and sustain employment. The restoration of competitiveness is the only way a small open economy like Ireland can benefit from the global economic recovery when it occurs. Getting back on track competitively will also help to restore our reputation overseas by boosting Irish exports and encouraging foreign direct investment.

Competitiveness has many dimensions

The National Competitiveness Council (NCC) was set up in 1997 to assess the factors that determine competitiveness and identify the actions most urgently needed to maintain and enhance that competitiveness. The Council has always acknowledged that competitiveness is not just about costs and prices, although these are very important issues. The NCC defines national competitiveness as:

> all those factors that impact on the ability of the enterprise base in Ireland to compete in international markets in a way that provides the Irish population with the opportunity to improve their quality of life.

Successive annual reports from the Council have warned about competitiveness difficulties since the beginning of this decade. In its 2003 Competitiveness Challenge report the Council stated:

> Ireland's immediate competitiveness priority must be to slow the growth of prices and costs ... there are also, however, more deep seated structural factors behind the cost escalation which if left unchecked pose a more fundamental threat to Irish national competitiveness ... these include public sector inefficiencies and the legacy of a generation of government regulations in product and service markets that act to inhibit competition.

But critically, at the core of the Council's assessment of the challenge facing us is the necessity to restore the competitiveness of our exporting sectors and our attractiveness for inward investment.

Loss of competitiveness since 2000

Much of the Irish economy's current problems stem from our loss of competitiveness which has been around for much longer than the economic recession. Both the IMF and the OECD have acknowledged in their respective reports on the Irish economy that Ireland faces a significant competitive disadvantage. The IMF Report (June 2009) calculated that Ireland's competitiveness is about 15 per cent above its long-term average when the real exchange rate, allowing for modest improvements in productivity, is taken into account. Both believe that competitiveness can (and must) be restored by lower wages and stronger competition, particularly in the non-traded sector, which will lead to reduced costs.

The generally accepted measures of competitiveness are the Central Bank's Harmonized Competitiveness Indicators.[23] The data show that the overall competitive position of the Irish economy deteriorated by 35 per cent between January 2000 and April 2008 reflecting a combination of higher consumer price inflation and an appreciation of the euro against our trading partners. Ireland's current price deflation has improved matters somewhat with the loss in competitiveness reduced to 30.5 per cent between January 2000 and May 2009. However, when the measure is deflated

The IMF Report (June 2009) calculated that Ireland's competitiveness is about 15 per cent above its long-term average when the real exchange rate, allowing for modest improvements in productivity, is taken into account. Both believe that competitiveness can (and must) be restored by lower wages and stronger competition, particularly in the non-traded sector, which will lead to reduced costs.

Figure 1 Measures of the Competitiveness of the Irish Economy: Harmonized Competitiveness Indicator for Ireland 1995 to May 2009 (1999 Q1=100)

by producer prices, it is evident that producer prices moved in line with those of our trading partners since 2005. The real issue concerns the impact of Irish consumer price inflation. Since 2005 it moved way out of line with our partners. This reflects the impact of labour market pressures which led to wage rates and other prices rising very rapidly since that time.

The priorities for making Ireland competitive again

The most recent report from the NCC[24] identified a number of policy priorities, some of which appear in my list of priorities below.

Restore stability to the public finances

This task will take a number of painful years. While this process has already commenced it is essential that Government continues to take the necessary decisive action on cutting expenditure as identified in the report of An Bord Snip Nua, starting with the 2010 Budget. With revenues projected to account for almost 35.6 per cent of GNP and Government current expenditure expected to represent 43.4 per cent of GNP in the April Budget for 2009[25], this situation is not sustainable.

It is essential that Government continues to take the necessary decisive action on cutting expenditure as identified in the report of An Bord Snip Nua, starting with the 2010 Budget.

Broaden the tax base

In view of the severe decline in tax revenue in 2008/2009, there is a need to broaden the tax base which has been progressively narrowed over recent decades. Any review of the tax base needs to ensure first and foremost that the current system is optimal, fair and equitable. Having done so, starting from the premise that a successful economy requires high quality public services, then faced with fewer/scarce resources, there is a need for some combination of increased taxes, wage cuts or productivity increases to finance those public services. The report for the Commission on Taxation is expected to recommend a restructuring of the tax system although some tax increases are also expected to be recommended. The NCC has consistently recommended the introduction of a property tax based on capital values. The latter would also serve to address the serious gap in the revenue base of local authorities which has arisen due to the recent dearth of development contributions as a result of the lack of new construction activity around the country. However the introduction of a property tax system needs to be well thought out and planned before it is introduced and must be fair and equitable.

The NCC has consistently recommended the introduction of a property tax based on capital values.

Current expenditure adjustment must start with largest components

In respect of current expenditure the largest elements of the current expenditure programme are the public service pay and pensions bill, at almost 39 per cent of the total projected revenues this year and Social Welfare (€21 billion), at almost 41 per cent and rising. If real progress is to be achieved on cutting expenditure and restoring stability to the public finances, both of these areas have to figure prominently in the measures put forward. Moreover, there is a need to recognize that the competitiveness of the economy is a function of both the public and private sectors. Thus there is a need now to carry out an up to date benchmarking exercise comparing wages in the public and private sectors and with public sector wages in our competitors. The recent National Employment Survey[26] reported that hourly earnings in the public sector were 48 per cent higher on average higher than in the private sector. This gap may have widened further since the survey was undertaken (October 2007) notwithstanding the introduction of the public pensions levy this

The recent National Employment Survey reported that hourly earnings in the public sector were 48 per cent higher on average higher than in the private sector.

year, given reductions in private sector pay in the meantime. This suggests there is justification for pay cuts in the public sector.

Capital expenditure – need to focus on productive investment

I agree with the NCC view that there needs to be a serious review of the investment priorities identified in the 2007-2013 NDP. That review should be based on proceeding only with capital projects which:

- earn an economic rate of return above their costs,
- add to the productive potential of the economy,
- are employment intensive, and
- minimize the external leakage of funds.

Investment in productive infrastructure is a key element in building a competitive economy, supporting the indigenous sector while helping to attract inward investment.

Ensuring the banks channel credit to viable businesses

With regard to the banking crisis, a number of recent surveys suggest that the flow of credit to business continues to be restricted notwithstanding the range of measures to support the financial sector over the past ten months:

- The Small Firms Association – one in four SMEs are not getting enough credit with the refusal rate highest (30 per cent) for firms with less than 10 employees.[27]
- IBEC – businesses are suffering badly from the financial crisis and the sharp devaluation of sterling. 31 per cent of respondents in a survey of 278 companies indicated that the availability of working capital in their company had decreased while 38 per cent reported that the cost of finance had increased.[28]
- The Construction Industry Council – inability to secure finance is the main reason for the delay/postponement of projects.

The core issue here is to restore a properly functioning credit

In order to restore the competitiveness of our exporting sectors, policies need to focus on getting Irish costs and other charges down to or below the levels of our trading partners if Irish firms are to improve their relative position with regard to cost competitiveness.

market so that businesses can get access to finance at a reasonable cost.

Restoring cost competitiveness

In order to restore the competitiveness of our exporting sectors, policies need to focus on getting Irish costs and other charges down to or below the levels of our trading partners if Irish firms are to improve their relative position with regard to cost competitiveness.

The NCC has done much work in the area of costs over recent years and is currently working on its fourth assessment of the costs of doing business in Ireland.[29] Four key inputs are examined – labour, land/property, utilities and business services (e.g., accounting and legal services) – across a sample of firms covering eight sectors of the economy. Across these eight sectors, labour costs account for 59 per cent of total costs.

The ongoing analysis by the NCC highlights a number of areas where our cost competitiveness is improving, notably on the moderation in the growth of labour costs relative to the average in the euro area, which has already been referred to, and a decline in the cost of office rents by 25 per cent in 2008. However, in other areas the costs faced by Irish firms are reported to be persistently high.

It is essential that competition in non-traded services sectors of the economy is encouraged, as this will be the best way of bringing down costs to business and consumers. In this regard, the recommendations of the Competition Authority with respect to a number of sectors, such as professional and legal services, should be used to increase competition and support the adjustment needed on prices and wages.

Need immediate coordinated plan of action

While many solid recommendations have been made over the past decade by the NCC and indeed by other agencies, there is an urgent need now to bring about a greater coherence and coordination of actions to support national competitiveness and the transition to the next phase of Ireland's economic

We have many policy priorities covering the ambit of financial, fiscal and competitiveness issues. There is a real urgency now to tackle each one of them. That requires all parties to be on board, namely trade unions, employers and politicians.

development. We have many policy priorities covering the ambit of financial, fiscal and competitiveness issues. There is a real urgency now to tackle each one of them. That requires all parties to be on board, namely trade unions, employers and politicians. If we delay in tackling the underlying problems responsible, we could see an even more protracted economic downturn.

Competitiveness is a Meaningless Concept

David Begg
General Secretary, Irish Congress of Trade Unions

Formerly worked with ESB. General Secretary of the Communications Workers' Union (1990-7). In 1997, assumed position as Chief Executive of the international humanitarian organization, Concern Worldwide. Appointed General Secretary of ICTU in 2001. Director of the Central Bank since 1995. Governor of Irish Times Trust, member of Government Taskforce on Active Citizenship, member of National Economic and Social Council and sits on Executive Committee of the European Trade Unions Confederation (ETUC).

Since October 2007 the value of the world's stock market has halved. The banking system has imploded. Inflation of 4.5 per cent has turned into deflation of the same magnitude. Global Capitalism, on the precipice of collapse, has been rescued by the state. In Ireland the crisis has been exacerbated by the exposure of a nexus of bankers and developers whose activities have mortgaged the future of our children, perhaps of several generations.

Against this background the question for debate, 'Can we get back to being competitive again', seems a tad incongruous. It implies a return to business as usual. This is illusory. The world of the last three decades has gone. Neo–liberalism has failed. The important question is what will replace it. In any event much that is expounded by way of competitiveness theory is suspect. This was eloquently explained in a book entitled *Just Capital* written by the then head of the Confederation of British Industry (CBI) and current chairman of the Financial Services Authority (FSA), Adair Turner, some years ago. His sceptical view of the subject was stated thus:

> By 1995 the CBI had carved out a name for itself as an advocate of competitiveness: In becoming its Director

> **The world of the last three decades has gone. Neo–liberalism has failed. The important question is what will replace it. In any event much that is expounded by way of competitiveness theory is suspect.**

General, in a sense I became the high priest of a cult whose beliefs I thought rather confused, but which I could not reject outright without causing more confusion, ineffectiveness and indeed, offence.[30]

Further on he wrote:

The use of the word 'competitiveness' pollutes and confuses real, important debates about real, important issues of Public Policy. It confuses the debate about the appropriate size and functions of the state, about the economic implications of different levels of tax and public spend.

Similar scepticism has been expressed by Paul Krugman who wrote in *Pop Internationalism:*

It's time to start telling the truth: Competitiveness is a meaningless concept when applied to National Economies. And the obsession with Competitiveness is both wrong and dangerous.[31]

Speaking specifically about the Irish economy Seán Ó Riain notes that:

The difficulties of the Irish economy are less a matter of 'competitiveness' than of the failure to build a deeper and more inclusive form of autocentric development around the development network state.[32]

Nevertheless the solution canvassed by establishment figures in Ireland for our current economic troubles is focused on competitiveness. The argument made is that we must reduce our cost base by cutting wages across the board by 15 per cent and by imposing swingeing cuts on public expenditure. If we do, so the argument goes, we will not only compensate for our inability to devalue our currency in line with sterling but we will be poised to increase our exports when the recovery begins.

There are a few problems with this analysis. First, the implementation of retrenchment on this scale would be hugely deflationary. I am not aware of any country ever having deflated its way out of a recession. Personal consumption typically amounted to about 60 per cent of GNP over the years. It rose at a rate of 9 per cent each year between 2005 and 2007. In 2008 it rose by 2.1 per cent but in quarter 1 of 2009 it fell by 10 per cent. The competitiveness solution being canvassed, through wage and public spending cuts, will impart a further dangerous

The competitiveness solution being canvassed, through wage and public spending cuts, will impart a further dangerous deflationary shock to the domestic demand side of the economy.

deflationary shock to the domestic demand side of the economy. One of the lesser known statistics of this global economic crisis is that shipping rates between China and Europe temporarily fell to zero dollars in early 2009. As consumer demand in the west dried up and exports dwindled, brokers actually waived the transport fee and only charged a minimal handling cost. According to the World Bank, exports from China, Japan, Mexico, Russia and the United States fell by 25 per cent in the year leading up to February 2009. In this bleak trading environment it is difficult to see how we could get even a dead cat bounce out of our exports by cutting wages.

Actually, when compared to other countries, Ireland's export performance does not indicate that we are uncompetitive. Our exports dropped by 5.9 per cent this year as against a drop of 16.5 per cent in Germany, 15.9 per cent in Italy and 9.8 per cent in the UK.

Actually, when compared to other countries, Ireland's export performance does not indicate that we are uncompetitive. Our exports dropped by 5.9 per cent this year as against a drop of 16.5 per cent in Germany, 15.9 per cent in Italy and 9.8 per cent in the UK. Moreover, we are heading towards a balance of payments surplus in 2009. According to the Global Competitiveness Index for 2008 – 2009 both Germany and the UK have higher ratings than Ireland.

The point is that we know that pro-cyclical deflationary policies will drive down the domestic demand side of the economy but there is no evidence to suggest any immediate boost to exports. But what about the prospects of benefiting from a recovery in world trade by improving competitiveness? There is much talk about 'Green Shoots.'

It is necessary to understand that there are two major causes for the collapse in world trade. One is the implosion of the Global Financial System. If it is the brain of the global market then the whole system is still in intensive care. The other is the imbalances in trade, savings and currency reserves that globalization has built up between East and West. In reality we are in a space where Europe is depending on America to create the recovery and America is waiting on China to redress the imbalances by fostering domestic demand in its own economy.

Consider, for a moment, how realistic a prospect this is? Chinese policy is to peg its currency against the US dollar, allowing a microscopic rise in the value of the renminbi over time. To change that policy, and allow a massive fall of the dollar against the renmimbi, would be a massive act of self-sacrifice by China and a massive signal that it intends to move away from an export-led strategy towards developing its home markets.

Many academic discussions of the imbalances tend to assume that the US, or the IMF, would in some way dictate to China the course of rebalancing. But China has already unleashed the world's biggest state spending programme in response to the crisis, pitching 15 per cent of its GDP into a stimulus package in November 2008. But creating a mass consumer market in China to buy the goods that were once exported to the US and Europe would involve turning Chinese workers from the low-paid wage slaves of the world into the consumer spenders of the world. It seems to me to be a big ask which at best is unlikely to resuscitate global trade any time soon. So when economists make these demands for sacrifices by ordinary mortals they need to be interrogated as to the practicality of what they propose.

None of these people predicted the recession and now we know that one of the most vocal was actually encouraging the banks in their irresponsibility. Insofar as the McCarthy Report is seen to be a blueprint for the type of public expenditure cuts which would aid competitiveness I want to make a passing reference to it.

It will hardly be disputed, I assume, that its impact too will be highly deflationary, contributing to the difficulties I have outlined. But there is a more fundamental point to be considered. A very astute observer of my acquaintance described the report as being like watching Plato's Guardians redesign the Republic from a blank slate.

There is something of an anti-politics feel about this. Without wishing to question either their integrity or their ability it is a fact that the two key figures on this Committee (An Bord Snip Nua) are a banker and an economist of the neo-classical school. Their approach seems to embody the key features of the system which has just failed us. If pro-cyclical fiscal policies were a cause of our compounding the crisis in the first part of this decade it is difficult to see why we should expect to find our salvation in them now. For me there is also a philosophical issue. I believe that affairs should be organized in such a way that the economy is embedded in society and not the other way round. The propositions contained in the McCarthy Report appear to be concerned solely with economic issues and have little regard to their social consequences. It is an approach, therefore, which is the very antithesis of what I think it should be.

To sum up, then, I believe with Krugman that competitiveness is an important issue for individual companies, perhaps even for sectors of the economy, but it is a meaningless concept at the level of a country.

The propositions contained in the McCarthy Report appear to be concerned solely with economic issues and have little regard to their social consequences.

First, we could correct the infrastructural deficits which are the legacy of a previous period of disinvestment in the 1980s. These include public transport, roads, hospitals, schools and broadband. We will never have a better opportunity to do this in a cost effective way and at the same time save a significant part of the capacity of the construction sector which is fast unravelling. Second, it is clear that normal commercial activity cannot take place without a functioning banking system. Third, we have to try to keep people in employment and upgrade their skills. In this regard it is instructive to note that the consistently most successful countries are the Scandinavians who make the highest investment in human capital. Fourth, we need to broaden our tax base to fill the gap left by property related transaction taxes and for the purpose of sustaining public services.

This approach is encapsulated in a proposal for a social solidarity pact constructed by Congress several months ago. It is a matter of regret to us that it failed to gain sufficient traction so far. It is only by uniting the country behind a vision of the common good that we can begin to rebuild. Unless we can achieve this, restoring competitiveness will be the least of our problems.

What happens from here on in is a political question of the highest importance. The Trade Union movement in Ireland, like in the rest of Europe, is founded on social democratic principles. The state model which Ireland has followed is captured well by Seán Ó Riain:

> Development states expose more clearly the political choice between Neo-liberalism and social democracy. In a time when Neo-liberalism promises financial speculation, impoverishment, corporate criminality, and permanent war, the choice is clear between social democracy and barbarism.[33]

It is a sentiment with which I entirely concur.

Results are Needed Now – Not More Reports

Brendan Tuohy

Former Secretary-General, Dept. of Communications, Marine and Natural Resources

Holds degree in civil engineering from UCC and post-graduate qualifications in environmental engineering and management from TCD. Was Secretary General of the Dept. of Public Enterprise and prior to that Assistant Secretary in that Department and its predecessor, Dept. of Transport, Energy and Communications. Was a member of the National Economic and Social Council and the United Nations Task Force on Information and Communications Technology for Development.

Introduction

Public sector reform has become a very topical and urgent issue with a growing realization that significant and urgent reform is required to enhance the effectiveness and efficiency of the public service. I will look briefly at the various public sector reform initiatives that have been taken over the past years in Ireland and then, looking to the future, I will suggest a few initiatives that could have significant impact if properly implemented.

Public sector reform initiatives

In looking back at previous efforts at reform in the public sector, it might be worth grouping the reforms into five different periods:

- The Report of the Commission on the Civil Service (Brennan Commission) which was established to inquire into and report on the recruitment and organization of the civil service with special reference to the arrangements for ensuring efficiency in working.[34] It reported in 1935 and concluded that the system was satisfactory overall.

Serving the Country Better (White Paper published in 1985) was aimed at improving the efficiency and effectiveness of the public service and recommended the introduction of management systems and corporate planning together with personal responsibility for results, costs and service.

- The Public Service Organization Review Group (Devlin Report), which looked at the organization of the Departments of State, including the appropriate distribution of functions as between both Departments and between Departments and other bodies.[35] It reported in 1969 and recommended the division of each Government Department along policy development (Aireacht) and execution lines including the establishment of executive agencies and the establishment of a new Department for the Public Service (DPS). While the DPS was set up, the other main recommendations were not implemented.

- Serving the Country Better (White Paper published in 1985) was aimed at improving the efficiency and effectiveness of the public service and recommended the introduction of management systems and corporate planning together with personal responsibility for results, costs and service. The proposals were never even debated in the Dáil or Seanad and, because of the worsening economic situation, the emphasis changed to controlling numbers and reducing costs. Some changes occurred including the integration of the DPS into the Department of Finance (1987), decentralization of over one thousand civil servants (1988), establishment of an Efficiency Audit Group (1989), introduction of performance-related pay for assistant secretaries (1990) and the introduction of administrative budgets for Government departments (1991).

- The Strategic Management Initiative (SMI) was introduced in 1994 and it drew on the international reforms that were occurring in the public services, many of which were based on greater managerialism, greater emphasis on organizational issues and strategic planning and greater use of market mechanisms for delivery of services. The initiative was driven very much by senior civil servants, with support from Taoiseach Albert Reynolds TD. The initial scope broadened to become the Public Service Modernization Programme.

- A range of initiatives were launched over the subsequent years, such as, Delivering Better Government (1996), Quality Customer Service (1997), SMI Implementation Group (1997), Review of Public Expenditure (1997), Public Service Management Act (1997), Freedom of Information Act (1997), Privilege and Compellability of Witnesses Act (1997), Report of the SMI Implementation Group, partnership structures agreed, proposals for multi-annual budgets and administrative budgets approved, Delivering Quality Public Service (1999), regulatory reform measures including 'Reducing Red Tape: An Action Programme of Regulatory Reform in Ireland' (1999) and OECD Report (2001), annual reports on implementation of modernization programme published, system of performance management and development (2000), Statements of Strategy (2001), Benchmarking Report (2002), Civil Service Performance Verification Group, Customer Action Plans and Charters (2003), Decentralization plans for 10,000 public servants, Civil Service Code of Standards and Behaviour (2004), Public Service Management and Recruitment and Appointments Act (2004) and Civil Service Regulation Act (2005).

Two reviews were published of the SMI process – an independent review by PA Consulting Group (2002)[36] and a special report by the Comptroller and Auditor General (2007).[37] The PA Consulting Report concluded that 'the civil service in 2002 is a more effective organization than it was a decade earlier.' It also noted that the programme is far from complete and that deeper engagement by politicians is critical.

The C&AG concluded that

> while initiatives have been coordinated, the achievement of results has been incremental and institution specific... and there is a need to review the extent to which the modernization programme is impacting on value in the form of improved services or more efficient processes.

The fifth phase of the reform process started with an organizational review programme coordinated by the Department of An Taoiseach and a system-wide review of the Irish public service that was undertaken by the OECD (in 2006). This review

The PA Consulting Report concluded that 'the civil service in 2002 is a more effective organization than it was a decade earlier.' It also noted that the programme is far from complete and that deeper engagement by politicians is critical.

was established (i) to benchmark the public service in Ireland against other comparable countries and (ii) to make re-commendations as to the future direction for public service reform in order to deliver world-class services to the citizen within existing resources and to contribute to sustainable national competitive advantage.

The final OECD review was published in 2008[36] and it concluded that (i) Ireland has a relatively low level of public service employment in international terms, (ii) Ireland is on-track in terms of public service reform, (iii) the Irish public service has given Ireland a competitive advantage by providing high quality services, but with slowing growth and global competitiveness, it needs to work smarter.

It went on to make some recommendations, stating that there is a need: (i) to focus on delivering the best service to citizens; (ii) for a more integrated public service, (iii) for a networked approach to working across current structures to allow greater connectivity between sectors, (iv) for greater mobility and flexibility of staff across the public service; (v) a senior public service entity to provide a single public service leadership cadre.

It further recommended that there is a need: (i) to move towards a performance focus and greater prioritization within budgetary frameworks; (ii) for improved governance and performance dialogue between central civil service and the wider public service, including clear guidelines for establishing new agencies and for operating existing ones; (iii) to use eGovernment more widely to achieve a more citizen-centred approach; (iv) for a strong leadership role for the centre of Government.

The Government established a Task Force on the Public Service. It was asked to prepare for consideration by Government a comprehensive framework for renewal of the public service, which takes into account the analysis and conclusions of the OECD Review, as well as lessons drawn from the Strategic Management Initiative, the Organizational Review Programme and the Efficiency Review Process. The Task Force reported in November 2008[39] and the Government issued a Statement on Transforming the Public Services[40] at the same time. In this statement, the Government states that 'the Report sets out a three-year framework, which Government has adopted, for what is, in fact, a radical transformation of the Public Service.' The Statement also announces a number of other reports that will be completed over the coming months including a Special Group on Public Service Numbers and Expenditure Programmes (June 2009), Value for Money and Policy Reviews (2009-2011) and a procurement initiative.

Summary of the experience of public sector reforms

The table below summarizes very briefly my analysis of the experiences over the years.

Time period	Extent of reform
Pre-1985	Very limited reform
1985-1994	Slow build-up with limited reforms
1994-2005	Some changes broadly in line with international trends but nothing very radical
2006-2009	Wide range of initiatives with greater political oversight, overseen and controlled by Department of An Taoiseach; limited open external engagement; very unwilling to be critical or surface serious problems; no real sense of urgency; no willingness to be radical.

Figure 1: Summary of the experience of Irish public sector reforms

The more recent reforms raise issues that bear further consideration. For example, has the overriding need to maintain social partnership and the continuing (many times protracted) search for consensus slowed the reform process and prevented *required* more radical reforms? Would the process benefit by much greater external inputs and oversight, particularly from people who are well experienced in major organizational reforms?

The Process of Public Sector Reform

There is a growing concern about the role of the public sector and and its effectiveness, efficiency, cost and the value for money being achieved by it. In any reform process, there is a need to make the case for reform, to articulate a vision of the future (that will detail in broad terms what the public service will look like in 5-10 years time) and to outline some significant impactful initiatives that will be completed within specified time periods. Organizational structures and processes should be put in place to lead the reform process and there is a need for significant external oversight by experienced practitioners of major organizational reforms.

> There is a growing concern about the role of the public sector and and its effectiveness, efficiency, cost and the value for money being achieved by it.

In the present situation, the case for reform is clear and there is a very visible 'burning platform' as the Government is currently borrowing approximately €400 million per week and the cost of the public service just cannot continue to be met from the revenues available to the Exchequer. The public are also demanding that the public service becomes more responsive, more accountable (including much greater personal accountability) and that it deliver more cost-effective, efficient and internationally competitive public services. So, there is a compelling case not just to reform the public service to make it more cost effective but that we also use the opportunity to make some significant and impactful structural and institutional changes that will help enable the country reposition itself for the future so that it can compete effectively in an international context.

As we look at the future choices available to the public service, there are two broad directions in which it can proceed.

Some comments on the future of public sector reform

The Government's *Statement on Transforming Public Services* is a good document – and it follows on many other reports and sets up some groups to report in the future. But, drawing on experience of previous efforts at public sector reform, I would like to make a few comments.

The Old Public Service continued	A New Public Service
Failure to deliver to expectations	Delivering beyond expectations
Weakening public service values and weakening respect for the public service	Strong core values of public service and heightened respect from the public
Increasing cost of the public service with increased waste and duplication and no contestability of services	Cost effective, innovative, recognized internationally as best-in-class and all services contestable with others
Many demoralized and frustrated staff with key people over-worked and operating in institutions not fit for purpose	Staff enjoying their jobs and working in a public service with institutions fit for purpose
Poor management with little delegated authority, limited staff training and development, too many generalists, not enough expertise in areas, underperformers being carried by good staff, little movement between public and private sectors	Good managers empowered to take decisions, dealing effectively with under-performance, staff trained for their jobs, culture of learning and openness to new ideas, expertise available, total movement of staff at all levels between all the public service and also with the private sectors
Deteriorating working relations between senior civil servants and Ministers, poor oversight of Executive by Oireachtas, inefficient Oireachtas and other public bodies, poor governance of State bodies	Good working relations between senior civil servants and Ministers, good oversight of Executive by Oireachtas, effective Oireachtas and other public bodies, good governance of State bodies
Leadership failures	Leadership renewal

Figure 2: The Choices for the Public Service

Reports are not results. There are more than enough reports available over many years that have analysed the issues in detail but they have not been implemented or only some parts of them have been implemented. It is results that are needed now and not more reports.

It rarely works to put new wine in old wineskins

Leaving in place the current structures to deliver the changes required will simply not work as the system is incapable of

The Report of the Special Group on Public Services Numbers and Expenditure provides an opportunity to look at different units of analysis not just within organizations but across Government Departments and agencies to see what changes could take place to enable the provision of better and more cost effective services.

delivering the reforms from within. In other successful public sector reforms, it was the establishment of external oversight bodies, accompanied by the recruitment of new senior people into the organization, that drove the reform process. For example, the establishment of the Police Service of Northern Ireland (with a recruitment of an external Chief Constable) together with the establishment of the Police Ombudsman and external oversight by the Policing Board, has worked very well. Similarly, the establishment of the Inspectorate of the Garda Síochána, with an external Chief Executive together with an Office of the Ombudsman for the Garda Síochána, and external recruitment into the top echelons of An Garda Síochána, has worked well.

The units of analysis must change

Currently, some reforms are taking place within organizations but there are very little cross-organizational reforms and the institutions do not easily accommodate such an approach. The Report of the Special Group on Public Services Numbers and Expenditure[41] provides an opportunity to look at different units of analysis not just within organizations but across Government Departments and agencies to see what changes could take place to enable the provision of better and more cost effective services.

Leaders drive change and leadership needs to be strengthened urgently

It is people, and particularly leaders, who drive change. There is a compelling need to broaden the leadership base of the civil service to include not only the wider public service but also the private sector and the not-for-profit sector. There are many hugely experienced and talented people who have led major organizational changes and whose talents could be very well used in the public service today. There is also a need to ensure that the current leaders in the public service are provided with suitable training and development so that they can acquire or develop the necessary leadership skills and expertise to drive the changes needed in the public service.

Public sector reform requires the following to succeed:

- An acknowledgement by all of the 'burning platform' and the absolute urgent need for radical change, not slow incremental change
- Strong political leadership, with renewed political oversight by Government and the Oireachtas and parallel dramatic changes in the political institutions
- A strong political mandate for urgent and radical public sector reform
- An enthusiastic and supportive public service, that is keenly aware of the growing gap between the conditions enjoyed by public servants and most others in the country and is willing to urgently transform the public service and be much more publicly accountable for the reforms.

Willingness to look at some of the non-discussable issues

A few of the key challenges facing the architects of public sector reform include the following:

- The current contracts enjoyed by public servants make it very difficult to drive change if the public servants themselves are opposed to it. I would suggest that consideration be given to changing the contracts of all public servants to renewable 5 year contracts so that each public servant is offered a 5 year contract and, subject to satisfactory performance over each 5 year period, the contract is renewed. If performance is not satisfactory, a process of performance development and improvement can be completed over a specific period but, if this process does not yield the required results and after due process, the contract is not renewed.
- There is a need for far greater personal accountability with consequences (including more public accountability) for public servants so that they can discuss and account for their decisions (and failure to take decisions) and be held accountable for what they do. At the moment, there is very little personal accountability.

The current contracts enjoyed by public servants make it very difficult to drive change, particularly with a sense of urgency, if the public servants themselves are opposed to it.

There is a need to appoint a Minister for Public Sector Reform with a specific brief to ensure that the process of reform is driven at Government level and that the structures of Government are fit for purpose and capable of tackling vital national strategic issues.

- The need to reform the operation General Council which decides on many of the conditions affecting civil servants.
- The urgent need for contestability for the majority of services offered by the public services so that the true costs (and corresponding quality levels) of the services can be compared to best in class. Oversight of this contestability/procurement process should involve a group composed of a majority of people from outside the public service and the process should be very transparent.
- The need for urgent reform of the political institutions to make them fit for purpose.
- The need to address the reform programme beyond the traditional public service including, in particular, ensuring independence yet accountability of independent regulators and the judiciary and the effective governance of the many State and local authorities' bodies and companies.
- There is a need to appoint a Minister for Public Sector Reform with a specific brief to ensure that the process of reform is driven at Government level and that the structures of Government are fit for purpose and capable of tackling vital national strategic issues. The Minister will require the visible strong support of the Taoiseach and Minister for Finance and should have responsibility for human resource management; training and development; Senior Executive Service and leadership development across the public service; organizational development; ethics, values and customer services quality control; procurement and information and communications technologies for the public service.

Conclusions

There have been some significant initiatives in public sector reform, particularly over the past decade. There is now a need for more radical reform and greater urgency in delivering significant results. Possibly some cross-party political support would ensure that the necessary reforms happen soon.

Unions Must Have Key Role in Transformation

Peter McLoone
General Secretary, IMPACT Trade Union

Born in Donegal. Former psychiatric nurse, he now heads Ireland's largest public sector union, IMPACT, with over 46,000 members in health, local government, education, civil service, semi-state companies and the voluntary sector. President of ICTU (2005-7), he is a member of the ICTU Executive Committee and its General Purposes Committee. He is also Chairman of ICTU's influential Public Service Committee. Played a key role in establishing the public service Benchmarking Body and was main negotiator on benchmarking. Member of Labour Relations Commission since 2000.

Reform – old objective

Two years ago, I spoke at this Summer School on the same subject of public service reform. On that occasion, I argued that trade unions needed to become advocates of real reform in the public services. I begin by saying that my strong belief in the positive role that trade unions can play in reform has not diminished. Indeed, it has been strengthened by the astounding events we have experienced over the last nine months.

This failure of public service leaders to put themselves in the citizens' shoes has had the inevitable result that it has become virtually impossible to convince the public of our desire and ability to reform. This despite (and sometimes, one thinks of the creation of the HSE) the massive changes that have happened in internal public service procedures, industrial relations, structures and systems. And despite, it should be said, the very real increases in the range, quantity and quality of the public services we provide to a larger and increasingly complex and demanding society.

Lest I be accused of simply pointing the finger at the failure of others, I must also acknowledge that my call in 2007 for trade unions to lead the change agenda has been accepted more in principle than in practice. In this respect we lag behind many of

This failure of public service leaders to put themselves in the citizens' shoes has had the inevitable result that it has become virtually impossible to convince the public of our desire and ability to reform.

What we face in the public service is massive downsizing in expenditure and numbers employed, accompanied by a huge increase in demand, as more and more people become dependent on the services we provide.

The *initial* challenge is to maintain services at the same level while reducing costs. Next, it requires us to *improve* and *expand* services, while continuing to reduce costs.

our trade union colleagues in Europe and this must change the mindset of politicians, management and staff about the scale and implications of the problem – if public service unions are to achieve even our most basic function of protecting our members' direct interests in the present crisis.

Transformation – today's imperative

In many parts of the private sector, we are seeing 'downsizing' on foot of a <u>collapse</u> in demand. What we face in the public service is massive downsizing in expenditure and numbers employed, accompanied by a huge <u>increase</u> in demand, as more and more people become dependent on the services we provide. Change is not necessary because we have a 'bloated', overstaffed, inefficient or, by and large, overpaid public service. A little over a year ago, the OECD, which trade unions would perceive as an ultra-orthodox body, representative of national Governments and favouring 'market' solutions to public service delivery, found the <u>opposite</u> to be the case. This report, which was welcomed by Government, opposition, newspaper editorials and most commentators, concluded that Irish public servants were delivering high quality services with fewer resources than comparable countries.

In my 2007 presentation, I said that public services are what define a society and give it its humanity. When you strip away all the economics, the number-crunching, and the 'slash and burn' opportunism that characterizes far too much of this debate, that remains the fundamental truth; a truth that will be tested by the decisions and actions we, as politicians, managers, commentators, citizens and workers, take over the next few months. If those of us who believe in quality public services fail to take the initiative, it will pass to others, possibly even external forces, who would be happy to see our public services effectively destroyed. That is why we need to understand that, unlike all previous initiatives, the challenge we now face is not to *reform*, and certainly not to simply take out the axe in order to balance the books, but to completely *transform* our public services. What does that transformation mean? Let me put it as starkly as I can. The *initial* challenge is to maintain services at the same level while reducing costs.

Next, it requires us to *improve* and *expand* services, while continuing to reduce costs. Then, it demands that we better *integrate* services, again with fewer resources.

Unions' proposition

It is an understatement to say that this demands a major change in the mindset of politicians, management and staff about the scale and implications of transformation, and what it will mean for our work and the way we do business. In this context, the thoughtful citizen will be very wary of the concerted vilification of those who work to deliver public services, and the systematic attempt by some managers and politicians to sideline their unions. This is extremely dangerous, not least because unions must have a key role in delivering the message of transformation, and finding the solutions on the ground, if a cooperative rather than a confrontational approach to this major challenge is to be found.

This is what I, and other trade union leaders, have been trying to do in recent discussions with Government. Our objective is to create the conditions in which you will get, at worst *cooperation with*, and at best, *enthusiasm for*, the challenge among those who work each day to deliver public services.

Both IMPACT and the ICTU Public Services Committee have put a simple proposition to the Government as a first step to making this a reality. We have recognized that the collapse in Government revenues is real and that, as a result, radical transformation is required to protect and enhance our education, health, local services, public administration, and all the other services on which all, or most, of us depend. We have reminded the Government and senior officials that public servants are not the greedy, lazy bogeymen of newspaper myth. They are human beings who, like any other human beings, do their best each day to provide decent services within the resources, structures and constraints they are asked to operate within.

They are not overpaid fat cats either. For the most part, our public servants are not highly paid. Months ago, I sought a simple commitment that there will be no further cuts in public service pay and pensions. We also called for an agreed framework for dealing with jobs and employment issues in the public service, to avoid the failed policies of the 1980s, when cuts and embargoes

Our objective is to create the conditions in which you will get, at worst *cooperation with*, and at best, *enthusiasm for*, the challenge among those who work each day to deliver public services.

They are not overpaid fat cats either. For the most part, our public servants are not highly paid.

imposed by central diktat, critically damaged many services,created decades-long specialist shortages, and caused many of the problems that service users and taxpayers are still grappling with today.

Escaping 'Bermuda triangle'

But this is high-risk territory. Let me use an analogy. All the stakeholders, politicians, managers, service users, taxpayers and workers, run the risk of disappearing in a 'Bermuda triangle' with three axes:

Axis 1: The Government, or the Department of Finance, want to reduce spending by €X (where X is as much as four or five billion). That requires huge cuts in payroll spending, which means cuts in jobs, pay, pensions, or some combination of the three.

Axis 2: Public servants and their representatives will not accept further cuts in their core pay or pensions, and they want to retain secure tenure for existing staff (i.e., no involuntary redundancies). Aside from the question of morale, which I have alluded to, any attempt to impose further cuts in these areas will inevitably lead to industrial action, which will massively disrupt services in the short term and, as we know from our experience of the 1980s and 1990s, make any real reform utterly impossible.

Axis 3: The public wants and expects improved services even, or especially, if demand increases and budgets reduce.

Right now, senior management strategies to deliver these apparently conflicting objectives are being presented as a generalized wish-list, disconnected from staff and the services to which they relate. It goes back to my opening point. For the guts of a decade, my trade union colleagues and I have grappled with the problem of trying to negotiate national agreements on abstractions like 'redeployment,' 'flexibility,' 'extended working days,' 'outsourcing,' 'shared services,' 'centralized procurement,' and a myriad of other measures so ill-defined, in terms of real service delivery on the ground, that they sometimes appear to have simply been plucked and

> **Public servants and their representatives will not accept further cuts in their core pay or pensions, and they want to retain secure tenure for existing staff (i.e., no involuntary redundancies).**

Xeroxed from an undergraduate business studies text-book.

Of course, these things can be real and meaningful. But they can only be real for any member of staff when they are applied to their personal working arrangements, and when the changes to these working arrangements are fully understood by them. This is now the central dilemma which needs to be resolved in balancing national and local negotiations with unions to deliver a real transformation agenda.

I believe the dilemma *can* be resolved by *devolving* the detail of change and transformation. Give the available budget to those who have operational responsibility for managing and delivering services, and let the people who know the services, and know the communities they serve, agree the changes and flexibility needed to ensure the best possible range and quality within the financial constraints, and with frameworks that protect services and the staff who work to provide them.

Ask the individual service providers, be they local authorities, health agencies, schools or other organizations (the unit of reference is a matter of detail, albeit an important one), to prepare transformation plans (local frameworks) that can attempt to reconcile the apparently conflicting objectives. That is, transformations that can, as far as humanly possible, deliver the services people want and expect within government spending objectives. It is at this level that 'redeployment', 'flexibility', 'shared services' and so on can really be translated into changes in working arrangements and work practices for individual members of staff, which relate to operational realities while delivering the basic guarantees that unions have been arguing for.

Other options

There is another course of action being contemplated and advocated; a course of action that has nothing to do with reform or transformation. It is simply to cut, cut services or, better still, cut the pay of public servants. Often ideologically-driven advocates use the simple language of 'balancing the books,' and see the maintenance of a range of quality public services as at best secondary, at worst irrelevant, to this imperative. Their contempt for the ordinary working people who deliver services fairly drips from the airwaves and Sunday newspaper pages, to which hard-working public servants have little or no access beyond the

Their contempt for the ordinary working people who deliver services fairly drips from the airwaves and Sunday newspaper pages, to which hard-working public servants have little or no access beyond the heavily edited letters page.

heavily edited letters page.

It is no accident that this chorus of criticism has increased in volume and intensity in the wake of the present economic crisis. I believe this is designed to do two things. First, the immediate objective is to divert blame and accountability away from the real culprits in our current economic catastrophe, the unregulated, greedy elite, and their increasingly confident cheerleaders who created the crisis here and abroad. Second, the long-term objective is to ensure that, once the taxpayer has cleared up the wreckage of this recklessness and greed, they can go back to 'business as usual', a finance-driven, casino capitalism that, for millions or ordinary working people and their families, has delivered little but reduced living standards, disappearing pensions and mass un-employment. The unavoidable logic of their position is that that the greedy and selfish individuals and organizations that created this recession, should emerge from the crisis stronger and richer than before.

... the immediate objective is to divert blame and account- ability away from the real culprits in our current economic catastrophe, the unregulated, greedy elite, and their increasingly confident cheerleaders who created the crisis here and abroad.

Choice

It is increasingly clear, indeed it is crystal clear, that their main target is a substantial reduction in public service pay, on top of the so-called pension levy already implemented. It is equally clear that they have more than one ear in Government, whose refusal to rule out public service pay cuts speaks volumes. If the Government attempts to go down the alternative road, of imposed cuts in pay and pensions, or compulsory redundancies, there will be a reaction which will include sustained, widespread and painful industrial action, including strikes. I do not believe there will be many, if any, winners if this choice is taken, least of all among the people who, more than ever, depend on our public services.

Genuine Workplace Change a Win-Win Option for All

Danny McCoy

Director-General, Irish Business & Employers' Confederation
(IBEC)

Born in Tuam, Co. Galway, held lecturing posts at Dublin City University, University College London, University of Oxford and TCD. Member of the National and Economic and Social Council (NESC), the Commission on Taxation, the National Statistics Board, the board of FAS (National Training Body), the Foundation for Fiscal Studies and the Statistical and Social Inquiry Society of Ireland. Formerly, Director of Policy with IBEC, was appointed Director-General in 2009 having joined the organisation in 2005. Previously, was a Senior Research Officer at the ESRI and economist at the Central Bank.

It was obvious for a number of years that Ireland's competitiveness had become seriously eroded. The difficulties facing the traded sectors of the economy were ignored by policy makers, however, in the face of buoyant employment growth and tax revenue arising from the overheating domestic economy. As ECB President Trichet recently pointed out, it is clear that Government and others mistook this bubble for a structural improvement in the Irish economy. All stakeholders now accept that economic recovery can only be achieved through a restoration of competitiveness and reinvigoration of net trade, resulting from growth in the exports of goods and services.

Competitiveness is essentially determined by three main factors – the trade weighted exchange rate, our cost base, and productivity. In past crises Ireland has been able to address much of its competitiveness problems through currency devaluation, this is now clearly not an option and all our efforts must focus on controlling costs and boosting productivity. At a business level what really matters is how the unit costs of the goods and services we sell compare to those of our competitors when we get them to export markets. A range of factors will impact on unit costs – innovation, process improvements,

All stakeholders now accept that economic recovery can only be achieved through a restoration of competitiveness and reinvigoration of net trade, resulting from growth in the exports of goods and services.

workplace flexibility and, of course, wage costs are all important factors.

A number of other EU countries have overcome significant competitiveness challenges in recent decades and it is useful to examine how this was achieved. In the early 1990s both Sweden and Finland suffered severe financial and economic crises, similar to what Ireland is currently experiencing. Over recent months a number of commentators here have pointed to the lessons to be learnt from how these countries addressed their difficulties. A key factor in their economic recovery, however, is the degree to which both countries relied on currency devaluations to restore competitiveness. Finland, in particular, also made another important decision at the height of its economic crisis which greatly strengthened its competitive position. Its programme for fiscal consolidation involved spending cuts in all major programme areas with the exception of one – science, technology and innovation. In fact, at a time when its public finances were in disarray it proceeded with plans to increase investment in R&D. This paid rich dividends in the following years as the resulting competitiveness benefits positioned the country strongly to take advantage of the global economic recovery.

Albeit due to different reasons, Germany experienced a similar bout of weak competitiveness in the mid-1990s. In the run-up to monetary union currency devaluation was not desirable. The path to recovery therefore involved an extended period of minimal nominal wage growth and productivity improvements which ultimately resulted in significant real unit labour cost reductions. Stronger wage growth in other countries meant that an effective nominal pay freeze was sufficient for Germany to restore its competitive position. Nevertheless the adjustment took a decade to complete and resulted in a significant erosion of real living standards. Per capita GDP in Germany was 113 per cent of the EU average in 1992 but had fallen to 101 per cent by 2002. It subsequently improved somewhat but much of the benefits of recovery have been temporarily stifled by the current global economic downturn.

The challenge facing Ireland is much more daunting than it was for Sweden, Finland or Germany. Firstly, there is no currency devaluation option. Secondly, the poor short-term

Finland, in particular, also made another important decision at the height of its economic crisis which greatly strengthened its competitive position. Its programme for fiscal consolidation involved spending cuts in all major programme areas with the exception of one – science, technology and innovation.

international economic outlook and the prospect of global deflation mean that the German option of a nominal wage freeze is unlikely to yield sufficient benefits. Thirdly, the Irish economy is much more open and suffers or gains more with changes in competitiveness.

In recent months many economists have argued the case for a sharp reduction in nominal wages in Ireland. Labour costs here have grown far more rapidly than in our main trading partners in recent years and are currently well above the EU-15 average. The timing for such an adjustment is also right as consumer prices are set to fall by about 5 per cent in 2009 and will decline further in 2010, thereby cushioning the impact of wage cuts on living standards.

Over the past decade Germany demonstrated how com-petitiveness could be restored with minimal nominal wage increases during a period of moderate inflation and relatively strong wage growth in its trading partners. In order for Ireland to achieve a similar improvement in competitiveness at a time of price deflation and exceptionally low wage growth in other countries cuts in nominal wages are inevitably required.

At the core of Ireland's competitiveness difficulties is the trend in the cost of doing business here vis-à-vis that in two of our main trading partners – the UK and the US. In 2000, average labour costs in Ireland were 40 per cent lower than those in the US and 17 per cent cheaper than the UK. A combination of euro strength and high wage growth in Ireland resulted in a complete reversal of the competitive position by 2008 when average labour costs in Ireland were 11 per cent above that in the US and 19 per cent higher than in the UK. The competitive position against the UK has worsened considerably further since Autumn 2008 as the value of sterling has remained weak and is now 20 per cent lower than it was 18 months ago. Such a competitive disadvantage is simply not sustainable in the medium term. The advantage provided to the manufacturing sector in the UK as a result of its recent competitive devaluation is such that it is difficult to envisage how the export manufacturing sector, in particular, can be sustained in the short-term in Ireland without some support. Empirical data show that it takes about 12 months before the full impacts of currency movements are felt in the real economy. The window for action to address the problem is therefore rapidly

Over the past decade Germany demonstrated how com-petitiveness could be restored with minimal nominal wage increases during a period of moderate inflation and relatively strong wage growth in its trading partners.

closing.

A co-ordinated policy of wage reductions across both the public and private sectors would provide a significant boost to Ireland's competitive position. At the very least we must set a target of returning our unit labour costs to the EU average. A reduction in wages would result in similar declines in both consumer prices and business costs, further reducing the cost of living and addressing Ireland's high cost of doing business. A policy of wage reduction could of course have significant downsides – it would involve considerable pain for house-holds, particularly those with high debt levels; would further erode income tax revenues; and could possibly lead to a damaging deflationary spiral. Irrespective of the policy pursued, however, it is inevitable that living standards will fall. A reduction in wages and prices would help preserve employment in the short-term and would leave Ireland well positioned to benefit from improved export opportunities over the coming years. Business is under no illusions as to the potential negative implications of falling wages for domestic demand and enterprise activity but given the exceptional importance of the export sector to the Irish economy, this is the least bad option we have.

Wage cuts would undoubtedly help restore our lost competitiveness but wage cuts in isolation will not fully address our difficulties. The unit cost of our goods and services can also be reduced in other ways. Education and training, R&D, provision of world class infrastructure, reasonably priced energy, and flexible work practices are all critical from a competitiveness perspective. In a time of exceptional stress for the public finances, it is not going to be possible to address these issues simply through the provision of additional resources. The McCarthy Report sets out a painful programme of adjustments for all sections of society – every household, every worker, and every business will have to adjust to a radically changed public expenditure environment. In short, as a society we are going to have to do more with less in order to limit the damage to our living standards and return to a path of sustainable economic growth.

The issue which I now wish to turn to is that of work place flexibility and productivity. Reducing unit output costs does

A combination of euro strength and high wage growth in Ireland resulted in a complete reversal of the competitive position by 2008 when average labour costs in Ireland were 11 per cent above that in the US and 19 per cent higher than in the UK.

not always have to involve cuts in wage rates. Through improved work practices, process improvements, and work-place innovation, unit costs of production can be substantially reduced. This does not only apply to the widget manufacturing company – all services, businesses, and the public sector can achieve similar improvements in productivity levels. The biggest obstacles to achieving such productivity improvements are management competency and workplace culture. In times of plenty many organizations were not run as efficiently as they could have been. For private sector businesses, profits often flowed even when companies were not operating at their optimum. In the public sector, the 'use it or lose it' approach to budgeting meant that value for money was often a secondary concern. In the current economic climate there is no room for sub-optimal management. World class management practices are needed to ensure that businesses remain viable and that as much employment as possible is preserved. In the public sector, managers must rise to the challenge of ensuring that lower levels of expenditure do not result in poorer quality provision of front line services.

During the Celtic Tiger years, many workers were envious of the large profits made by some sectors of the economy. Employment opportunities were plentiful and job security no longer carried the value of previous times. Workplace cultures were impacted by the excesses of society in general. The current challenges we face provide an opportunity for everyone to bring a renewed commitment and energy to our workplaces. Through working smarter and more flexibly, all employees can help improve the productivity level of their organization. If this culture change can be achieved right across the economy, the boost to national competitiveness would be substantial. Up to now change has been slow and cumbersome especially in the public sector and in unionized employments in the private sector. There is no doubt that this has impacted negatively on competitiveness and employment preservation. Finding success again will result from people co-operating, both at national and enterprise level, to compete effectively on global markets. The reality is that non-union companies can implement change much faster and more effectively. This is the key to success. All too often employers in unionized environments find that the implementation of change costs too much and takes too long because of inflexibility. Unions must recognize that, unless they become champions for change,

In short, as a society we are going to have to do more with less in order to limit the damage to our living standards and return to a path of sustainable economic growth.

World class management practices are needed to ensure that businesses remain viable and that as much employment as possible is preserved.

more businesses will fail, more jobs will be lost, and the economy will continue to decline.

There will be no quick fixes to Ireland's competitiveness problems. Like the challenges we face in the banking sector and with the public finances, we are facing a hard slog over the coming years in order to undo the damage of recent excesses. It is impossible to ignore costs, including labour costs, in the competitiveness debate but it would also be wrong to suggest that reducing wages would be a panacea. We must take a wide-ranging view of competitiveness and all of its determinants. Genuine workplace change with a view to boosting productivity can be a win-win option for businesses, employees, Government, and society at large.

Our ability to embrace change across the economy will be a key determinant of our future success. Up to now change has been slow and cumbersome and this has restricted our ability to reach our potential.

Our ability to embrace change across the economy will be a key determinant of our future success. Up to now change has been slow and cumbersome and this has restricted our ability to reach our potential. Change is the only constant and it must be rapidly embraced. If through working together we resolve to get our costs in order and bring a new enthusiasm for change and success to our workplaces, I am confident that Ireland's economic fortunes can improve dramatically in the coming years. Resolving our competitiveness short-comings will also be essential in our efforts to tackle the unemployment crisis – a more competitive economy will provide better employment opportunities and higher and more equal living standards for everyone.

Chapter 7

IRISH EDUCATION AND THE ECONOMY

ONLY THE BEST WILL BE GOOD ENOUGH
Don Thornhill
Chairman, National Competitiveness Council (NCC), former Sec. Gen. Dept. of Education & Science and former Chairman, HEA

UNIVERSITIES: THE HEART OF INNOVATIVE IRELAND
John Hegarty
Provost, Trinity College Dublin

EDUCATION IS KEY TO RECOVERY
Brian Hayes TD
Fine Gael Spokesperson, Education & Science

Only the Best Will be Good Enough[42]

Don Thornhill[43]
Chairman, NCC, former General-Secretary, Dept. of Education & Science and former Chairman, HEA

Graduate of UCD with a BSc and PhD (Chemistry) and TCD (MSc (Econ)). A former top civil servant, Chairman of the Irish Payments Services Organisation, member of the board of Forfás, Irish Taxation Institute and Science Foundation Ireland. Former Chairman of US/Ireland Fulbright Commission and former Board member of the Irish Management Institute and Digital Hub Agency. During career in public service, centrally involved in many policy developments which transformed the Irish economy and society, particularly education and research. Completed seven year term as executive chairman of the Higher Education Authority (HEA) in January 2005. Secretary General of the Dept. of Education and Science from 1993 to 1998 and also worked in the Dept. of Foreign Affairs and Dept. of Finance and in the Office of the Revenue Commissioners. Elected member of the Royal Irish Academy and an honorary life member of the Royal Dublin Society.

Introduction: Education is a vital activity and policy domain

We should aim to have one of the best education systems in the world. Our future prosperity depends on the quality of our knowledge and human capital. The success of our economy and of our businesses will depend on our ability to trade successfully in international markets with ever more knowledge intensive products and services. Education and research are the key policy means of enabling us to increase our knowledge and human capital.

Education is about much more than economics. It is a transcending area of policy encompassing values across the social, economic, moral, ethical, religious, civic and cultural domains – as well as in sport and physical education. Education is also the key to addressing economic and social disadvantage. The emphasis in this paper on the role of education policy in contributing to economic recovery should not be interpreted as

Education and research should be priority areas for investment and policy attention even during this time of acute fiscal stress. If we are seen to falter, particularly in relation to our commitment to investment in third and fourth level education and research, we will lose the valuable momentum built up during the last decade.

implying that I see education policy as having only an economic purpose. Quite the contrary, I believe that the policy recommendations in this paper will also contribute to more effective outcomes across the full range of concerns of education policy.

> **The Council takes the view that Ireland needs one of the best education and research systems in the world in order to drive and sustain economic recovery.**

Education and research should be priority areas for investment and policy attention even during this time of acute fiscal stress. If we are seen to falter, particularly in relation to our commitment to investment in third and fourth level education and research, we will lose the valuable momentum built up during the last decade. This is not an argument for exempting Exchequer spending on education from the major fiscal adjustments which are needed. It does mean that Education should be a policy priority and that we give continuing attention to improving the effectiveness of our system and to ensuring excellent outcomes.

NCC statement on education and training

> **The availability of computers in Irish schools is low relative to leading countries and ICT is not effectively integrated into teaching practices on a system-wide basis.**

The National Competitiveness Council (NCC) published a paper on education earlier this year.[44] The Council takes the view that Ireland needs one of the best education and research systems in the world in order to drive and sustain economic recovery.

The NCC paper makes recommendations across the full landscape from pre-school education to fourth level including R&D. It highlighted the importance of pre-school education, the need for persisting with the investment strategies set out in the Strategy for Science, Technology and Innovation, a renewed focus on mathematics and science education in secondary schools, integrating IT into education, a comprehensive loan scheme for third level students and a review of the inadequate and inequitable student grant system. This paper is consistent with but moves beyond the recommendations in the NCC report.

Our education system performs well – but needs to do better

Results of international benchmarking exercises include the following:

- The OECD PISA studies on Scientific, Reading and Mathematical Literacy of 15-year-olds indicate that Irish students at this age score well internationally on reading, reasonably well in science and just about average on mathematics.[45]
- 11.5 percent of Irish 18-24 year olds have not completed the Leaving Certificate or equivalent which compares favourably with the EU-27 average of 15.2 percent.[46] Non-completion results in higher risk of unemployment. Even though our performance is better than the EU average we need to strengthen efforts to prevent early school leaving.
- In research performance, Ireland's global citation ranking had improved from 27th place in 2003 to 17th in 2008 and Irish universities are moving up the world rankings.
- The time devoted to science teaching at primary level, at just half the OECD average, fits poorly with the need for high quality learning outcomes in mathematics and sciences.[47]
- We allocate fewer resources to ICT in education than other countries.[48] The availability of computers in Irish schools is low relative to leading countries and ICT is not effectively integrated into teaching practices on a system-wide basis. There is an urgent need to improve ICT infrastructure across a range of areas including broadband speed and access, technical support and school networking.
- According to OECD data, Irish rates of expenditure per student are below the EU and OECD average at primary, secondary and tertiary levels and to date Exchequer spending on pre-primary education has been very modest. In that regard the recent Government decision to reallocate some of the funding for Child Benefit into pre-primary education is very welcome. In 2005 expenditure on all levels of education accounted for 5.4 per cent of GNP (4.6 per cent of GDP) compared to an OECD average of 5.8 per cent and an EU-19 average of 5.5 per cent of GDP.[49] This, of course is reflected in high teacher/student staff ratios and bigger class sizes than in many OECD countries.

Funding is important but excellent teachers, policies, processes and the support of families and society matter even more in achieving strong educational outcomes.

Playing to our strengths – three guidelines for public policy

The recent NCC report concluded that

> In Ireland, strong educational outcomes have been achieved with relatively modest public financial resources. Funding is important but excellent teachers, policies, processes and the support of families and society matter even more in achieving strong educational outcomes.[45]

This is consistent with the view that while inputs are important, higher expenditures will not guarantee successful outcomes.

Pupil/teacher ratios are a relevant example. The available evidence does not support a popularly held view that the lower the ratios the better the quality of educational outcomes. Reducing class sizes is expensive and can deflect scarce resources from other more effective strategies such as ensuring our teachers can avail of frequent professional development and providing students and teachers with suitable physical and technological infrastructure (e.g., school buildings, science labs, sports facilities, adequate computers and broadband access).

An excellent education system requires excellent teachers.

Against this background, and given the need for significant reductions in public expenditure[46] there is an urgent need to establish policy strategies which will ensure excellent outcomes and effective expenditure of Exchequer funds as well as providing opportunities for teachers and others working in education to use their skills and commitment to maximum effect.

My own view is that we need to strengthen the following three positive features of our system:

1. The high status and quality of our teachers
2. Parental commitment and interest in education which is supported by the presence of significant exercise of choice as compared with other countries
3. Funding mechanisms which support these two features.

There are three critical policy guidelines which would strengthen these features:
1. Pay relentless attention to teacher quality
2. Provide choice for parents and students by stimulating competition and contestability between schools and other educational institutions; but balance this with appropriate co-operation
3. Government's role should be to
   a) Provide funding using financial mechanisms which promote and incentivize excellent outcomes
   b) Regulate quality
   c) Set policies

Guideline 1: Pay relentless attention to teacher quality

An excellent education system requires excellent teachers.

Ireland is well placed internationally for teacher quality – a situation envied by other countries. The Irish primary teacher cohort is drawn from the top 14 per cent of CAO applicants. At secondary level, almost all graduates accepted onto the Higher Diploma in Education (H.Dip.) courses now have a First Class or 2.1 Honours degree.

Good pay and conditions contribute to making teaching an attractive and prestigious profession.

Department of Education and Science figures show that primary school teachers earn on average €57,000 per year which compares favourably with other sectors in the economy.[53] Irish teachers are well paid by international standards and relative to other occupations in Ireland even when adjustments are made, as in Figure 1 over, for higher Irish price levels.[54] Using purchasing power parities, Irish teachers enjoy a premium over the EU-15 average of 24 per cent at primary level, 18 per cent at lower secondary level and 11 per cent at upper secondary level.

It is important that teachers are rewarded well. What did disquiet me, though, when I worked in the Department of Education and Science were the many rigidities in the system – which I believe are neither in the interests of education or of teachers themselves. These included what was then the

What did disquiet me though when I worked in the Department of Education and Science were the many rigidities in the system – which I believe are neither in the interests of education or of teachers themselves.

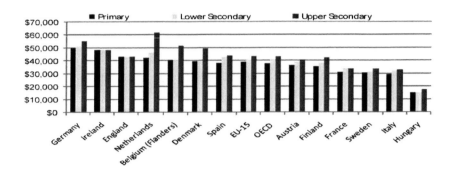

Figure 1: Teacher Salaries after 15 years of experience, 2006
<u>Source</u>: OECD, *Education at a Glance*, 2008

overwhelming importance of school-based seniority for promotion in most schools.[54] Also the initial opposition from teachers to whole-school assessment by the Inspectorate of the Department, the reluctance to engage with parents, through for example parent-teacher meetings, other than at times which suited teachers more than other working adults – and what seemed to be an almost obsessive focus on ensuring that time spent on professional development would be compensated for by teaching time off in lieu. These behaviours are legacies of another era and were accompanied by a mindset which sought additional payment for any structural change, and are unaffordable. These inefficiencies and their costs are described in the Bord Snip Nua report.[55] The report also refers to a number of payments for what are variously described as 'management and further administrative duties' and other allowances which are paid to teachers. The consequence of this is that what might be seen as 'piece work arrangements' now constitute a significant part of teacher pay. This is not consistent with the professional role and status of teachers. I agree with Colm McCarthy and his colleagues that future contract arrangements for teachers should include a total statutory working time which would provide for activities such as school planning, parent/teacher meetings, in-service training and development, supervision of students and middle-management duties where and when appropriate as defined by school management. This would strengthen the leadership role of school principals who carry most of the burdens of management and legislative compliance. In many cases this leaves them with insufficient time to focus on learning outcomes.

Principals should be able to distribute responsibilities and tasks within the school team to those best fitted to carry them out.

There are other important roles for public policy in promoting teacher quality:

- **Entry into teaching should attract candidates for teacher education and academic careers from among the most talented people in the population.**
- **Teacher education and training should be of high quality and should include considerable teaching practice under supervision of experienced teachers.**
- **Professional and in-service development should be frequent, continuing and progressive during a teacher's career.**
- **There should be reasonable arrangements in place to allow teachers, whose performance is not satisfactory, to leave the profession with dignity and with preparation for changing career.**

Guideline 2: Provide choice for parents and students

The availability of choice for students and parents is a powerful stimulus for improving the quality of educational outcomes. Choice can enhance the responsiveness of schools and other institutions to meeting the challenges of different needs and aptitudes and of a changing environment.

We tend not to think of our educational system as being one which offers choice – except perhaps at third level. Yet compared to other countries (where defined school catchment areas are often rigorously administered) parents of school going children in many parts of Ireland can select between two or more schools. Organizations and groups can establish primary and second level schools provided they meet a number of essential conditions.[56]

Yet compared to other countries (where defined school catchment areas are often rigorously administered) parents of school-going children in many parts of Ireland can select between two or more schools. Organizations and groups can establish primary and second level schools provided they meet a number of essential conditions.

These characteristics of choice and contestability contribute significantly to achieving good outcomes. We are I suspect at an early stage in what might be an important debate about school ownership, particularly in the light of a possible evolution of the role of the Catholic Church in primary and secondary education. It is important that the further development of primary and post primary schooling in this country retains these vital characteristics of choice and contestability and that we do not replace them with a monopoly ownership and management position.[57]

Guideline 3: Government's role should be to:

- Provide funding using financial mechanisms which promote and incentivize excellent outcomes
- Regulate quality
- Set policies

Capitation funding is also differentiated – for example in targeting special needs and at third level in taking account of the differences in teaching costs between subject areas.

The management of schools and higher education institutions is best done by the entities themselves. The vital roles for Government are in policy, funding, and regulation – particularly in regard to quality and outcomes.

Funding

The mechanisms used are important. Ideally, Exchequer funds should follow the students. In this way institutions that are perceived to be successful gain from enrolling more students and others are challenged to perform better. It is one of the strengths of the Irish system that this is by and large how voluntary schools (through capitation funding and pupil teacher ratios) and universities (through a unit cost mechanism) are funded and the allocation of Exchequer funds to the Institutes of Technology is progressing in that direction. Capitation funding is also differentiated – for example in targeting special needs and at third level in taking account of the differences in teaching costs between subject areas.

In addition to the foundation capitation funding, incentive funding can be made available to schools and colleges where they meet or exceed targets set in consultation with government or public agencies. The capitation based funding can also be supplemented by competitive funding mechanisms where institutions, or groups of institutions, compete with one another for funding for new and developmental projects. This can be particularly effective for targeting resources to meet particular policy objectives such as skills needs and research and development.

Quality

Quality assurance and improvement should be at the centre of public policy concerns. At third level the work which has been done in the construction of the National Framework of Qualifications (NFQ) is a considerable achievement. The Minister's proposals to consolidate the quality assurance and certification bodies into a single organisation is the logical next step. At first and second level the Whole School Evaluation approach and particularly the publication of the Inspection reports is being applied by the Inspectorate of the Department of Education and Science with increasing effectiveness and confidence.

Setting policies

Government is a vital trustee of the education system and has the lead role in setting policies. This covers a wide range of areas including funding, curriculum and the determination of policy priorities. I have touched on many of these throughout the paper but there are two, international education and policy on research and development, which in my view are immediately related to the contribution of education to restoring economic growth and where careful policy attention is required.

Internationalisation of Education: Seizing the Opportunity

The internationalization of education presents significant growth opportunities for Ireland in terms of exporting a high quality service. Strategically managed, the attraction of overseas students to Ireland could have a range of educational, economic, social and cultural benefits. It is an important source of foreign earnings, employment and Exchequer revenue.

We are missing out on opportunities to generate foreign income and employment and need to make further progress in

For Ireland, the human and social capital content of the overall sources of growth accounted for 83 per cent of our wealth – as compared for example with 80 per cent for most of the richer countries and as low as 73 per cent for Canada and as low as 55 per cent for the poorer countries.

terms of developing our education system as an international service which will enhance its capacity to meet domestic needs.

Investing in research, development and innovation - this is not a time to falter

Our prosperity depends critically on knowledge and education. A 2006 World Bank report,[54] apportioned the sources of wealth of countries between three categories of capital – human and social, production and natural resources. For Ireland, the human and social capital content of the overall sources of growth accounted for 83 per cent of our wealth – as compared for example with 80 per cent for most of the richer countries and as low as 73 per cent for Canada and as low as 55 per cent for the poorer countries. Until the 1990s the increasing numbers graduating with first degrees, diplomas and certificates from our universities and the former regional technical colleges and DIT provided the human capital which brought Ireland up the value chain of increased value added and prosperity. The entry of the post-Communist countries, China and India and other countries into the world trading system plus our own increasing costs mean that we have to continue to move up the value chain of production.

Exports are the foundation for our economic growth. We rank among the most export-dependent economies in the world and in turn FDI companies account for 80 per cent of our exports. The perception by these companies of Irish policies is of vital concern to us. They have seen us as a location characterized by the assurance of high levels of policy consistency – on corporate taxation since the late 1950s, on increased access to education since the late 1960s and more recently in investment in research, development and innovation. Our policy makers have understood that investment in these strategies is a marathon not a sprint. Any, serious deviation from this, particularly any pause in our commitment to investment in science, technology and innovation will have major damaging effects on our international competitiveness and will seriously impair national recovery.

Universities: The Heart of Innovative Ireland

John Hegarty
Provost, Trinity College Dublin

Born in Claremorris, Co. Mayo and educated at St Patrick's College, Maynooth and NUIG (PhD). A post-doctoral fellow at the University of Wisconsin and research fellow at Bell Laboratories, New Jersey (1975-86). Professor of Laser Physics at TCD (1986-2001) and Head of Department of Physics (1992-5). Was an adjunct professor at University of Georgia (1990-5), visiting professor at University of Tokyo and Sony Corporation (1995). Dean of Research TCD (1995-2000). Appointed Provost in 2001. Member of Royal Irish Academy, American Physical Society, American Optical Society, Institute of Electronic and Electrical Engineers and Fellow of TCD. Has published extensively on laser physics in national and international journals.

As the head of a University whose mission it is to prepare for the future, I would say that recovery, when it happens, will be in a different Ireland. It will be an Ireland in which all organizations of the state will have transformed themselves willingly or by necessity. In the process, we will have to think the unthinkable, imagine what was not imagined before, and try the untried. If we are smart, we will build on the good things that have developed this country over the last 20 years while abandoning those that have brought collapse.

As many of the stalwart policies and visible edifices of the Celtic Tiger have disintegrated, education stands out as one pillar whose importance is greater now than ever before and for which people rightly have great expectations. I believe that our education sector must step up to the plate in new ways and lead the way to a stronger, more creative, Ireland in many respects. Today, I will talk of Higher Education and the role of the University in particular.

If we are smart, we will build on the good things that have developed this country over the last 20 years while abandoning those that have brought collapse.

Need for innovation reflects traditional values of the University

In stating that the University and all other institutions must be innovative and imaginative in responding to the national need, I would argue that this is in line with one of the age-old values of the University: the inculcation of critical thinking by challenging accepted notions – in other words, thinking what was unthinkable before, imagining the unimagined, and taking risk in the process.

I argue that the mission of the university in the Ireland of the 21st century must be three-fold: Teaching, Research and Knowledge Transfer, including commercialization and employment creation.

I would like to give a few examples of what I see as true innovation and use them as indicators for how we might plan and accelerate innovation across the whole system. All my examples are Trinity related but every university in Ireland could recite their own. I argue that the mission of the university in the Ireland of the 21st century must be three-fold: Teaching, Research and Knowledge Transfer, including commercialization and employment creation. I also argue that the University is a community, not a business, in which students and staff alike are always exploring, learning and challenging, and in which there is the freedom conducive to spontaneous and unconventional thinking.

Institutions joining forces – the TCD/UCD Innovation Alliance

The first example relates to an announcement last March by Trinity and UCD in response to the Government's Smart Economy policy. We took the unprecedented and radical step of joining forces to accelerate the creation of innovative new businesses and jobs over a 10-year period. We did this, conscious that some of our predecessors might be turning over in their graves, but also conscious that a new approach to the creation of high quality jobs from excellent research and by skilled graduates was exactly what the country needed. We were also mindful that together our universities account for about 50 per cent of research investment in Higher Education, of research students, patents and new companies. Furthermore, there was an onus on us to demonstrate that investment of public resources in knowledge and skills would be matched by accelerated translation o f that knowledge and those skills back into wealth and wisdom.

The essence of our joint action is a transformation of the Masters and PhD programme into one that better prepares students for a career outside of academia. While we expect these students to be at the cutting edge of knowledge, we also want them to have acquired skills in entrepreneurship and innovation that will enable them to be creators of jobs and innovative practices in enterprise – rather than being job seekers and passive employees.

Teaching entrepreneurship and business awareness is not a simple task. We envisage a programme of mentoring by experts from industry and the venture capital and policy-making communities, in which students are taken out of their normal environment, working together in teams across disciplines and across the two institutions on special projects. I believe that the students will relish the experience and will gain tremendously from it in terms of maturity, confidence and creative collaboration. On graduation, these students will constitute a new engine for innovation and enterprise not witnessed in this country before.

We are also taking an entirely new approach to how we manage intellectual property arising from research so that it yields a much higher level of licensing, company formation, new processes and products in existing indigenous companies, and a more effective anchoring of international companies in Ireland against intense competition. The output from research in terms of patents, spin-offs and licences is comparable to that of MIT if you relate it to investment. It is no accident that 40 per cent of IDA-induced foreign investment in Ireland last year was R&D based, rather than coming from traditional manufacturing and services. I can foresee this increasing in the future. Our model of partnership has a number of key assumptions – that we have the best academic staff and research facilities. That implies investment.

The model spelled out here is at odds with that advocated by An Bord Snip Nua which views universities as they were 20 years ago, largely undergraduate in nature. But it is a model consistent with government policy – the Smart Economy framework, the OECD and the EU, and furthermore with US President Obama's view of the role of American universities which featured strongly in his stimulus package. Reversal of investment in research and

While we expect these students to be at the cutting edge of knowledge, we also want them to have acquired skills in entrepreneur-ship and innovation that will enable them to be creators of jobs and innovative practices in enterprise – rather than being job seekers and passive employees.

higher graduate education will, in my view, effectively suggest that 'Ireland is closed for business'.

Commercialization is a partner of good research and teaching – the case of Opsona

The first example is in the Sciences and demonstrates how Science, Art, Intellectual Property, New Business and Student Inspiration can all work together. In 2004, a new company, Opsona Therapeutics, was launched by 3 immunologists from our Schools of Biochemistry and Immunology and Medicine. Their 6-year research on the immune system produced a family of potential anti-inflammatory drugs dealing with diseases such as rheumatoid arthritis, MS and irritable bowel disease. The founders have published their results in the best scientific journals, patented their ideas, and raised over €30 million venture capital funding for their company. Through their research agreements with Wyeth and Merck-Schering Plough, they are chasing a $450 billion market and are targeting a further $300 million investment. Opsona is the biggest company spinning out of a university in Ireland in the Lifesciences and it could well be the next big biotechnology company in the world. Of course through our new Alliance with UCD we want to accelerate the formation of many such companies.

It is no accident that 40 per cent of IDA-induced foreign investment in Ireland last year was R&D based, rather than coming from traditional manufacturing and services.

There are a few interesting features about the new venture that are worth noting. First, the company is a product of the highest quality research by world class academics funded by SFI. Second, they are training the next generation of researchers who will set up their own companies or be hired by companies like Opsona. Third, the researchers are some of our best and most inspiring teachers – just ask the undergraduate students. Fourth, they are engaged in helping the public, and especially 15-25 year olds, to understand science. A recent exhibition on infection and the spread of disease in the Science Gallery at Trinity drew over 40,000 visitors in three months.

Here is a case which combines everything seamlessly – brilliant academics reaching out to the second level and the public, inspiring our undergraduates, making breakthrough discoveries in research, creating a new business, and training the people who will do likewise. Knowledge transfer, often narrowly defined as Innovation, is the 3rd arm of the university – it arises *naturally* from good teaching and research. The three reinforce each other.

Breakthroughs from unexpected quarters – a case in the Humanities

The second example of innovation is in the Humanities. In Trinity, we are embarked on a ground-breaking project to unleash the power of the 18th century Long Room Library by the use of technology and digitization. The 1641 Depositions Project is an interesting example. In 1641, the outbreak of a rebellion by the Catholic Irish is alleged to have begun with a general massacre of Protestant settlers and has been the cause of much bitter historical controversy ever since. The 1641 Depositions are the witness testimonies of the Protestant settlers gathered by government-appointed commissioners after the Rising. All 19,000 pages have been in the Trinity Library since 1741. Our goal, with funding from the IRCHSS, is to digitize these unique testimonies and make them available to scholars all over the world for analysis.

The most advanced digitizing technology is unable to interpret such complex information. IBM would like to understand the mental process involved in deciphering the testimonies and simulate it with entirely new innovative technology.

This illustrates how breakthroughs can come from the most unlikely quarters. The Humanities meeting the Technologies can spark the most extraordinary developments and the University is an ideal meeting place for both.

Access/NIID

The final example of innovation relates to access to education. While every 3rd Level institution has programmes to reach out to those who are disadvantaged in our society and who have not been well represented before, the best way to address disadvantage is at pre-school and primary level. We are conscious however that already in this recession, there are thousands of people losing their jobs who will need access to

Reversal of investment in research and higher graduate education will, in my view, effectively suggest that 'Ireland is closed for business'.

The Humanities meeting the Technologies can spark the most extraordinary developments and the University is an ideal meeting place for both.

upskilling and reskilling courses. Higher Education is responding to this new demand in addition to all of the other demands. I would like to focus, however, on a special area of disadvantage.

A decade ago, a number of enthusiasts in Trinity along with some involved parents set up a pilot scheme for those who suffer intellectual disadvantage such as Down Syndrome. The goal was to develop within the university a programme of education that might transform the lives of these special people and to develop, through research, best practice in this area. Today we have a National Institute for Intellectual Disability (NIID). The impact has been extraordinary as a poem by Helen Donnelly, an NIID student with Down Syndrome, demonstrates:

> As one door closes after me
> I open a door to the future
> Full of challenges and experiences
> Bravery, determination.
>
> The next door I open
> Is a bumpy road ahead
> And it becomes steeper
> And harder to walk.
>
> Until I reach the top
> Then I come down followed
> By a smooth path along the way.

Helen could be talking of the challenges facing this country and I hope that we are as successful in moving forward as she was.

My point in alluding to the NIID is that we need to question assumptions about the capacity of human beings to learn, and to broaden the concept of who benefits from education. It is innovation in action.

University as a community

The University is often viewed as a knowledge factory with students receiving knowledge and staff dispensing it. There is a tendency to forget that universities are *living communities*. As in the monasteries which preceded them, community life

Opsona is the biggest company spinning out of a university in Ireland in the Lifesciences and it could well be the next big bio-technology company in the world. Of course through our new Alliance with UCD we want to accelerate the formation of many other such companies.

involves time for reflection as well as action, in which everyone learns by being challenged inside and outside the lecture theatre; in which the qualities of wisdom, leadership, and civic engagement are honed; in which knowledge is advanced and made to work for the benefit of society; in which teaching, research and innovation are partners; in which there is engagement with enterprise, the public and government; in which the only benchmark is quality; and finally, in which there is an expectation of delivery of something special and unique to society that is beyond the ordinary.

The basis for innovation and new thinking is already in place in Ireland's Higher Education Institutions. We need to *accelerate* the qualities and outputs that I have been talking about while drawing inspiration from traditional values, and we need to justify our claim to freedom by taking risk and showing impact. There is now an opportunity to do so and I am confident that Higher Education will not be found wanting. While we are busy cutting everything in the short term, we need to be careful that we do not stunt the factors that will drive recovery and sustainability in the medium to long term, in the face of intense global competition.

While every 3rd Level institution has programmes to reach out to those who are disadvantaged in our society and who have not been well represented before, the best way to address disadvantage is at pre-school and primary level.

Education is Key to Recovery

Brian Hayes TD
Fine Gael Spokesperson, Education & Science

Born in Dublin and educated at St. Joseph's College, Ballinasloe, Maynooth College (BA) and TCD (H.Dip.). Formerly a secondary school teacher and National Youth and Education Officer Fine Gael. First elected to Dáil Éireann in 1997. Served in Seanad Éireann (1995-7) and Fine Gael Seanad Leader (2002-2007). Former Party Spokesperson on Health and Children. Re-elected to Dáil for Dublin South-West constituency in May 2007.

Introduction

We have had ten years of soft option politics.

It would be good for the country if we could agree with the Government on a new model for the funding of higher education. This would send out positive signals internationally.

An important symbolic event, the Anniversary of the Dáil, marking ninety years of continuous democracy in this country took place in January. The reason I mention this is that not since Independence has our country faced such enormous challenges as today. People are seeing a real fall in their living standards. This is no mere economic decline or adjustment. What is required in response is a fundamental transformation in how we organize society, how we deliver public services and how we reposition our education system to meet the challenges that lie ahead.

Between 2007 and 2010, our national debt will have trebled, not even taking the activities of NAMA into account. A total of 500,000 people will be out of work by year's end. The dilemma for this Government is that they led us into this crisis and people find it difficult now to take prescriptions from them. While there were indeed some international factors responsible, the public do not buy that. We have had ten years of soft option politics.

How should the opposition respond?

It would be easy to sit back and oppose for opposition sake but now, as the biggest party following the local and European elections, Fine Gael has a responsibility as well as a new mandate. The onus is on us. We cannot be the party of 'No' but have to be the party of solutions. Our own supporters expect it. The day of Punch and Judy politics is over. Real cooperation is required but the fact is that Fianna Fáil do not 'do' cooperation. On the day Brian Cowen was elected Taoiseach, he evoked the memory of Seán Lemass. Well our Taoiseach is no Seán Lemass but the most tribal FF leader ever. If he wants cooperation he must show the opposition that he is open to suggestions from our side of the House.

We must also do our job and scrutinize Government policies but at the same time seek agreement where it is possible. An area with potential for cooperation is higher education reform. It would be good for the country if we could agree with the Government on a new model for the funding of higher education. This would send out positive signals internationally. The financial crisis in our university sector must be resolved. For instance, there are top-up fees in the North which has given a huge competitive advantage to Northern Ireland universities over the past number of years.

We must not go back to the 1980s when the PAYE sector was overburdened with fees while the self-employed could cook their books and the rich could take out covenants. I am a defender of fees abolition since participation rates went up from 44 per cent to 65 per cent and the numbers in higher education rose from 120,000 to 170,000. I propose that students pay up to 30 per cent of the fees when they can afford it. There should be no upfront fees or barriers preventing students going to college. The Universities and IOTs should compete for money based on a change agenda. There are tests colleges should meet such as a new approach to quality, number of students from poorer backgrounds attending, and whether courses are meeting labour market demand.

We must have higher education reform allied to new resource contributions. We cannot have one without the other. We must not go back to the simplistic idea that the percentage of a new amount of money be given to the higher education sector. This is not going to work and is not sensible in the long run. We must demand greater coordination between the Universities and the IOTs and between the Universities themselves. There is far too much of a 'me too' attitude in higher education, with replication

> **The numbers in higher education rose from 120,000 to 170,000. I propose that students pay up to 30 per cent of the fees when they can afford it.**

> **There is far too much of a 'me too' attitude in higher education, with replication of courses in every college.**

of courses in every college. This has got to come to an end. It would make more sense if colleges specialized in core subjects as a means of becoming world leaders in a particular area. A new national technological university must grow out of the IOTs. Contracts for academic staff also need to be reviewed.

I think it is very important to take higher education out of the Department of Education and Science, possibly the most dysfunctional department in the land. Higher education has grown far too large and a new department called the Department of Learning, Training and Enterprise is needed. The existing department would become the Department of Schools where it would focus on key issues involving the primary and post-primary sector.

Response to An Bord Snip Nua

I would also like to comment on the Report of An Bord Snip Nua. It highlighted waste and duplication and it is right andproper that no department can be immune to what the Minister for Finance has called 'these adjustments'. The idea that the Department of Education budget can be ring-fenced without any changes to it and other departments have to find savings is absolute nonsense. I think we have to be up-front and honest about this rather than pretending that we can ringfence everything within the Budget.

What we have to ring-fence is the front-line staff. Teachers are the essential 'hardware' in education. I want to make it absolutely clear that I will not support any reduction in the number of teachers in our primary and post-primary system under any set of circumstances. It is crazy at a time where we are likely to have some 50,000 net additional children coming into the primary school system over the next few years that we are talking about taking teachers out of the system. The same is true of talk about taking teachers out of post-primary schools when we are trying to provide a range of choices within post-primary schools to meet the curricular needs of these students.

It would be stupid to suggest that each department find a blanket 3 or 4 per cent savings. In my view, each department needs to go through its budget and weed out what is not essential. There are many agencies that could be merged or amalgamated. We have far too many VECs, for instance, in this country. In a population the size of Greater Manchester, it makes no sense to have 33 separate education authorities. Every problem that a Minister for Education has had for the past ten years was solved by setting up a new agency. That has got to change if we are serious about prioritizing front-line services.

I want to say to the partners in education that there is far too much territorialism in Irish education. While choice is very good, we have 35 separate partners in education. While all bring a unique contribution to bear, I get the sense that people are obsessed with their own area and they do not see the bigger picture. This is the same for unions as for political parties. We have got to make sure that we deal with this issue of territorialism once and for all. I will make a simple proposal. We have An Bord Snip Nua Report identifying potential savings in the Education Budget. I think the Joint Education Committee of the Dáil and Seanad should take September and October to invite in the partners in education to get their views on the basis of what they are for, not against. We need an honest public debate between now and October on efficiencies and economies of scale in education. I think it is possible that we can arrive at a consensus on cost savings within the Education Budget. We could get agreement, perhaps not on everything, but I certainly think we could get agreement on the essential savings required to get us through the crisis.

Education is key to recovery

There are a number of points I want to make about education as the key to economic recovery. One is money. We do not spend enough on education in this country largely because of history. In the past, we got education free of charge from the religious and this is now coming to an end. What we do spend is spread too thinly across the entire system to make much of a difference. We also have a view of education that it is merely for people from the ages of 5 to 21. But if you are in your 40s and you want to go back to college or in your 60s and want to retire and do something else, you do not really fit in. Really successful economies encourage lifelong learning, the notion of education as something which takes place throughout your life. We have to radically change that if we are serious about the challenges

I will not support any reduction in the number of teachers in our primary and post-primary system under any set of circumstances.

We need an honest public debate between now and October on efficiencies and economies of scale in education. I think it is possible that we can arrive at a consensus on cost savings within the Education Budget.

facing the economy. The other thing is we need to decentralize power to schools. There is a 'Stalinist' attitude in the Department of Education and Science, really a department of schools which handles everything from window frames to circulars on nuclear winters. The place is extraordinary and very frustrating to deal with at the best of times. What we need is a radical programme of decentralization within our schools. Frankly, it is a joke that principals spend so much time form-filling. Show me the bad principal in a good school. There is no such place. Good schools follow good principals. Give a school a budget and let it decide what is important. For instance, if it wants to prioritize say science or music it must have the flexibility to do so.

The key thing we have got to do right now is to concentrate on the quality of teaching, the quality of the experience of students and the quality of leadership in schools. These are the most important ingredients. I am great fan of what Tony Blair did in education. He increased money going into education in the UK but in return demanded accountability and standards. I think the issue of accountability is the aspect of education we need to put centre-stage right now if we are going to meet our economic challenges, primarily because the experience of a teacher in front of a class is an absolutely pivotal experience deciding whether or not success can be engendered in that child.

Finally, there has been a lot of negative comment, various tabloid attacks, since the publication of the Report of An Bord Snip Nua, on teachers. I am fed up with it. We need the best, brightest and most ambitious to go into teaching. High achieving teachers need to be rewarded. It is a privilege to go round to schools and see such wonderful teachers. Of course there are some who should not be there at all. With 40 per cent of the membership of the INTO joining in the last ten years, this offers an extraordinary opportunity for radical change within the profession as well as radical change in the perception of the profession. Bashing teachers, a sideline of particular newspapers, is not going to get us through this. We need people on a reform programme to make sure that the quality product we have is supported in the years to come.

Really successful economies encourage lifelong learning, the notion of education as something which takes place throughout your life.

High achieving teachers need to be rewarded. It is a privilege to go round to schools and see such wonderful teachers. Of course there are some who should not be there at all.

Chapter 8

ENERGY AND THE ECONOMY – NEW APPROACHES?

WE MUST PREPARE FOR A DIFFERENT ENERGY DIET
Jeremy Gilbert
Former Chief Petroleum Engineer, British Petroleum

RENEWABLES – KEY PART OF WAY FORWARD
Pádraig McManus
Chief Executive, Electricity Supply Board (ESB)

ENERGY – DETERMINING FACTOR IN RECOVERY
Simon Coveney TD
Fine Gael Spokesperson, Communications, Energy & Natural Resources

ENERGY – OPPORTUNITIES AND CHALLENGES
Paul Dowling
Chief Executive, Airtricity

We Must Prepare for a Different Energy Diet

Jeremy Gilbert
Former Chief Petroleum Engineer, British Petroleum

Born and educated in Dublin. Degree in Mathematics from TCD. Joined BP in 1964. Worked in Libya, US, Kuwait, Abu Dhabi and Iran. In 1979, moved to Aberdeen and later managed all BP's UK petroleum and reservoir engineering activities. Worked in San Francisco from 1986 as Vice President-Production of BP Alaska Exploration before returning to UK in 1988 as Technical Manager for development of Wytch Farm field. Appointed BP's Chief Petroleum Engineer in 1989 and later, Resource Development Manager. Retired in 2001. Now Managing Director of Barrelmore Ltd., Irish company providing reservoir engineering advice, audit and training support to the international oil industry. Was Chairman of Heriot-Watt University's Industrial Advisory Board, and member of Imperial College London and University of Alaska Industrial Advisory Boards.

We read continually of the way in which Ireland might become a world leader in developing and applying new sustainable energies. Wave power on the west coast, tidal power where currents are strong, wind generation on hills and mountain ranges, and electricity from waste digesters. All of these potential sources do indeed exist and in the long term may provide reliable and economically-viable power to our industries, cars and transport. But we need to wake up to the near certainty that these new and exciting sources are unlikely to become significant providers quickly enough to solve the problem which I believe will face us over the next decade as world supplies of oil reach a peak and begin to decline. We are going to regret that concentrating on other problems which we have encountered over the last decade has meant that we have not given the attention we should have to finding and developing large-scale sources of energy other than oil.

This problem will be particularly significant for Ireland because of our overwhelming dependence on imported oil. Some two thirds of our overall energy usage is derived from oil,

We are going to regret that concentrating on other problems which we have encountered over the last decade has meant that we have not given the attention we should have to finding and developing large-scale sources of energy other than oil.

The rate of oil discovery peaked in about 1970 and has declined steadily ever since. Meanwhile, our consumption of oil has steadily risen with average year-on-year increases of about 1.5 per cent. Since about 1980 the world has been consuming more oil each year than it has discovered.

Depletion of the world's oil fields is in itself enough to make likely a peaking in oil supply in the very near future.

virtually all of our transport depends on oil as a fuel and, of course, all of this oil is imported. Ireland is critically dependent on easy access to reasonably-priced oil imports. Our already-fragile economy will be severely tested if world oil prices increase significantly over the period in which we seek to move away from our dependence on oil.

While there is considerable controversy over the reasons for both the increases and the huge variations in oil prices that we have seen over the last year – and over the last few months in particular – I believe that oil prices will soon start to rise consistently and will reach levels exceeding those we saw in mid 2008. I believe this because my experience suggests that we are close to the point at which world oil supply will be unable to match world oil demand. The result will be competition for supplies, with the world's richer countries initially being able to buy most of what they need at the expense of their poorer neighbours, but the shortage of supply and increased unit cost soon having a serious impact on every country.

I am certainly not saying that the world is about to run out of oil. Far from it, we have a century or more of substantial production to come. But the oil production levels we can anticipate during this century will decline steadily, despite the demands of a growing world population for more energy to support increasing standards of living.

Around the world we find that more and more countries have reached the stage where their production has peaked and begun to decline; indeed, production is in decline in at least 60 of the world's 99 producing countries. While many of these were only small producers even when at maximum the list also includes countries like the US, UK, Norway, Iran, Indonesia. Even if we look at the OPEC and FSU countries, only six of the 28 have managed to increase production since 2005. In general, it seems that a country's production rate will begin to decline when about 60 per cent of its original reserves have been produced.

The rate of oil discovery peaked in about 1970 and has declined steadily ever since. Meanwhile, our consumption of oil has steadily risen with average year-on-year increases of about 1.5 per cent. Since about 1980 the world has been consuming more oil each year than it has discovered. Over the last decade we have been using about 4 barrels of oil for every barrel we have discovered. The early years of this century have shown a slightly better reserves replacement record but this appears to have been a short-lived anomaly. There is no reason to assume that the declining rate of discovery can be reversed despite new and better technology being available

This situation, living on the exploration successes of the past, cannot continue forever! It is inevitable that available supply is going to reach a peak and then begin to decline. The challenge facing analysts is to predict when that peak will occur and, even more important, what the decline rate will be subsequent to the peak. Calculations of future oil production would yield uncertain results under the best of conditions. In practice, lack of good data – for political and commercial reasons – make it very difficult for independent analysts to do their work. However, what many independent experts perceived as bias and obvious errors in predictions which have been made over the last decade by prestigious agencies, such as the US Geological Service (USGS) and the International Energy Agency (IEA), have led study groups and universities to undertake the huge task of assembling the necessary data and using statistical methods to estimate world reserves and future production rates. The most extensive of these studies has been made by the Association for the Study of Peak Oil (ASPO), a group founded in Ireland by Dr Colin Campbell.

ASPO's estimates of existing reserves, country by country, and of volumes yet to be found are regularly updated as new information becomes available. Given the secrecy which surrounds oil industry data, the information is not always timely or plentiful but it does result in a description of world oil reserves which is unbiased and open to audit. In brief, ASPO's studies suggest that with about 1100 billion barrels (Bstb) of regular oil already produced, we can expect about 750 Bstb of further production, taking into account about 120 Bstb of yet-to-be-found oil. Remaining non-regular oil reserves probably amount to about 600 Bstb. This independent analysis has suggested that most published estimates of reserves and production are very optimistic. In particular, it seems that OPEC-provided estimates of their remaining oil is about 300 billion barrels less than they have led us to believe and that the potential for recovery from

Increased expenditure on fuel can be expected to rapidly result in reduced economic activity on a broad front.

At very least we need now to begin reducing our energy expenditure by forcing more efficient usage.

non-OPEC fields may be as much as 600 billion barrels less than the USGS predicted in their major 1995 report which has been the basis for many projections of future supply. When these estimates of reserves, already discovered and yet-to-find, are used as the basis for supply calculations it seems that the time of peak production has just occurred or will be reached within the next few years.

Depletion of the world's oil fields is in itself enough to make likely a peaking in oil supply in the very near future. The probability of this occurring is increased by lack of investment to bring forward production from remaining reserves. This effect is sometimes explained by thinking of fluid draining from a tank: it is not just the volume of the tank which is important when considering how fast it will drain, it is also the throughput of the tap. Until a few years ago the world production capacity was significantly larger than demand. There was always spare capacity and this was managed by the oil producers to share the market and, to some extent, to control prices. Since about 2007 this spare capacity has disappeared. Investment in new fields and new production facilities has not been sufficient. This situation has come about mainly because over the last three decades there has been a reversal in the control of the world's oil fields and in the investment pattern of those controlling field development.

In this short paper it is not possible to discuss in detail the contribution towards meeting oil demand that might come from what are called 'unconventional sources'. Sadly, I do not believe that any of these sources offer an immediate solution to the problem which is facing us. While there are indeed many billions of barrels of oil-in-place in oil sands, in so-called oil-shales and in heavy-oil fields, it is clear to most experts that none of these sources is going to deliver significant volumes of oil in time to have any influence whatsoever on the timing of the supply peak. Indeed they will have little influence for many years on the slope of the subsequent decline curve. Estimates of production from the Canadian oil sands, the largest deposits in the world, have been regularly reduced in recent years as the environmental consequences of proceeding with development there have

Our already-fragile economy will be severely tested if world oil prices increase significantly over the period in which we seek to move away from our dependence on oil.

been recognized and problems of meeting input water and natural gas volume requirements have emerged. Far from the 5 million barrels per day (MMbd) or more output which had been predicted only five years ago it now seems that we will be fortunate if output ever exceeds 3 MMbd. While this may seem a significant volume it has to be seen in the light of overall production of 85 MMbd, an annual decline of at least 5 MMbd and demand increasing at 1 per cent per year or more.

The demand level for oil will ultimately be determined by economic activity, by changes in living standards, by transportation changes, by population growth and of course by the success of efforts to move away from oil to other more sustainable fuels. Given the pattern of oil usage, by category and by area, and the rates of change in population and living standards it seems virtually certain that while demand may not increase as rapidly as in the last few decades it is not going to fall. Estimates which have suggested demand may reach 120 MMbd may be too high but it is hard to believe that with a return to even limited economic stability and growth demand will not increase above current levels.

As a supply-demand gap opens prices will rise to force a match. Initially the reduction in demand will come primarily from those countries which can least afford to pay the higher prices. Experience from 2008 and earlier price-driven demand reductions suggests that electricity, agriculture and local transport will be the first activities to be hit; the poorest people will feel the impact most. In richer countries like Ireland, with poor public transport facilities and many people who must drive to work or school, such people will find it hard to cut back on driving. Increased expenditure on fuel can be expected to rapidly result in reduced economic activity on a broad front.

It is not for a petroleum engineer to predict how the community will react to quickly increasing petrol prices and the inevitable parallel increases in electricity and transport charges. As someone who has spent a working life planning and optimizing the development of oil fields I can only try to explain how real the threat of a declining oil supply is and encourage political leaders to give urgent attention to the development of alternative fuels, ideally fuels which are sustainable and do not pollute. I know, principally from work done over the last few years by Dr Robert

The rate of oil discovery peaked in about 1970 and has declined steadily ever since. Meanwhile, our consumption of oil has steadily risen with average year-on-year increases of about 1.5 per cent. Since about 1980 the world has been consuming more oil each year than it has discovered.

We talk about encouraging purchases of electric cars, of building more energy-efficient housing, of taxing aircraft fuel but movement on all of these is slow.

Hirsch, that the time required to scale up the embryo technologies which appear good candidates is of the order of about 15 years from the time at which we make a serious start.

At the very least we need now to begin reducing our energy expenditure by forcing more efficient usage. We talk about encouraging purchases of electric cars, of building more energy-efficient housing, of taxing aircraft fuel but movement on all of these is slow. Politicians are reluctant to take actions which will alienate them from their constituents who have little awareness of why we must spend now to avoid critical problems some years hence. Even if there were to be immediate implementation of policies on such items the long life of existing devices means that it will be many years before an effect on consumption occurs.

There is little indication that Ireland, or the rest of the world, is close to taking actions which will have a long-lasting and significant impact on the demand for oil. I do not believe that nature is going to give us the 15 years needed to develop alternatives. Hence I am very pessimistic about the world's ability to balance its energy budget over the next two or three decades. Ireland's appetite for oil will not be met over this period. We must prepare for a different energy diet – and time is very short for what will be a huge change.

Renewables – Key Part of Way Forward

Pádraig McManus
Chief Executive, Electricity Supply Board (ESB)

Born in Kildare and educated at Naas CBS and UCD (BE in electrical engineering). Joined ESB in 1973 and spent fifteen years with the company's international businesses, later becoming Managing Director of ESB International and Commercial Director of ESB. Various management positions in ESB (1983-2002). Appointed Chief Executive in 2002. Fellow of the Institute of Engineers, Board Member of the Irish Management Institute and Vice Chairperson of Business in the Community Ireland. Was recently appointed to the Board of Trustees of The Conference Board.

Climate Change, security of electricity supply and price stability is the main rationale underpinning the need for renewables. A lot of R&D is going into technologies such as solar, bio-mass, wave and tidal, even heat pumps. However, the one that is racing ahead at the moment is wind technology. In wind, Ireland has about 1,000 MW of wind connected at the moment. By 2020 it is estimated that it will have 5,000 MW.

If we develop renewables, we have security of supply and eventually get away from what has strangled us for years, namely total dependence on imported fossil fuels.

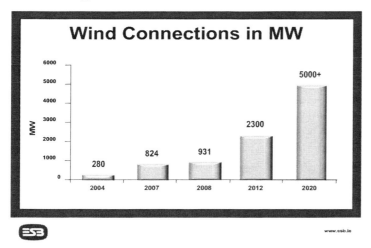

Figure 1

The whole issue about renewables is that Ireland does not have any natural source of energy. We do have peat that we have burnt for a long time. People, however, have mixed views on that, and it has a limited life span. Everything else is imported. There is no other European country that is so dependent on imported fossil fuels as we are. Over 90 per cent of our electricity is generated from imported fossil fuels, and the absolute reality of that, even though we are in recession, is that fuel will go up again. In our sector you cannot look at one, two or three years ahead. You have to look and plan long term. So when fuel goes up, and emphasis on the environment drives up the cost of carbon, renewables come into their own and become competitive.

We need to be connected to the UK grid to make it one grid, and I believe that will happen.

You cannot build an electricity infrastructure overnight. You have got to plan for the long term. If we develop renewables, we have security of supply and eventually get away from what has strangled us for years, namely total dependence on imported fossil fuels. If you have a native source of energy for electricity it gives price stability in the long term. So today you may say that the price of fuel is way down and that wind cannot compete and that is true but we cannot look at those things in the short term. What we are aiming to do is to make ESB produce electricity by 2035 without producing CO_2. And although Europe has set 2050 as its target, we are well ahead of that. We have set interim targets for 2012 and 2020 when we will make substantial cuts in CO_2. We have also committed to having 33 per cent of our portfolio by 2020 in renewables.

The whole drive towards renewables makes sense for the ESB, in terms of carbon, environment, security of supply, having our own source of energy and stability in pricing. The amount of renewable has to go hand in hand with interconnection. We have been talking about interconnection for years. In 2003, I offered to build the interconnector to the UK and hand it over lock, stock and barrel to whomsoever the Government designated, but there were concerns about the whole issue of dominance and it did not happen. We are still talking about it. We now have a renewed target of 2012. For us to develop that amount of wind on our small system we need interconnection. We need to be connected to the UK grid to make it one grid, and I believe that will happen, but it needs to happen faster.

Everybody has a keen interest in pricing, which I will now examine. How the market works in Ireland is that we have a pool, a load of generators and suppliers. We also have a grid that just moves electricity from one place to the other. It is a very complex arrangement and the technicalities of it are complex but the simple message is that people make electricity and sell it to a pool. Suppliers buy it and then sell it to customers. It is a pool system. The ESB cannot for the moment buy it. But it is my hope that one day we will be able to do so. If so, we will be able to drop the price of electricity but because competition is growing we are not allowed to do that now.

Since we import all our fuel we are totally dependent in terms of our electricity price on how the international price of fuel varies. It fluctuates a lot. People actually lock in because the amount of money involved in buying fuel is so enormous. When it comes to summer time people lock in for the following year and a lot of the annoyance around the issue with big suppliers is that if you lock in at a high price then you are locked in – it is like locking in your mortgage at a fixed rate.

Other countries have nuclear, hydro or combinations of both, and in the commercial sector while we are above the European average, we are not much above it.

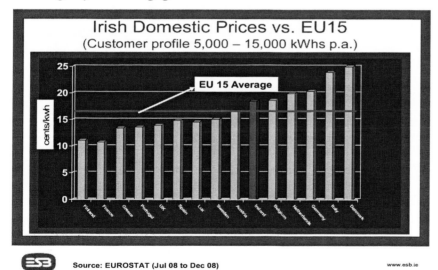

Source: EUROSTAT (Jul 08 to Dec 08)   www.esb.ie

Figure 2

Generally when people lock in at a fixed rate and it goes

against them they are not pleased, and then it is everybody else's fault but their own! So if you lock into a contract for one year or two years it is the very same as locking in your mortgage on a fixed rate. There is no way out of it until your contract runs out. There is a myth that the price of electricity in Ireland is amongst the highest in Europe. The first thing to clarify in relation to that is that of the 2 million customers in Ireland, 300,000 of them do not use electricity so they pay just a standing charge. If you include those in the lower use you are going to get a completely distorted view of what the electricity price is so you have got to look at the average. If you look at the average, you will see that even though domestic prices in Ireland are above the average, they are barely above the average. Countries like Belgium, Netherlands, Germany, Italy and Denmark have much higher prices in the domestic sector than Ireland.

The whole emphasis in terms of price, with due respect to hard pressed people who have to pay their domestic bills, should be on trying to support the job creation sector.

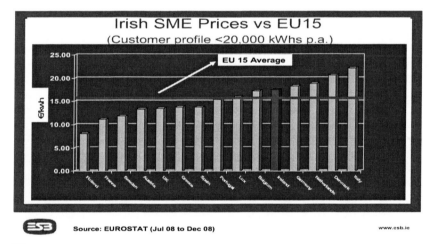

Source: EUROSTAT (Jul 08 to Dec 08)   www.esb.ie

Figure 3

The very same applies in the commercial sector. Countries like Belgium, Netherlands, Denmark, Italy are above or similar to Ireland in that particular sector. Other countries have nuclear, hydro or combinations of both, and in the commercial sector while we are above the European average, we are not much above it.

Back in the 1990s there was virtually only one supplier and that was the ESB. At that time we were not investing in renewing the network, but the prices were the lowest in Europe and everybody still harks back to that time. One of the things we did but

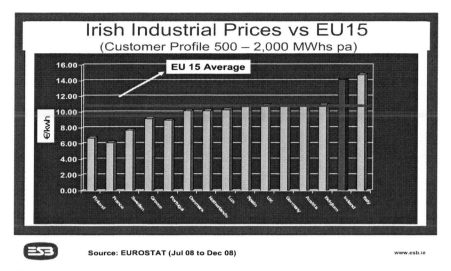

Source: EUROSTAT (Jul 08 to Dec 08)   www.esb.ie

Figure 4

which nobody ever knew because there was only one supplier, is that we skewed the tariff towards the industrial sector so that we could keep the industrial or job creating sector at its lowest possible price level. Now that we are in the open market it has to be open book and everything is done according to regulations, and that is why you have that cost reflective tariff as they call it. People may not have known that we actually dealt with this in our own way in the 1990s when there was just one supplier. Recently, it has been suggested that we load the domestic sector to bring down the tariff to the industrial sector. I am not proposing that we do that because we are so dependent on imported fossil fuels, but we should be more protective of the industrial jobs creative sector. The whole emphasis in terms of price, with due respect to hard pressed people who have to pay their domestic bills, should be on trying to support the job creation sector.

The ESB is one of the most successful companies in Ireland, It is now the second most valuable company in the State after CRH. The banks used to be well ahead of us but they are certainly not any more. So it is incumbent on us, I believe, to be a creator of employment in sectors where we actually need to grow and this is what we are doing. The contribution that ESB makes to the Irish economy every year is of the order of €2.5 billion comprised of

If you look at the average, you will see that even though domestic prices in Ireland are above the average, they are barely above the average.

purchases, payroll, taxes, rates, foreign sales to ESB international and dividends.

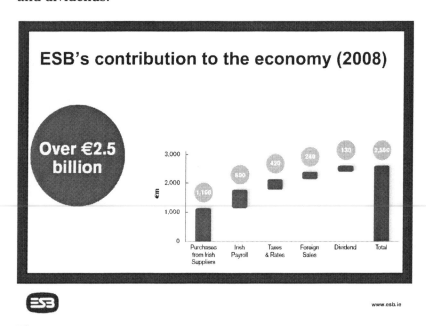

Figure 5

There is a lot of anxiety that we might stop our capital investment programme. We are not going to do that. We have invested heavily in the network over the last number of years, resulting in reductions in outages, and we are going to continue to invest. We have one of the most automated networks across Europe at the moment and that is going to be a big advantage to us as we get into the smart grid area. All across Europe there has been huge under investment in the electricity sector. It is a big problem, but we are going to continue with our programme.

Our key focus now is on helping job creation. Electric vehicles, a smart grid network, home energy efficiency programmes and a major eco investment fund, along with the redevelopment of ESB's head office in Dublin could lead to major job creation. Energy is potentially a major source of employment and a recent stimulus package announced by the ESB outlined the creation of 3,700 new jobs. The ESB is also training 800 apprentices and 300 young professionals and graduates. As well as creating

As well as creating jobs, we are committed to finishing the training of FÁS apprentices.

jobs, we are committed to finishing the training of FÁS apprentices. The first 100 have actually gone through and are now qualified apprentices. These are people who were let go from other employment before their training was finished. We are working with FÁS to manage this. We are also, instead of taking on the normal number of 45 apprentices, taking on 100 for the next number of years and developing this into a 6 year programme. We will train those people over that period of time to bring them up to University entrance level and, after two years, 50 will go back to college to do engineering and 50 will continue with their trade.

An area where we see big opportunities are electric vehicles. We are working closely with people from Southern California Edison because they are the leading utility in terms of smart metering and the development of electric vehicles. Electric vehicles were blocked in the past, largely by the motor industry, but it is not going to happen this time. It is going to be slow, but we are going to be supporters in rolling out the infrastructure to make sure that it works this time round.

In relation to home energy efficiency we have ambitious targets and we have already started a programme for providing home audits for people. We will audit the house free of charge and do what is needed to do to raise efficiency levels in accordance with the standards that have been set out. All the banks have now committed to Government to support this sector and are prepared to play their part in it. It is a programme that we feel is going to grow over the next number of years.

We have an investment fund that we started because we were inundated with people who said that if the ESB was only with me I could create, say, a solution in wave technology. So we have set up this fund and intend to invest in new technologies. Not all of them will work but we believe that some of them will. The whole smart grid and smart network is something that is developing. It is going to create a lot of employment in terms of the additional infrastructure that has to be developed.

In summary, renewables are a key part of the way forward. Because of the way fossil fuels are going, we have no other alternative but to be in there. In time it will pay back handsomely in terms of having security of supply, a source of electricity for ourselves on the island, providing stability in terms of price.

The contribution that ESB makes to the Irish economy every year is of the order of €2.5 billion comprised of purchases, payroll, taxes, rates, foreign sales to ESB international and dividends.

In relation to home energy efficiency we have ambitious targets and we have already started a programme for providing home audits for people. We will audit the house free of charge.

Energy – A Determining Factor in Recovery

Simon Coveney TD

Fine Gael spokesperson, Communications, Energy & Natural
Resources

*Born in Cork, holds a BSc in Agriculture and Land
Management from Royal Agriculture College, Gloucester-
shire. Also educated at Clongowes Wood College, Co.
Kildare, UCC and Gurteen Agricultural College, Co.
Tipperary. First elected to Dáil Éireann in by-election for
Cork South Central in October 1998, following untimely
death of his father, Hugh. Member of various Oireachtas
Committees including Family, Social and Community
Affairs, Education and Science, Communications Marine
and Natural Resources and Strategic Management Initiative
Committee. Elected to European Parliament in June 2004 as
Fine Gael candidate for the Ireland South constituency. In
May 2007, re-elected in General Election and resigned seat
as MEP. Was member of Cork County Council from 1999 to
2003.*

Today I challenge all stakeholders in the Energy sector, but particularly the Commission for Energy Regulation (CER), Government and Semi-State companies such as the ESB and Bord Gáis, to prioritize achieving significant reductions in the relative cost of energy in Ireland.

Energy policy is a key component in providing a more
competitive and attractive environment for doing business. It
can also be central to an exciting new stimulus plan for an
economy that needs reform. I will focus on two issues relating
to energy policy. The first is the cost of energy in Ireland, in
particular electricity, and its impact on competitiveness and
job losses. The second addresses how, with big thinking and
State leadership, the energy sector can play an exciting role in
repositioning the Irish economy and a good news story for
employment, sustainability and the driver of economic
growth.

Effect of Energy Prices on Economic Competitiveness

The cost of doing business in Ireland is clearly too high, and it
is costing jobs every day. High energy, utility, and labour
costs drive businesses out of business and out of Ireland.
Either way, the consequences are dire for the hundreds

who are losing employment every day. If you think I'm exaggerating, here is what the IMF said in June: 'In recent years, Ireland has become the most expensive location in the Eurozone'.

Certainly this is the case when it comes to energy costs. Irish electricity prices are above the EU average in all bands, ranging between 12 per cent to 38 per cent above the EU average. Domestic household electricity is also the most expensive in the EU. So let us be clear on this: energy, particularly electricity, but also gas, is too expensive in Ireland. Today I challenge all stakeholders in the Energy sector, but particularly the Commission for Energy Regulation (CER), Government and Semi-State companies such as the ESB and Bord Gáis, to prioritize achieving significant reductions in the relative cost of energy in Ireland.

The truth is that in the Irish energy market, consumers and businesses continue to pay the price for facilitating new entrants into a competitive market place, yet we see no direct benefits of competition in terms of lower energy costs. It is about time we made competition work, by measuring its success, not by the number of new players in the market, but by how the energy market is delivering to consumers and energy users.

So what can be done in practical terms to bring down prices? The most significant factor affecting energy prices in Ireland is global oil prices, due to Ireland's high dependence on imported fuel and the knock-on impact oil prices have on other fuel prices, in particular natural gas and as a consequence electricity. The unprecedented increases granted by the CER this time last year were warranted due to the cost of a barrel of oil reaching $147. But since then, the price of oil has dropped and stabilized at around $60 a barrel, a drop of 58 per cent since July 2008. At the same time the cost of wholesale gas in the UK has dropped by over 60 per cent. However, in April 2009 regulated prices were only reduced by 12 per cent for gas and 10 per cent for electricity by the CER. I have consistently said that this price reduction was nowhere near what it should have been to deliver fair value for consumers.

Electricity pricing is more complex than gas and I would like to explore a number of ways in which we might be able to reduce prices by reforming the way energy prices are regulated.

> We have the ridiculous situation where Bord Gáis and Airtricity are offering households significantly cheaper electricity than the ESB, 10 per cent to 15 per cent cheaper, yet the ESB are not allowed by the CER reduce their prices to compete.

> Households and businesses paid in excess of €220 million extra last year for carbon on their electricity bills. This is carbon tax by stealth.

Fixed maximum price vs. setting ceiling

Current legislation orders the energy regulator to set an actual price for electricity and gas in Ireland for households, and in the case of gas, small businesses also. I believe this needs to change to allow the CER to set a maximum price rather than setting the actual price.

We have the ridiculous situation where Bord Gáis and Airtricity are offering households significantly cheaper electricity than the ESB, 10 per cent to 15 per cent cheaper, yet the ESB are not allowed by the CER reduce their prices to compete. So we have spent ten years trying to deliver a competitive market place for households and now that we have real competition, the regulator is keeping ESB prices artificially high. The reason given is that Bord Gáis and Airtricity need to be allowed to get a sizeable foothold in the market before the ESB is allowed to compete on price. This is nonsense and consumers are paying too much for their ESB bills as a result.

Carbon Charging: scandalous rip-off of consumers!

After 2012 all electricity generators will have to purchase what are called carbon credits for every ton of carbon emitted while generating power. However, from 2008 to 2012 the Government is giving 'carbon allowance credits' for free to all generators as we prepare for full carbon trading. This approach seems reasonable until you consider that power generators are required to charge energy users for the full value of carbon emitted during generation. So generators get the credits for free, but they charge full price for those credits when billing consumers. As a result, the average electricity bill for families and businesses in 2008 had a 10 per cent increase directly attributable to carbon charges, even though there is no added cost for electricity generators attached to carbon credits. Households and businesses paid in excess of €220 million extra last year for carbon on their electricity bills. This is carbon tax by stealth.

It is estimated that over the life time of the current phase

My party, in Government, wants the opportunity to totally restructure the semi-state sector, so that the country creates a portfolio of state owned companies fit for purpose in a modern new economy, equipped for all the new challenges we face.

of the carbon allowance credit plan (2008-2012) electricity generators could make unearned gains of almost €1.6 billion, on the back of Irish electricity users. To its credit the ESB offered to give back €300 million to offset rising energy prices in the first half of 2009. However unfortunately, they have declined to commit to refunding any of this carbon windfall profit in 2009 or in the future.

Fine Gael would merge Coillte and Bord na Móna to create a strong, strategically placed bio-energy and land management company.

The CER is clearly uncomfortable with this situation, but has stated repeatedly that it is for Government to change policy in this area. I am increasingly of the view that we should consider removing carbon charging from electricity bills altogether until 2012, when all generators will have to pay for carbon allowances anyway under the EU carbon trading mechanisms. We in Fine Gael have called on Government to recoup this unearned windfall profits through a tax/levy on generators but have got no response. Getting rid of carbon charges, on a temporary basis, until 2012, would reduce electricity costs by between 7 per cent and 10 per cent overnight.

When it comes to energy projects we should think big and the State should be taking the lead. Fine Gael has recently launched a policy document entitled 'Rebuilding Ireland'. It maps out how, with ambitious thinking and genuine reform, we can fund an €18 billion stimulus package aimed at building the modern infrastructure upon which we can grow a new economy. This project will not solve all our economic woes, but it can provide real cause for optimism.

Not only will we need to employ tens of thousands of people in the construction phase of such a plan, but more importantly we can create the opportunity for hundreds of thousands to benefit from the new infrastructure proposed. We are primarily talking about a massive investment programme in telecommunications infrastructure, water infrastructure and most importantly energy infrastructure though a modern Smart Electricity Grid.

This stimulus package can be funded without increasing national debt. Instead we propose to fund the investment programme though capital raised by new and existing commercial state companies. My party, in Government, wants the opportunity to restructure the semi-state sector, so that the country creates a portfolio of state owned companies fit for purpose in a modern new economy, equipped for all the new challenges we face.

The State has created state companies in the past that have delivered hugely successful projects through the expertise and ambition within such companies. The ESB was set up in 1927, as the State was trying to find its feet and reinforce our national independence. Two years later, in 1929, the Shannon scheme at Ardnacrusha began construction. The State committed nearly a third of our entire income to complete a highly controversial piece of energy infrastructure that proved such a success in giving the New Ireland the capacity to generate our own power. It is still operating today. Likewise with rural electrification thirty years later; the ESB again delivered for the State.

We are at another Ardnacrusha Moment as a country. We must be prepared to commit to ambitious projects that can create the basis for economic growth. Any country that simply tries to hold onto the status quo when under pressure will shrink and continue to suffer. The great competitive advantage that a small country like Ireland has is the ability to adapt and transform ourselves quickly. We must use that ability now. The opportunities in the energy sector are exciting with the right leadership from Government. Let me give you some examples of what I would like to do:

- Fine Gael would merge Coillte and Bord na Móna to create a strong, strategically placed bio-energy and land management company. This company would own almost 10 per cent of the land mass of Ireland and could over time manage the transition from peat to wood biomass as a fuel source, using Coillte wood and Bord na Móna power stations. It would develop an ambitious roll-out of combined heat and power (CHP) plants in public buildings across the country. Do you know that the state currently spends €300 million a year on imported fossil fuel to simply heat public buildings? That money should and can stay in Ireland.
- Fine Gael wants to create a new state company called Smartgrid that would be independent of ESB Networks to own and manage a modern electricity network capable of facilitating micro generation in people's homes, a vast electric transportation

> **We as a nation spend €6.5 billion every year on imported fossil fuels to generate power and heat and to drive our transport fleet. With the right thinking and proper planning we can spend the vast majority of this sum of money here in Ireland, if we exploited our own natural and renewable resources in an intelligent way.**

charging infrastructure for electric vehicles, new energy storage projects and much more. Much of this is already happening through GRID25 and ESB commitments, but it can be more ambitious.

- Fine Gael wants to rationalize and sell off assets that are no longer of strategic interest to the state within our state owned companies. It is immoral to be holding on to assets that we do not need, when there are new projects that need finance and at a time when we are cutting back on vital public and social services because of lack of resources. Selling Bord Gáis Energy (BGE), for example, has been mentioned as an obvious opportunity for Government to raise much needed funds. Why does the State need to hold ownership of a second large energy company, competing with the ESB? It is my view that we should ensure that all gas pipeline infrastructure remains in state ownership, probably under the management of Smartgrid or EirGrid as lots of synergies exist between gas and electricity infrastructure. However the state could raise up to a billion euro by selling the remaining assets in BGE, without compromising pipeline infrastructure.

- Selling Bord Gáis Energy (BGE), for example, has been mentioned as an obvious opportunity for Government to raise much needed funds. Why does the State need to hold ownership of a second large energy company, competing with the ESB? It is my view that we should ensure that all gas pipeline infrastructure remains in state ownership, probably under the management of Smartgrid or EirGrid as lots of synergies exist between gas and electricity infrastructure. However the state could raise up to a billion euro by selling the remaining assets in BGE, without compromising pipeline infra-structure.

I will leave you with one final thought. We as a nation spend €6.5 billion every year on imported fossil fuels to generate power and heat and to drive our transport fleet. With the right thinking and proper planning, we can spend the vast majority of this sum of money here in Ireland, if we exploited our own natural and renewable resources in an intelligent way. We can create the smart electricity grid that facilitates power generation from wind, wave, biomass, waste, micro generation and conventional plant and distribute it in a more cost effective way. We will be forced to do this anyway, as the world moves past 'peak oil', and imported carbon based fuel resources become more scare and more expensive.

Energy, its generation, distribution, cost and management, will be one of the key determining factors as to when and how Ireland picks itself up from the mire of recession and becomes a country and economy to be proud of again.

Energy – Opportunities and Challenges

Paul Dowling
Chief Executive, Airtricity

Has a BSc in engineering from DIT and an MBA from TCD. A chartered engineer, worked with Bord na Móna from 1990 to 1997, managing wind projects and creating engineering business by selling contract fabrication and maintenance services. Former board member of British Wind Energy association. Joined Airtricity as Chief Operating Officer in 1997 and appointed Chief Executive in 2008.

Within the global economic system, energy is a fundamental enabler of economic activity. As an isolated economy, on the periphery of Europe, with more than 90 per cent fuel import dependence, discussions regarding energy in Ireland must first be contextualized in relation to global trends. Let us start by exploring changes in demand in the world economy in the last 20 years. Gross demand for energy is growing globally, increasing 13 per cent from 1988 to 1998. Between 1998 and 2008 gross demand grew even faster at a rate of 26 per cent.

The demand centres for energy are also changing. The US and Europe have shown relatively modest energy growth of 4 per cent and 2 per cent respectively over the past ten years. In contrast, China over the same period has seen demand grow by 118 per cent. By 2008 the BRIC (Brazil, Russia, India and China) economies have increased their consumption to 30 per cent of the world's energy. A major shift is therefore underway whereby developing economies are becoming the key new energy consumers.

As with most commodities the price of energy is a balance between supply and demand. In the West we have been influenced by the activities of cartels such as OPEC who limit supply and in so doing maintain high prices. While to-date this has shaped supply in response to demand and subsequently price, it is likely that in the future new global consumers of energy will have a more important impact. Indeed it could be said that Chinese and Indian energy policy will have more of an impact on energy prices in Ireland than the activities of OPEC.

By 2008 the BRIC (Brazil, Russia, India and China) economies have increased their consumption to 30 per cent of the world's energy. A major shift is therefore underway whereby developing economies are becoming the key new energy consumers.

We have an energy system in Ireland that is now 91 per cent dependant on imported fossil fuels. In the European context we also have one of the most carbon intensive economies in the EU. The current over-dependence on imported fossil fuels in the Irish energy market does not bode well for the future competitive-ness of the Irish economy.

We are now in an era where population growth combined with rising living standards/expectations in developing economies and the transfer of manufacturing from the West to these economies is driving an explosion in energy demand globally. With regard to global energy sources, over the last ten years oil supply has increased by 10 per cent, gas by 35 per cent, coal by 49 per cent, nuclear by 12 per cent and hydro by 22 per cent. At a time when the global imperative is to abate the climate change impact of anthropocentric greenhouse emissions we are burning more carbon intensive fossil fuels, coal in particular.

In Ireland there has been much more substantial growth in energy demand, rising over 23 per cent in the last 10 years. The mix of fuels has seen coal reduced but with a rapid expansion in both oil and gas. We have an energy system in Ireland that is now 91 per cent dependant on imported fossil fuels. In the European context we also have one of the most carbon intensive economies in the EU. The current over-dependence on imported fossil fuels in the Irish energy market does not bode well for the future competitiveness of the Irish economy. In the long term fossil fuel prices will rise due to increasing demand from countries like China, scarcity of easy to find resources and the inclusion of the cost of carbon in energy prices.

Our immediate competitive position in relation to our EU neighbours is poor, a situation compounded by our diseconomies of scale. For example, in the electricity market the Single Electricity Market (SEM) established between the Republic of Ireland and Northern Ireland, is one of the smallest electricity markets in the EU. Along with Italy and Slovakia, Ireland has the most expensive electricity for industry. In the current international climate of high fossil fuels prices the markets with the lowest costs for electricity in the EU are those with significant renewable energy such as Norway and Sweden or significant nuclear generation such as France.

What does Ireland need to do over the coming years to deal with this situation? One strategy is to do nothing, maintaining the current status quo of fossil fuel import dependency. This strategy would have merit if we could reasonably expect a world of cheap fossil fuels and no penalties for carbon emissions. However, the long term availability of cheap fossil fuels and no penalties for carbon pollution is no longer a reasonable assumption.

The most likely trends, as we have already begun to see in recent years, are higher and more volatile fossil fuel prices coupled with increasing charges associated with carbon emissions. In this world, Ireland's current fuel mix leads to a permanent competitive disadvantage in energy terms within the EU. We need, therefore, to focus our efforts in mitigating this disadvantage, transitioning from a high to a low carbon and low import dependent economy. In the absence of a substantial find of low cost fossil fuels in Ireland, we are starting from the current position of large scale importation of fossil fuels. In this scenario we have to minimize the usage of fossil fuels and make sure they are used in the most efficient manner possible.

Along with Italy and Slovakia, Ireland has the most expensive electricity for industry.

While much of the energy debate in Ireland tends to focus on electricity, the transport and heat sectors are also substantial and growing consumers of energy. While I do not propose to address heat and transport in any detail it is important to observe the convergence that is happening between these two sectors and electricity. In the drive to decarbonize energy consumption transport and heat will likely become key demand centres for electricity generated from low carbon sources.

The electricity sector, therefore, is the one that we in Ireland need to focus on. Comparing the historical global growth of energy with the historical growth in the use of electricity we see some interesting trends. In the last 10 years energy usage in the world has increased by 26 per cent while the use of electricity has grown by 40 per cent. In the EU where energy usage has grown by 2 per cent in the last 10 years, electricity demand has grown by 16 per cent. Indeed, in Ireland energy demand has grown by 23 per cent but electricity demand is up by 41 per cent. Around the world there is a move to higher value forms of energy such as electricity that provide power in a form that can readily be used by most domestic appliances and most industrial machinery. Simultaneously, the electricity system itself is becoming more efficient at converting energy into electricity and minimizing the losses.

In Ireland it makes most sense to focus most of our national

In Ireland it makes most sense to focus most of our national efforts at making the electricity system more efficient and cost effective. In doing so we are also focusing our efforts on the sector that we expect to be the key infrastructure in the low carbon economy of the future.

efforts at making the electricity system more efficient and cost effective. In doing so we are also focusing our efforts on the sector that we expect to be the key infrastructure in the low carbon economy of the future. Ireland has the second highest emissions of CO_2 in the EU-27. We are 60 per cent higher than the EU-27 and 54 per cent higher than our neighbour Great Britain. To improve this situation we have two options:

- Reduce overall energy consumption in Ireland relative to our competitors
- Reduce the carbon in the energy we use within the Irish economy

These options are not either/or options but rather it is the confluence of both that will help Ireland on to the path of sustainable and competitive energy. In the first option, as energy is critical to economic activity we cannot do without, we must, however, learn to use it as efficiently as possible, thus reducing quantities consumed. A carbon tax, if properly applied and recycled within the economy, is a powerful market signal to achieve this goal and should be pursued by the Government. A targeted support framework is required to deliver investments that will lower fossil fuel consumption. A portfolio of options is available to improve carbon intensity including:

- Using gas instead of peat, coal or oil in the generation mix.
- Storing carbon produced in the production of electricity
- Building a nuclear power station
- Building renewable energy

The two most likely in the context of the Irish power system are (1) and (4) as storing carbon is still an unproven technology and nuclear energy is not on the political agenda in Ireland. Within (1) and (4) the option that gives Ireland the best long term position is the delivery of indigenous renewable energy in the form of on-shore and off-shore wind energy. Ireland has one of the best wind resources available in

Europe. If we look at development across Europe we see that in the last 10 years wind energy has grown from 6,500 MW to some 65,000 MW installed across the EU-27. It is clear that wind energy is growing rapidly. Ireland with some of the best resources will be one of the cheapest places in Europe to generate electricity from the wind.

At a structural level we also have to deal with Ireland's diseconomies of scale. This is best explained by a quick comparison of the Ireland (Ire) and Great Britain (GB) electricity systems. The population of the island of Ire is 6.25 million and the population of GB is 60 million. The scale of the electricity market in Ire and GB reflect this difference in population. The installed capacity base of electricity generation in Ire in 2005 was 8,500 MW and for the GB market it was 72,500 MW. The maximum hourly demand in Ire was 6,400 MW in 2005 compared to a maximum hourly demand of 58,300 MW in GB. In very crude terms this means that the GB electricity system is about 10 times the size of the Ire electricity system and benefits from significantly better economies of scale.

Due to this scale differential it is possible to install larger more efficient generators on the GB system. For example the largest power station in GB is Drax at some 3,960 MW compared to the Moneypoint power station in the SEM at 900 MW. Due to the scale of the market it is also possible to build new capacity in larger unit sizes than is possible in the Ire power system. Furthermore, the scale of the generation market in GB does allow the market to support significant nuclear generation capacity.

Energy competitiveness is key to the Irish economy. If we focus on the historical performance of the electricity prices for industrial end users we get the following cost comparison:

While these obstacles are challenging Ireland is uniquely positioned. We have one of the best renewable profiles in Europe which not only provides solutions for electricity production but also as a replacement fuel in heat and transport through the medium of electricity.

Year	1997	2002	2003	2004	2005	2006	2007
Ireland	6.91	7.68	7.76	8.12	9.3	10.11	11.25
UK	6.04	6.4	5.63	5.01	5.93	8.22	9.74
% difference	14%	20 %	38 %	62 %	57 %	23 %	15%

Based on standard consumer (2GWh/year) on 1 January each year.
Source: *Eurostat*

It is clear that the Ire electricity market is not delivering the same costs as GB for industrial customers. On the path to delivering more competitive prices for Ireland the short-term political objective must be parity of electricity costs with GB for the industrial consumer. This is best achieved by establishing one single market between GB and Ireland similar to the SEM. For the Irish customer this will deliver economies of scale, improve competitive forces, increase customer choice and deliver parity in price with a leading trading partner. For the GB electricity customer it should enable lower cost renewable energy options, such as onshore wind, to be developed cost effectively.

Conclusion

As a small island, 90 per cent import dependent on price volatile fossil fuels, we are heavily exposed to the changing global demand for energy resources and ever increasing decarbonization ambitions. While these obstacles are challenging Ireland is uniquely positioned. We have one of the best renewable profiles in Europe which not only provides solutions for electricity production but also as a replacement fuel in heat and transport through the medium of electricity. Transitioning from our current fossil fuel dependence and maximizing our renewable resource, cost competitively, is challenging given our diseconomies of scale. Scale is the fundamental issue which can best be addressed by seeking to physically interconnect and harmonize our market with GB. In doing so economies of scale are resolved; our energy portfolio is expanded and more secure; and we can deliver electricity price parity with a key trading partner.

As a mutually beneficial arrangement I strongly encourage the Irish Government to open dialogue with our GB colleagues and pursue electricity market harmonization. This will deliver energy security, sustainability and competitive-ness to both jurisdictions while providing a sound foundation for future economic prosperity in Ireland.

Chapter 9

THE POTENTIAL OF AN ALL-ISLAND ECONOMY

WORKING TOGETHER ON ISLAND MAKES SENSE
Dara Calleary TD
Minister of State, Dept. of Enterprise, Trade & Employment

DEVELOPMENT OF AN ALL-ISLAND ECONOMY IS CRUCIAL
Martina Anderson MLA
Sinn Féin Spokesperson, Equality and Human Rights

Working Together on Island Makes Sense

Dara Calleary TD
Minister of State, Dept. of Enterprise, Trade & Employment

Educated at St Muredach's College, Ballina, Co Mayo, TCD (BA in Business & Politics). Elected TD for Mayo constituency at 2007 General Election. In 2009, appointed Minister of State at the Department of Enterprise, Trade and Employment with special responsibility for Labour Affairs. Has been a member of the Fianna Fáil National Executive since 1997 and served on party policy committees on Transport, Enterprise & Employment, Agriculture and Youth Affairs. Worked with Chambers Ireland from 1999-2006 and in Irish bankng. Son of Seán Calleary, TD for Mayo East from 1973 to 1992, who served as a Minister in three government departments, and grandson of Phelim Calleary, elected Member of 14th Dáil for Mayo North at the 1952 by-election.

Cross-border relations have never been better. Indeed, the changed atmosphere in terms of political discourse on these islands is one of the reasons we face into these challenging economic times with a sober sense of hope. In tackling the budgetary difficulties of twenty years ago, any politician suggesting that North/South cooperation might have a role to play would have been derided for their naivety and mocked for their optimism. The NO of that era has given way to an Obama style YES WE CAN attitude to tackle the problems of today.

Today, many of the men and women who got to know each other only as negotiators for peace – often to a backdrop of violence and recrimination – now meet as elected representatives to discuss where to build our roads, how to protect our children and what we can do to improve our broadband and energy services. Where once politicians, North and South, read about their differences in the newspaper, today they will pick up the phone, argue the options and agree plans to the mutual benefit of all those we represent. For that is the nature of what has been achieved in the North and throughout the island of Ireland:

> **Where once politicians, North and South, read about their differences in the newspaper, today they will pick up the phone, argue the options and agree plans to the mutual benefit of all those we represent.**

the victory of dialogue over distrust, what the journalist and writer Frank Millar has termed a 'triumph of politics'.

Industrial relations developments in the Republic and Northern Ireland continue to reflect elements of diversity as well as uniformity. It is just one hundred years ago since tripartite bodies were first established in Britain and Ireland in 1909 for the purpose of establishing minimum wages and other conditions for employees in certain low-paid and vulnerable employments. Problems of low wages and of unfair deductions, applied to homeworkers engaged in knitting, embroidery and lace-making here in Glenties, provided some of the political impetus for these social reforms. The poor employment conditions of many Donegal women engaged in this work was highlighted by Edwardian labour inspectors and in the stories of Patrick MacGill and the testimony of Paddy The Cope.

These wage-fixing bodies, which became known as Wages Councils, ceased to exist in Great Britain and in Northern Ireland in 1993. A decade earlier the Thatcher Government had also repealed the Fair Wages Act which permitted collective agreements to be extended to cover all employers within a particular sector. This brought to an end the means of making these sectoral agreements legally enforceable, along the lines of the Registered Employment Agreements established in the Republic under the Industrial Relations Act, 1946. It is hardly surprising, however, that industrial relations institutions and practices in the Republic have followed a different course of development over the past half century. Both Registered Employment Agreements and Joint Labour Committees – the counterparts in Ireland of the UK's former Wages Councils – continue to operate here alongside more recent reforms, such at the introduction of the National Minimum Wage in 2000.

> I would contend that it is time to consider whether an individual employer should be entitled to submit a claim to the Labour Court that for economic reasons he is unable to meet the terms agreed by Joint Labour Committees and under Registered Employment Agreements. The Government is committed to bringing forward legislation to modernize and strengthen these systems.

I would contend that it is time to consider whether an individual employer should be entitled to submit a claim to the Labour Court that for economic reasons he is unable to meet the terms agreed by Joint Labour Committees and under Registered Employment Agreements. The Government is committed to bringing forward legislation to modernize and strengthen these systems.

It may be necessary, however, to 're-balance' the existing mechanisms while providing at the same time for their continued effective operation in the face of renewed legal challenges. This would only bring both the Joint Labour Committee and Registered Employment Agreements systems into line with the procedures already established here under the National Minimum Wage Act, 2000. A reform on these lines would contribute to protecting employment in situations where employers are faced with severe economic challenges. It would also be a step towards unifying, simplifying and clarifying the complex structure of our industrial relations institutions in the Republic.

I referred earlier to how far we have travelled. A sign of that is The *Comprehensive Study on the All-Island Economy*, launched by the British-Irish Inter-Governmental Conference in October 2006, setting out an ambitious range of strategies and collaborative actions aimed at maximizing the competitive advantages of the island. Since restoration of the Northern Ireland Executive in May 2007, the Government has engaged constructively with Northern Ireland Ministers to agree a range of initiatives designed to boost economic activity on the island and eliminate market failure arising from the existence of the border.

We are working hard now to deliver on our shared priorities through the North/South Ministerial Council and through a range of other contacts between key decision-makers on the island. We are fortunate, in doing this, to have excellent North/South bodies like Tourism Ireland helping to brand the island so successfully overseas. And the role and strategic importance of InterTradeIreland has never been greater as it seeks, with our support, to ensure companies North and South are able to take advantage of the economic opportunities close to home in a period of global turbulence.

We are putting our money where our mouth is too, even in these difficult times. At our first North South Ministerial Council (NSMC) meeting following restoration of the Executive two years ago, we pledged £400 million to upgrade the A5 road to Derry and Letterkenny and the A8 road from Belfast to Larne. And at another NSMC Plenary meeting earlier this month, our fourth since restoration, Ministers agreed the details of a first Government contribution of €9 million towards preparatory work

The impact of the worldwide recession means that it makes sense that we work together on this island to optimize the use of the economic resources that are at our disposal, transforming North/South economic collaboration into a source of mutual competitive advantage.

We are also working to build an 'Innovation Island', one that is on the cusp of cutting-edge research and development.

In November last, ten programmes, involving research collaborations between Queens University Belfast, the University of Ulster and internationally recognized research centres in the South were approved for funding of £14.5 million by a panel whose members are representative of both jurisdictions.

as well as procedures for future payments. We are firm in our conviction that an integrated and connected island will have the best opportunity to fulfil its undoubted and enormous potential.

We are also working to build an 'Innovation Island', one that is on the cusp of cutting-edge research and development. We are looking forward to discussing our plans for this 'Innovation Island' with our Northern Ireland Executive colleagues and examining whether, together, we can make this vision a reality at home and a recognized brand abroad. In our increasingly inter-connected world, the brightest minds on both sides of our border must be given every incentive to collaborate in order to compete. That is why the Government and the Executive are each providing unprecedented sums for cross-border research and innovation, ensuring companies in both jurisdictions can make use of research excellence anywhere on the island.

We are now beginning to see the fruits of all-island cooperation in R&D. Significant progress has been made to date under the All-Island Innovation Voucher initiative. It is very heartening, also, to learn of the steady flow of collaborative research projects that are being approved for funding under the Innovation Fund. In November last, ten programmes, involving research collaborations between Queens University Belfast, the University of Ulster and internationally recognized research centres in the South were approved for funding of £14.5 million by a panel whose members are representative of both jurisdictions. The projects approved will cover a wide range of priorities including Future Energy Systems, Mobile Information and Communication Technologies, Major Chronic Diseases and Infections, Functional Foods, Nutrition and Bone Health, and Safe and Traceable Food.

In addition to the above developments, the potential for further North/South research collaboration continues to be realized through the US-Ireland R&D Partnership. Under this partnership, the governments of the US, Ireland and Northern Ireland are working together to advance scientific progress by awarding grants for research on a competitive basis in the thematic areas of Diabetes, Cystic Fibrosis, Nanotechnology and Sensors. The US-Ireland Research Partnership offers us an excellent model of collaborative research for mutual gain, with great potential to generate innovations to the marketplace and that lead to improvements in health promotion, disease prevention and healthcare.

We are collaborating to maximize our combined drawdown under the EU's Seventh Framework Programme, a €51 billion funding programme designed to promote research and innovation cooperation between Member States. Our Government has set a target of €600 million in funding over the programme's lifetime and we hope as much as possible of this can be drawn down by entrepreneurs and university researchers in both parts of this island.

InterTradeIreland, the North/South trade and business development Body set up under the Good Friday Agreement, is working to identify and to help realize opportunities to increase economic activity through increased levels of North/South trade and business co-operation. Its role is to encourage and support North/South co-operation to the mutual benefit of the two economies. The impact of the worldwide recession means that it makes sense that we work together on this island to optimize the use of the economic resources that are at our disposal, transforming North/South economic collaboration into a source of mutual competitive advantage.

There is enormous potential to expand our 'green economy', jointly harnessing our wind and ocean reserves and delivering energy security for the generations to come. We must build on the outcome of the all-island grid study launched last year and examine how, together, we can meet our ambitious targets for renewable energy and reductions in carbon emissions over the decade ahead. And, in all of this, we will be inspired by our success in delivering a Single Electricity Market for the island, a remarkable feat which has brought efficiency savings and enhanced competition to the benefit of consumers North and South.

I passionately believe that this is an area that should be exploited on an all-island basis and that we should work to remove any barriers to the development of our island as the alternative energy hub not just of Europe but of the World. Our shared wind and tidal resources are unmatched. I have spoken

There is a growing realization that in facing the challenges of our increasingly globalized world – whether those challenges are environmental or economic – we are stronger when we share, and weaker when we work alone.

already of our commitment to the development of an innovation island. By matching the natural resources with innovation, we can achieve much.

As well as exploiting new opportunities I feel that we have an obligation too – an urgent and compelling obligation – to explore ways in which we can save money by working together. We have made a good start on this. Patients in certain border areas can now access GP and cancer services in the other jurisdiction, for example. But there is so much more we can do together to provide closer and more accessible public services. And we must open our eyes as well to non-contentious and mutually beneficial ways in which we can pool our budgets, our talents and our time. If, for example, we are each trying to deliver a message about obesity or suicide prevention or road safety or any one of a number of issues, it surely makes perfect sense to sit down together, agree a campaign and save money by delivering a coherent message.

We will be inspired by our success in delivering a Single Electricity Market for the island, a remarkable feat which has brought efficiency savings and enhanced competition to the benefit of consumers North and South.

There is a growing realization that in facing the challenges of our increasingly globalized world – whether those challenges are environmental or economic – we are stronger when we share, and weaker when we work alone. And I know we also share a common ambition: to be part of an innovative and dynamic all-island economy, one that attracts investment, encourages our own entrepreneurs, and provides jobs. We all want our society to provide safety, security and quality public services. Now is the time to put our shoulders to the wheel.

It is beyond anyone's doubt that seismic and unprecedented economic questions are currently being asked. A critical new dimension working in our favour is that, by thinking on an all-island basis, we have an increasing number of answers within our grasp. In meeting the challenges of the years to come, the Government will work with the Northern Ireland Executive and social, cultural and business leaders like yourselves to provide the investment and economies of scale that will allow this 'Innovation Island' and hopefully this 'renewable energy hub' to emerge at the front of the international pack when the global economy recovers.

Development of an All-Island Economy is Crucial

Martina Anderson MLA
Sinn Féin Spokesperson, Equality and Human Rights

From Bogside area of Derry, attended Long Tower primary school and St. Cecilia's College. Served as Sinn Féin's political co-ordinator promoting, upgrading and mainstreaming All-Ireland agenda. Elected as MLA for Foyle in 2007. Appointed Party's Director of Unionist Engagement leading to first public meetings between Party leadership, churches and opinion-makers within unionism. Represents Sinn Féin on Policing Board and Committee of the First and Deputy First Minister. Selected as Party's candidate to fight next Westminster election.

I am pleased to be given the opportunity to outline my party's position on what needs to happen if we are to recover economically. Nobody will be surprised to learn that Sinn Féin's firm belief is that a sustainable economic recovery will require an all-Ireland approach and bilateral measures by both administrations, North and South. But that belief is not simply borne out of our political desire to see the reunification of Ireland. It is a practical, thought-out and common-sense approach to tackling our economic problems. It is the *only* long-term solution.

The simple fact is that we live on a tiny island and it just does not make sense to have two competing economies in a country this size. Since the Good Friday Agreement, trade between North and South has steadily increased. Thousands of people live their lives in one jurisdiction yet shop, study or work in the other. Partition creates impediments to economic development at a substantial cost to the economy.

And this is not just a Sinn Féin belief. It is a belief which is shared by increasing numbers of people – from all walks of life – right across this island. In recent weeks the IBEC-CBI Joint Business Committee sent a very clear message to both administrations on this island that a focused approach to

> In recent weeks the IBEC-CBI Joint Business Committee sent a very clear message to both administrations on this island that a focused approach to building an all-Ireland single economy is the best way forward for economic regeneration.

On this small island, we have a VAT rate of 15 per cent in the North and 21.5 per cent in the South. With such a disparity, it is little wonder that border businesses in particular are being decimated.

Working in collaboration Dublin and Belfast can eliminate waste and duplication thereby freeing up essential resources for frontline services and building social and economic prosperity for all.

building an all-Ireland single economy is the best way forward for economic regeneration. Other business leaders across Ireland also accept that the all-Ireland dimension makes sense. They realize that two separate economies on an island of under 6 million people, now more than ever, will only serve to hamper efforts to revitalize the economy. They recognize that back to back development will lead only to wasteful spending on duplication of services.

Given the current global economic crisis, to have two health services, two education services, two transportation systems, two currencies and so forth on an island the size of Ireland is nothing short of economic madness. Continuous fluctuation between the two economies is also of no strategic benefit to anyone. It is time that the political administrations started to heed the message from the business community. We should be examining new avenues of all-Ireland co-operation and the establishment of a strong all-island economy.

The historic lack of joined up thinking from successive British and Irish governments has resulted in viable businesses floundering on both sides of the border in the face of constant fluctuations in the areas of VAT, corporation tax, excise duty and currency variation. This is a reality which is recognized by other nations in Europe. That is why countries like France, the Netherlands, Belgium, Germany, Poland and the Scandinavian nations ensure that VAT rates between neighbouring states are harmonized. Ireland is the only place to buck that trend. On this small island, we have a VAT rate of 15 per cent in the North and 21.5 per cent in the South. With such a disparity, it is little wonder that border businesses in particular are being decimated. For too long it has been a merry-go round of boom and bust for businesses on both sides of the border.

And I have to take particular issue with people like Brian Lenihan who famously accused Irish shoppers of being unpatriotic by spending their money in the North. It is to rein in the banks and financial institutions that the Government of which Brian Lenihan is a member should be focused. It was his Government's economic policies combined with the corporate greed on behalf of banks and developers which created this ludicrous situation and to try and put further financial pressure on ordinary struggling families is disgraceful. If Government Ministers want to show that their patriotism is more than just skin deep then they should begin the process of building an all-Ireland economic and political framework. That is the only way we are going to secure the economic future of Ireland. I believe the case has already been made on this issue. Working in collaboration, Dublin and Belfast can eliminate waste and duplication, thereby freeing up essential resources for frontline services and building social and economic prosperity for all.

We have witnessed the creation of the all-Ireland single energy market which provides for a competitive, sustainable and reliable electricity and gas market across the island. It is accepted that it will eventually deliver long-term economic and social benefits to communities right across the island. Tourism Ireland is an all-Ireland body designed to efficiently promote Ireland abroad and has had much success in source markets across the globe. The tourism sector remains of critical importance to Ireland's economic well-being and the service sector relies heavily on it. InterTradeIreland established by the Good Friday Agreement to develop North/South business opportunities has, since 2003 assisted businesses across the island in creating hundreds of jobs and generating hundreds of millions of Euro in trade. We have seen a strategic all-Ireland collaborative approach with billions of Euro committed to developing the road infrastructure across the island. Nobody would argue that this does not make good economic sense.

If we are to emerge from this economic crisis, we need to build on that kind of co-operation, not retreat from it as some would advocate for what I can only believe are selfish, political and unsubstantiated reasons. To those northern politicians who for narrow party political reasons are advocating cutting back on all-Ireland projects I would urge them to just consider the following. The Irish Government's proposed National Asset Management Agency (NAMA) will control an estimated €15 to €20 billion of assets in the North making it the largest single investor in the North. How it plans to manage these assets will have a massive impact on the North. We need an agreed plan not only to manage these assets but to build and manage the island's economy. Both jurisdictions face public spending cuts with An Bord Snip Nua in

The Irish Government's proposed National Asset Management Agency (NAMA) will control an estimated €15 to €20 billion of assets in the North making it the largest single investor in the North. How it plans to manage these assets will have a massive impact on the North.

the South and an expected public spending cut following the next Westminster Election in the North. We simply cannot afford the luxury of two separate administrative systems for an island our size. This is not an ideological position but a very practical one. The systems we have are loaded with inefficiencies and waste.

In Ireland we will face into this economic crisis together by deciding that we are going to direct significant resources to sustaining existing jobs. Such an approach will not require that we abandon our efforts to attract FDI, but it will recognize that in the immediate and short term there is little prospect for such investment on a significant scale. I would contend then, that we should 'Invest in Recovery' by identifying and resourcing initiatives that will sustain existing employment, because in the event of an economic upturn, jobs that are lost now will be all the more difficult and expensive to reinstate in the future.

We should be looking at co-operation and integration in other sectors such as through Universities Ireland in the area of third level education with a particular focus on the Knowledge Economy.

We should be looking at co-operation and integration in other sectors such as through Universities Ireland in the area of third level education with a particular focus on the Knowledge Economy. We should be building an all-Ireland agricultural sector to fully exploit Ireland's unique comparative advantage in grass-based agriculture. There is scope for all-Ireland agriculture, as a single unit, to negotiate a common Irish position within the CAP, or within the EU Common Fishery Policy. We should be fully exploiting the opportunities afforded in the higher value food processing industry such as niche markets like organic farming, in which both parts of Ireland remain far behind compared to their EU counterparts. The GM-free market is another example of neglected growth and development in a partitioned Ireland. The potential of the fishing industry and development of our unique resources for aquaculture, fishing and fish processing, and marine based facilities, is another. There are many, many more – not least of all the need to introduce a single currency across the island.

Sinn Féin recognizes the potential to create jobs in the agri-food sector. My party colleague, Arthur Morgan TD, is currently drafting a report on how to expand employment in the agri-food sector for the Oireachtas Committee on Enterprise, Trade and Employment. If we are to recover economically and as a nation, the administrations, North and South, need to build on the lessons learned from the co-operation which has already shown considerable success.

And I totally reject the recent statement by Minister of State Martin Mansergh TD that the recession makes Irish unity less attractive. Does Martin Mansergh really believe that Ireland is the only country on earth that could not sustain itself as an independent sovereign nation? I believe it is clear from everything that I have already said that the reverse is actually the case. It is about time that Irish political leaders threw off the yoke of inferiority and started projecting a positive, can-do image of Ireland, that will motivate instead of deflate peoples' aspirations. With all due respect, I do not believe any of us should take political or economic advice from an administration that refused to take heed of the economic danger signs and led us into the biggest economic disaster in history. The reality is that the full potential of the island in terms of economic development cannot be realized while we have division, duplication and disruption because of a British imposed border. Real economic recovery will require an all-Ireland approach. To use the old adage – 'united we stand – divided we fall'.

If we are to recover economically and as a nation, the administrations, North and South, need to build on the lessons learned from the co-operation which has already shown considerable success.

Chapter 10

LISBON – IMPLICATIONS FOR IRELAND

IRELAND NEEDS EUROPE BUT EUROPE NEEDS IRELAND
David O'Sullivan
EU Director-General, Trade and former Sec. Gen. EU Commission

IRELAND MUST PROTECT STATUS WITHIN EUROPE
Angela Kerins
Chief Executive, REHAB

LISBON IS A MATTER OF TRUST
Pádraig MacLochlainn
National Campaign Director, Sinn Féin

A YES VOTE IS IN OUR INTEREST
Mícheál Martin TD
Minister for Foreign Affairs

WE NEED EUROPE MORE THAN EVER
Lucinda Creighton TD
Fine Gael Spokesperson on European Affairs

REJECTING LISBON IS NOT REJECTING EUROPE
Patricia McKenna
Chairperson, People's Movement and former MEP

A NO VOTE WOULD IMPACT ON INVESTMENT
Ruairí Quinn TD
Labour Spokesperson, Education & Science and former Leader, Labour Party

Ireland Needs Europe but Europe Needs Ireland

David O'Sullivan

EU Director-General, Trade and former Sec.-Gen.
EU Commission

Grew up in Dublin and educated at St Mary's College, Rathmines. Graduated with a BA in Economics and Sociology from TCD and awarded a Diplôme des Hautes Etudes Européennes from College of Europe, Bruges. Worked in Dept. of Agriculture and Dept. of Foreign Affairs. Joined European Commission in 1979 working for Directorate General for External Relations. Was member of Cabinet of Commissioner Peter Sutherland. In 1989, became head of unit in the task force for human resources, education, youth and training. From 1993 to 1996, Deputy Head of Cabinet to Commissioner Pádraig Flynn. From 1996 to 1999, Director with responsibility for policy coordination at European Social Fund, subsequently Director responsible for management of resources, and then Director-General for education, training and youth. In 1999, was appointed Head of Cabinet of Romano Prodi, then President of the European Commission and in 2000, to top post of Secretary General. Since 2005, has been Director General for trade, playing a key role in WTO talks.

In 1972, during the referendum campaign for Ireland's accession to the then EEC, I was canvassing for the Yes vote at the Front Gate of Trinity College. A good friend and debating partner stopped in surprise when he saw me. We knew each other well and held similar views on many of the issues of the day. He said to me, 'So, you think it was all a waste of time, then?'

I immediately understood his point. He thought joining the EEC meant Ireland giving up its hard won independence. But I was shocked because, for me, the direct opposite was true: joining the EEC as a sovereign European state, separate from the United Kingdom, was the ultimate expression of our independence.

I was brought up in a nationalist tradition, proud of the state and what it represented. I lived through the difficult times of the

An independent Ireland was there not to opt out of the world but rather to opt in and bring our distinctive point of view to bear in a meaningful way on the problems of the world. Only in this way, for me, would our independence have true meaning.

As I watched the 25 flags of the enlarged Europe unfurl, it struck me that we had truly come such a long way from the rather isolated and insecure country of my youth. And we owe so much of that success to our engagement with Europe.

late 1960s and the 1970s when the struggle in the North revived old animosities. But I always believed that Ireland needed to reach out past, at times, the suffocating bilateral relationship with Britain to the wider world and, in particular, to continental Europe. For me, we had become independent not just to control our own destiny but in order to do something with that control. An independent Ireland was there not to opt out of the world but rather to opt in and bring our distinctive point of view to bear in a meaningful way on the problems of the world. Only in this way, for me, would our independence have true meaning.

In the 1950s and 1960s, the United Nations offered such a platform, skilfully exploited by people like Frank Aiken and others. We flexed our muscles with a courageous vote about China's eventual membership of the UN. We led the debate on nuclear non-proliferation. We proudly sent our troops to fight in the Congo, and later in Cyprus and the Lebanon, in the name of global justice. Joining the EEC was, therefore, the next logical step in the process of Ireland finally taking its place amongst the nations of the earth, as Emmet once dreamed. Of course, none of us could have foreseen exactly what that decision would mean. If anyone had suggested then that thirty years later, there would a fully integrated single market in Europe, with a single currency, and full freedom of movement for people, or that the EEC, now known as the European Union, having already expanded to include the fledging democracies of Greece, Spain and Portugal, would be opening its doors to the newly liberated countries of Central and Eastern Europe, it would have seemed like an impossible dream.

Yet, when I was privileged to be present at the extremely moving ceremony at Áras an Uachtaráin on 1 May 2004 to mark the fifth and most momentous enlargement of the Union, that dream came true. I was doubly proud. Proud of what Europe had managed to accomplish through the re-unification of the once divided continent. But just as proud of the role Ireland was playing in the eyes of the world at that history making event. As I watched the 25 flags of the enlarged Europe unfurl, it struck me that we had truly come such a long way from the rather isolated and insecure country of my youth. And we owe so much of that success to our engagement with Europe.

Of course, there was the money. The immediate benefit of EEC membership was the protective mantle of the Common Agricultural Policy for our farmers long locked in the stifling embrace of Britain's cheap food policy. Then came the structural funds. In total, some €62 billion in receipts from the EU budget flowed into Ireland during the years 1973 to 2000, amounting at one point (1991) to 7.4 per cent of GDP.

It is easy to take this for granted but those financial flows provided the platform for the remarkable performance of the Irish economy during the Celtic Tiger years. Of course, Ireland only really began to make best use of those transfers after we turned our own economic policies around in 1987. The lesson of this is also clear: Europe can provide the ingredients of success but it requires our own efforts to translate that into a winning formula.

But the real benefit of membership came from the way it opened Ireland up to the world. This was true in so many ways. For the civil service, engagement with other administrations in Brussels necessitated a major process of modernization. This was not just true for the Department of Foreign Affairs which has become highly respected internationally but also of the 'home' departments who suddenly found themselves in regular meetings with colleagues from all over Europe. Students were offered new opportunities for studying abroad through the COMETT and Erasmus programmes. These were so successful that it is now almost commonplace for our students to spend a year in a university outside Ireland as part of their course. European health and safety legislation brought improved conditions for workers. Environmental legislation brought new environmental awareness. Women's rights improved dramatically and started a virtual revolution in the role of women in Irish society. Joining the EEC was like opening the doors and windows of a dusty house and it changed our lives forever.

Membership also transformed our relationship with the UK. It is in some ways ironic that we both entered the EEC precisely at a moment of renewed tension in our bilateral relationship caused by the conflict in the North. I am profoundly convinced it was in part because of our joint membership of the then EEC that we managed to avoid that relationship going wrong. The peace process would always have had its own momentum and its own

I am frankly astounded when people talk of the risk that Ireland might lose its identity in the process of European integration. Nothing could be further from the truth. Membership of the EU has given us an enhanced international profile and a new confidence in what it means to be Irish.

heroes but membership of the EEC provided both a framework and an incentive to find a peaceful and consensual solution to our common problems.

And, through EU membership, Ireland's international stature grew also. Membership of the EEC forced us to initiate a policy of official bilateral development aid for poor countries, something previously left to charities or missionary orders. Because we were part of the decision making process in Brussels, people suddenly cared about what Ireland thought about European or global issues. We remained a small country but one with influence beyond our size.

Ireland's attractiveness as a destination for Foreign Direct Investment stems directly from our EU membership which offers a gateway to a market of some 500 million consumers.

I am frankly astounded when people talk of the risk that Ireland might lose its identity in the process of European integration. Nothing could be further from the truth. Membership of the EU has given us an enhanced international profile and a new confidence in what it means to be Irish. Everything that this country achieved in order to justify the title of 'Celtic Tiger', the economic progress, the increased international profile, the enormous boost of self confidence, the liberation from Britain's shadow, the greater openness and pluralism of our society, all of this flowed directly from our engagement with Europe. Only the revisionists of the history of the last thirty five years could seek to convince otherwise.

Of course, a cynic might say, 'Ok, maybe Ireland needed Europe back then, but we have grown up now and we can afford to take a more independent stance'. So, why does Ireland still need Europe? Economically, it is clear that we still benefit hugely from EU membership, as well as from our membership of the Euro zone. Ireland's attractiveness as a destination for Foreign Direct Investment stems directly from our EU membership which offers a gateway to a market of some 500 million consumers. The Irish economy has been so successful at providing a transatlantic entry point into the EU that by 2007 the stock of FDI from the US alone was worth €20 billion.

Without membership of the Euro zone, the former Irish punt would have crashed through the floor creating a major crisis for the economy well beyond what we are currently experiencing.

The recent financial crisis and the recession it has provoked only further reinforce this argument. Without membership of the Euro zone, the former Irish punt would have crashed through the floor creating a major crisis for the economy well beyond what we are currently experiencing. Irish-based financial institutions are benefiting massively from liquidity provided by the ECB. They are currently receiving €130 billion in ECB loans, about 15 per cent of the €900 billion of ECB loans to the European banking sector. This is equivalent to 77 per cent of Irish GDP.

So Ireland still needs Europe, for lots of reasons. But the traffic is not all one way. Europe needs Ireland. We have brought a distinctive Irish perspective to the table in Brussels. As a former colony, we are uniquely sensitive to the development needs of the third world. We have pursued in Europe the commitment to a more just world that we began in the League of Nations and the UN. As an open, free-trading economy, we have defended the need for Europe to adopt the same policies. We have defended the need to protect agricultural production in Europe and nurture the rural community. We have been active in promoting workers rights and a just society. We have staunchly defended the enlargement of the Union to the emerging democracies of Central and Eastern Europe, including opening our doors to their workers, when others kept them shut. In all of this, we have been able significantly to influence the policies of the EU internally and externally.

In the meetings of the Council of Ministers, we are acknowledged as a voice of reason and compassion, even if occasionally very tenacious in defending certain national interests! Nothing to be ashamed of there! But we earned respect and credibility. We are at risk of losing that. The question is not, as was once famously suggested, whether we are closer to Boston than Berlin and certainly not – to paraphrase the iconic banner of James Connolly's Citizen Army – that we want neither Boston nor Berlin, but rather that we need both Berlin and Boston and, furthermore, that we need Beijing and Brazzaville.

Our struggle for independence was long and bitter. But surely we became independent not just to control our own destiny but also so that we could contribute to the betterment of the planet. One of our first acts of international engagement under the leadership of Éamon de Valera was to support the League of Nations. We were a fervent supporter of the UN in the last century. In the 21st century, the best way for Ireland to fulfil that

The big picture is that we can either play in the premiership and have real influence, or we can become permanent 'hurlers on the ditch', free to hold any views we wish but ultimately irrelevant.

historic destiny is through the European Union, through which we can sit at the highest tables of global decision-making and be sure that our voice actually counts, whether in the debates on climate change, the defence of fundamental rights or in the shaping of new global economic order that offers the prospect of prosperity for all coupled with policies that address issues such as poverty, disease and war. The big picture is that we can either play in the premiership and have real influence, or we can become permanent 'hurlers on the ditch', free to hold any views we wish but ultimately irrelevant.

Ireland needs Europe but Europe needs Ireland. The world needs Irish engagement through a Europe that can actually impact on the key decisions that will shape the coming century. My fervent wish is that we will continue to play an active and influential role in this marvellous adventure that is European integration and Europe's role in the world. I remain deeply convinced that what those who struggled for the independence of this country down the years would want is that we opt for openness and not reclusion, for engagement and not isolation, and for influence and not irrelevance.

In these unsettled times, Ireland needs above all to send out a positive message reaffirming our engagement with a Europe that has delivered the transformation of this country in the past and which continues to offer us the best prospect of a brighter future.

Ireland Must Protect Status within Europe

Angela Kerins
Chief Executive, REHAB

Former positions as Director of Group Development & Public Affairs and Chief Executive of RehabCare, health and social care division of Group. Chairperson of both the National Disability Authority and Disability Legislation Consultation Group. Member of the Department of Foreign Affairs/NGO Joint Committee on Human Rights, National Executive of IBEC, Broadcasting Commission of Ireland (BCI) European Platform for Rehabilitation and Advisory Committee of ComReg. Permanent Representative to Economic and Social Council of the United Nations and ECOSOC. In 2003, was awarded an honorary Doctorate of Laws (LLD) by the National University of Ireland in recognition of her work in disability sector.

I hope to offer an additional perspective on the Lisbon Treaty significantly influenced by my role as Chief Executive of the Rehab Group, an organization which spans Ireland, England, Scotland, Poland and the Netherlands, with a turnover of €215 million employing more than 3,600 people. Rehab operates in a wide range of industry sectors including manufacturing, packaging, logistics, waste management, gaming and lotteries, vocational training, employment services, healthcare, rehabilitation, advocacy and health promotion. More than 56,000 people directly use our services annually. We actively participate in European-wide organizations in the area of policy development, advocacy and quality and have NGO consultative status at the United Nations. While it is true that our activities are complex and diverse our overall mission is simple – it is about investing in people and changing perspectives.

Rehab's diversity makes me acutely aware of the benefits which EU membership has delivered across many sectors. I believe that Ireland must ensure that it protects its status within the EU as a progressive and leading state. I believe that a Yes vote in the Lisbon Treaty Referendum will be both good for Ireland and good for Europe.

Throughout the 1970s, 1980s and even the 1990s, Ireland took

Throughout the 1970s, 1980s and even the 1990s, Ireland took full advantage of every possible benefit of EU membership.

full advantage of every possible benefit of EU membership. We became experts in benefitting from EU support, developing capital infrastructure, building our intellectual capacity and developing our commercial and farming interests. We moved from a country which was hugely dependent on one market to an economy that took full advantage of our access to almost 500 million people. As a small island economy on the fringes of Europe, we knew what was good for Ireland and worked hard to maintain good relationships with European partners. Respect for Ireland and the quality of our representatives grew and now many current key senior officials in Brussels are Irish.

Furthermore, people became concerned about loss of national identity and many verbalized the concern of 'Brussels telling us what to do'.

However, Europe is not just about the economy. The EU has been the single most important catalyst for social cohesion in Ireland bringing groundbreaking improvements including the lifting of the marriage bar, equal pay, maternity leave, pension protection, equality of access to goods and services, worklife balance and reasonable accommodation for people with disabilities. The European Social Fund also financed the education and training of hundreds of thousands of our people.

Despite all this, our public's enthusiasm for the European project dipped. My own views are that the evolution from an economic union to become also a more political and regulatory union became a real cause for concern for many and the Commission failed to communicate effectively with its citizens. Furthermore, people became concerned about loss of national identity and many verbalized the concern of 'Brussels telling us what to do'.

In June 2008, we believed Ireland could stand on its own and basked in the glory of our golden time. Perhaps we were becoming victims of our own arrogance because in the same four weeks as we rejected the Lisbon Treaty, we sent a stuffed turkey to represent Ireland at the Eurovision!

I believe we as a nation woke up on the morning of 13 June 2008 with very mixed feelings. The Lisbon Yes campaign had failed miserably in a cocktail of complacency, arrogance, confusion and real concerns. We knew that this would become a significant problem for the country. Today, thirteen months on from the day Ireland voted No to Lisbon, our country's economy has altered significantly. Irish people are suffering not only due to the world recession but also due to the specific economic crisis that we find ourselves in. We are no longer part of a golden era. Every week thousands of people are losing their jobs as our national debt soars.

If we track the changes in the worldwide perception of our economy over the last few decades the difference is stark. In 1963, *Time* magazine ran a cover story of Lemass heralding the beginning of economic growth which read *'Ireland – New Spirit in the Ould Sod'*. We went on to be consistently used in the international press as a case study of a small economy done good. Then in April 2009, *The New York Times* ran an article which read *'Erin go Broke'*.

The *Economist Country Report* has also charted the rise of Ireland over the last twenty years starting with a cover headline in the 1980s marking the beginning of our rise which read *'Poorest of the Rich'*. A 1990s headline *'Europe's Shining Light'* heralded our rise and in 2004 a cover story read *'Luck of the Irish'*. It will be very interesting to see what the next *Economist* headline about us is.

While the Lisbon Treaty is not a panacea for economic recovery, its ratification is a very important step on the road.

While the Lisbon Treaty is not a panacea for economic recovery, its ratification is a very important step on the road. The position that Ireland takes on the second referendum will attract the eyes of the world. A Yes vote sends out a clear signal that Ireland is part of Europe. A No vote will raise a big question in the boardrooms across the world where Ireland's future as a safe and profitable place to invest in is being discussed.

In debating the treaty we should be careful not to make it out to be more than it is. Lisbon is a complicated corporate governance document. It is not exciting. It contains no seismic change. It is, in effect, dull but necessary, leading some who describe it – to borrow a phrase from Churchill – as 'a sheep in sheep's clothing'. All organizations must have corporate governance reviews and changes that allow them to run as effectively and efficiently as possible. This is, in effect, Europe's governance review.

Lisbon is a complicated corporate governance document. It is not exciting. It contains no seismic change. It is, in effect, dull but necessary, leading some who describe it, to borrow a quote from Churchill, as 'a sheep in sheep's clothing'.

The issues that have caused concern have been addressed. We now have a solemn declaration that addresses many concerns of our citizens. Issues relating to taxation policy, the right to life, education and the family, Irelands traditional policy of military neutrality and the position relating to having a Commissioner, have all been addressed.

Europe is competing against huge economies which operate as single entities. The changes brought about by the Lisbon Treaty will create a more agile, competitive Europe. For the good of the Irish economy and all European economies, Europe must maintain its dominant position, and continue to move, grow and evolve to stay ahead of the game. Effectiveness in decision-making is essential to enabling the Union to take advantage of the opportunities posed by the upturn, which will no doubt come.

The Lisbon Treaty is fundamentally about governance but also includes some very valuable provisions. It promotes democracy by increasing the role of national parliaments in EU decision making. It enables one million European citizens to come together to propose an issue to the Commission, it allows us to protect our tax base – a fundamental requirement of our recovery – and gives the Charter of Fundamental Rights legal status. All of these are progressive and democratic changes.

I see every day in Rehab the benefits of being at the core of Europe. Prior to our membership there were few services for people with disabilities. Rehab was the first organization in Ireland to benefit from ESF funding. With this support we built an Irish-based international organization providing world class services to people with disabilities. In fact, European resources supported the development of a vibrant, entrepreneurial, not-for-profit sector in Ireland over the last forty years.

We have also built up valuable networks and alliances across Europe to develop and share best practice. Our successful electronic recycling business is a direct result of the WEEE Directive, requiring manufacturers to recycle electrical goods. This provides sustainable jobs at market rates for people with disabilities and has to date provided 2,000 high spec refurbished computers with all the current Microsoft products to 1,600 schools at little or no cost.

Over the last five years alone, with support from the European Social Fund, Rehab's training and employment division has placed 3,000 people with disabilities in jobs. With unemployment among people with disabilities at nearly

It enables one million European citizens to come together to propose an issue to the Commission, it allows us to protect our tax base – a fundamental requirement of our recovery and gives the Charter of Fundamental Rights legal status.

Over the last five years alone, with support from the European Social Fund, Rehab's training and employment division has placed 3,000 people with disabilities in jobs.

70 per cent, efforts to reduce this rate are vital to ensure their economic, political and social integration. Our diverse workforce brings expertise from across Europe, importing cutting edge techniques and programmes to allow us to deliver best practice and quality. We are spreading best practice, too, in our manufacturing plant in Poland. We have introduced a unique integrated employment model which sees people with disabilities work side by side with non-disabled people. For Rehab, the continued prosperity of Europe and Ireland is crucial to our future. We are dependent on accessible European markets in order to continue to grow our business and commercial interests for the good of our philanthropic goals.

Along with all our other recovery measures, in Lisbon 2 we now have an opportunity to rebuild the trust which has been central to Ireland's success in Europe.

So, back to the future economic headlines for Ireland. What will the next *Economist Country Report* say? Will we be the country of recovery. Will the headline be '*Ireland is back*'? We now have a profound responsibility to ensure that international colleagues believe that Ireland is a good, sensible and safe place to do business. We must mobilize our innate ability to ensure that every opportunity to do this is grasped, every resource is utilized to its maximum, every goal is achieved and that we protect and foster our image of the highly educated, diverse, flexible and talented Europeans that we are.

We are dependent on accessible European markets in order to continue to grow our business and commercial interests for the good of our philanthropic goals.

Lisbon is a Matter of Trust

Pádraig MacLochlainn
National Campaign Director, Sinn Féin

Prior to commencing current full time role as a public representative, served on Irish National Organisation of the Unemployed (INOU) National Executive from 1997 until 2000 and represented organisation on National Rural Development Forum. Elected to represent Inishowen on Donegal County Council in 2004, narrowly missed out on Dáil seat in Donegal North East at 2007 General Election. Served on Sinn Féin Ard Comhairle (National Executive). Was appointed to board of InterTradeIreland.

We wanted a new Treaty that reflected the new social and economic challenges facing member states. The government has failed to deliver. Not a single full stop or comma or word has been changed in the Lisbon Treaty.

The government has announced the referendum date for Lisbon 2. On 2 October the people will go to the polls for a second time to vote on the Lisbon Treaty. On 12 June 2008, nearly one million people gave this government their verdict on the Lisbon Treaty. By rejecting the Treaty they gave the Taoiseach and the Minister for Foreign Affairs a strong and unequivocal mandate upon which to negotiate a better deal for Ireland and the EU with their European counterparts. The people wanted substantial change to the existing Treaty. We wanted a better deal. We wanted a new Treaty that contains the policy and political direction necessary to deliver a better Europe, a Europe that is democratic and accountable, that promotes workers rights and protects public services. We wanted a Europe that is positive and progressive.

As the global financial crisis began to unfold and the recession in Ireland deepened we also wanted a new Treaty that would challenge the failed policies of deregulation, centralization and unfettered markets, the fingerprints of which are all over the text of the Lisbon Treaty. We wanted a new Treaty that reflected the new social and economic challenges facing member states. The government has failed to deliver. Not a single full stop or comma or word has been changed in the Lisbon Treaty. The proposition that will go before the Irish people on 2 October will be the very same Treaty they rejected on 12 June 2008.

When you brush aside all the meaningless rhetoric about 'legally binding guarantees' what you have is nothing more than a series of clarifications on minor aspects of the Lisbon Treaty. So when we come to vote on the Lisbon Treaty in October we will be voting on exactly the same Treaty, with exactly the same consequences for Ireland and the EU, as we did on 12 June 2008. The promise of retaining our Commissioner must also be questioned. The agreement by the Council of Ministers tells us we will keep our Commissioner for an unspecified time. Unless this issue is written into an EU Treaty, the likely outcome is that the reduction in size of the Commission envisaged in Lisbon will be delayed 5 years until the next European Parliamentary elections in 2014.

This is an issue of trust. Would you trust this government to deliver on any commitment, be it on European or domestic matters? I certainly would not. On neutrality the clarifications tell us that Irish troops can only be sent abroad with the consent of the Irish government in the Council of Ministers and the Oireachtas. This we already know. But neutrality is not only what you do with your troops; it is also about the alliances you form, what you do with your resources, and what other member states do in your name.

Provisions for Permanent Structured Cooperation in the Lisbon Treaty create the real possibility that wars we do not support will be fought in our name and with our resources while the Mutual Defence clause creates obligations incompatible with any internationally recognized definition of neutrality. The government could have secured opt-outs from these contentious areas of the Treaty that deal with Common Foreign and Security Policy and Common Security and Defence Policy. After their people rejected the Maastricht Treaty in 1992 the Danish government secured a number of opt-outs before putting the Treaty to a second vote.

With regards to taxation the government has completely missed the point. Under the Lisbon Treaty, any move to a common corporation tax system across the EU would require a unanimous vote at the Council of Ministers. Anyone who read the Treaty could tell you this. Sinn Féin's concern on taxation rests with Article 48 of the Treaty. This article allows the Council of Ministers, by unanimous decision, to alter the text of existing EU Treaties. Today if the EU wanted to agree a common corporation

But neutrality is not only what you do with your troops; it is also about the alliances you form, what you do with your resources, and what other member states do in your name.

tax system they would have to do so as part of a broader Treaty revision process. This would require both unanimity at Council and ratification in each member state, including a referendum is this state. However, Article 48 allows the Council of Ministers to make significant changes to the Treaties by unanimity. EU leaders view national debate and referendums on issues of social and economic significance as 'cumbersome'. We view such processes as fundamental tools of a functioning progressive democracy. So Lisbon does not affect our tax sovereignty, but it makes it easier for the Council of Ministers to make the change in future, and without the inconvenience of a referendum.

So Lisbon does not affect our tax sovereignty, but it makes it easier for the Council of Ministers to make the change in future, and without the inconvenience of a referendum.

Again this is an issue of trust. Fianna Fáil, despite their assurances, could not be trusted on this or indeed any other matter of importance in my view. And let us remember the concerns the government has not even acknowledged in its clarifications. There is no mention of the reduced influence of smaller member states as a consequence of the new voting arrangements at Council; No mention of the 60 or so member state vetoes that will end; No mention of the controversial changes to international trade negotiations that were opposed by farmers and trade justice groups alike; No mention of the opening up of vital public services such as health and education to the vagaries of the market.

An Tánaiste Mary Coughlan said recently that saying Yes to Lisbon was necessary to secure Ireland's economic future. Let us remember that her former party leader and Taoiseach Bertie Ahern was one of the main authors of the Lisbon Treaty with input no doubt from his Finance Minister Brian Cowen. The Minister herself has lost over 200,000 Irish jobs since becoming responsible for enterprise, trade and employment. Their combined resumé on economic matters is not exactly inspiring. Ireland's place is at the heart of Europe. This is not in question.

The challenge facing Ireland and Europe is building a union that meets the needs of its peoples. We need a Treaty that delivers a better Europe for all member state citizens and it is in this context that Sinn Féin will continue to campaign for a better deal.

A Yes Vote is in Our Interest

Mícheál Martin TD
Minister for Foreign Affairs

Born in Cork and educated at Coláiste Chríost Rí, and UCC (BA). Completed MA in history at UCC before beginning career as secondary school teacher. In 1985, elected to Cork Corporation as Fianna Fáil candidate and served on that authority until 1997. Contested first Dáil seat in 1987 General Election but not elected. Eventually elected to Dáil Éireann for Cork South Central constituency at 1989 General Election. Served as Lord Mayor of Cork in 1992. Joined Bertie Ahern's new front bench in 1995 as Spokesperson on Education & the Gaeltacht. When Fianna Fáil returned to power in 1997, was appointed to newly-expanded position of Minister for Education & Science. In cabinet reshuffle in 2000, was appointed Minister for Health & Children. In 2004, did a straight swap with Mary Harney to become Minister for Enterprise, Trade & Employment. In a cabinet reshuffle in 2008 following election of Brian Cowen as Taoiseach, became Minister for Foreign Affairs.

More than a year has elapsed since the rejection of the Lisbon Treaty. What a different world we now live in! Events in the world highlight the vital importance of a strong European Union that is capable of dealing with the economic downturn and providing global leadership on issues such as climate change. I am convinced that ratification of Lisbon represents an important step towards resolving our present difficulties. Now that we have our legal guarantees in place to address concerns held last year there are plenty of reasons for approving the Lisbon Treaty.

Last week, it was revealed that almost 15 per cent of the loans given out by the European Central Bank to the European banking sector went to Irish-based institutions. That is a massive show of support for our banking system. The liquidity made available by the ECB has been indispensable to us as we strive to cope with the credit crunch and sustain jobs across the country. The ECB is now ensuring that our interest rates are at an all-time low. This is a powerful illustration of the extent to which the European Union is

It is not easy to convince people who are anxious about the future that the Lisbon Treaty should matter to them. But there is no doubt that our membership of the Eurozone has helped us weather the effects of this severe economic storm.

crucial to our collective economic well-being.

The referendum on the Lisbon Treaty will take place against a backdrop of unprecedented economic difficulties. Many voters who have lost their jobs, or have seen their salaries cut, will feel wounded by this experience and that is understandable. It is not easy to convince people who are anxious about the future that the Lisbon Treaty should matter to them. But there is no doubt that our membership of the Eurozone has helped us weather the effects of this severe economic storm.

Multinational companies view access to European markets as a key factor in their investment decisions. With only 1 per cent of the Union's population, Ireland attracted 25 per cent of all new US investment in Europe in the decade up to 2005.

When Ireland joined the EEC in 1973, our GDP per capita was 58 per cent of the European average. At that time, 54 per cent of our exports went to the British market, with only 21 per cent going to the rest of Europe. By the end of 2007, Irish GDP per capita had reached 144 per cent of the EU average. Only 18 per cent of our exports now go to the UK, compared with 45 per cent which go to the rest of the European Union.

Ireland's membership of the EU and participation in the Single European Market has been the most significant factor in ending our country's economic dependence on Britain. The Single European Market has helped indigenous Irish companies develop their export performance. Equally, it has helped Ireland attract a vastly disproportionate share of foreign direct investment, particularly from US companies. Multinational companies view access to European markets as a key factor in their investment decisions. With only 1 per cent of the Union's population, Ireland attracted 25 per cent of all new US investment in Europe in the decade up to 2005. Our capacity to continue bringing in investment will be crucial to our future prospects.

Since the establishment of the Single European Market in 1993, the stock of foreign investment in Ireland has increased by more than 400 per cent. The companies involved spend approximately €16 billion per annum in Ireland, have a payroll of approximately €6.7 billion, and paid about €3 billion to the Exchequer in corporation tax in 2007. Some 85 per cent of our manufactured exports are produced by companies that have come here largely as a result of Ireland's unhindered access to EU markets.

All the evidence demonstrates that our economy really took off when the European Union, on the basis of the Single

European Act, started removing barriers to trade in the early 1990s. Irish companies have been big winners from the single market. We have a relatively small population. Domestic demand for our goods and services will never be sufficient to sustain an advanced economy. The fact is that we export over 80 per cent of what we produce. The rules of the single market serve to smooth the way for our exporters as they seek contracts with customers across Europe. The euro means they know exactly how much they will be paid when a contract is fulfilled.

It is easy to cite statistics that highlight the benefits we derive from access to European markets. Behind these statistics, however, lie the stories of real companies that provide employment right across the country. The single market is crucial to the performance of Irish companies like EirGen Pharma and Creganna. These companies and many more like them depend for their very existence on our access to European markets. Our membership of the European Union has also made Ireland a magnet for foreign direct investment. Companies like Apple and Google did not come here because they liked our climate, but because we are seen as a country that is fully plugged into the European Union. It would be unwise to give them any reason to think otherwise.

I mention these companies because our membership of the European Union has been a significant factor in their decision to invest here. It is true, of course, that our corporation tax rate of 12.5 per cent is a major attraction for investors. Our legal guarantee which confirms that nothing in the Lisbon Treaty makes any change to the competence of the European Union in relation to taxation will be very reassuring for current and prospective investors in Ireland. Companies like Apple and Google and Microsoft tend to look at the long-term picture when taking strategic investment decisions. Any element of uncertainty about our future will tend to militate against decisions to choose Ireland as an investment location. Our competitors for foreign investment will be quick to exploit any suggestion of fading Irish commitment to Europe and to depict us as semi-detached Europeans.

When we go to the polls on 2 October we need to consider what signal we are sending to the people in places like Mountain View and Cupertino in California, to companies who have put their trust in Irish workers and Irish know-how. Prospective investors

Irish companies have been big winners from the single market.

Our legal guarantee which confirms that nothing in the Lisbon Treaty makes any change to the competence of the European Union in relation to taxation will be very reassuring for current and prospective investors in Ireland.

will want to know whether Ireland is destined to be an inward-looking or an outward-looking country. Our whole strategy, back to the days of Seán Lemass and Jack Lynch, has been to look outward and to embrace the economic opportunities available in Europe and beyond. It would be a tragedy if we were to put our future at risk by sending out a message that we are somehow retreating into ourselves and diluting our European engagement.

The agreement to retain our commission-er and the provision of legal guarantees on taxation, ethical issues and our traditional policy of neutrality represent a genuine effort to address the concerns that arose last year.

At each stage of Europe's evolution, we have kept faith with our commitment to working with our European neighbours in pursuit of our shared interests. At each stage, Ireland has benefited from the Union's advancement. We have thrived within the single market and we have gained greatly from our possession of a leading international currency, the euro. There are those who argue that it might have been better to stop the clock in 1972. Certainly, Ireland would be a less developed country today had the European clock been stopped in 1972. The reality is that the demands of today's world necessitate a reformed EU and the Lisbon Treaty is the means by which we can bring this about.

The European Union has, indeed, evolved since we joined in 1972. Back then there were only nine Member States; now there are 27. The Lisbon Treaty will improve the functioning of the Union. It creates a new role for national parliaments and extends the areas where the European Parliament is involved in the law-making process. It will improve the democratic accountability of a Union in which all decisions are taken by elected people whose only desire is to advance their peoples' well-being. All of this is welcome; none of this is radical. It represents a set of adjustments to the way in which the EU operates. These are designed to cope with the new challenges facing Europe. This means that the Member States control the Union and not the reverse.

But the Treaty does involve a degree of change and at a time of change it is legitimate to ask what this means. The Lisbon Treaty is designed to make the EU stronger so that it can cope more effectively with challenges such as climate change, energy security and conflict prevention.

The European Union has grown in many ways since 1972. It is older and bigger. It has much to its credit. But perhaps ours is the generation Yeats had in mind when he penned his memorable poem, 'What then?' Might he have been thinking of today's Europe when he wrote:

> The work is done, grown old he thought,
> 'According to my boyish plan;
> Let the fools rage, I swerved in naught,
> Something to perfection brought';
> But louder sang that ghost, 'What then?'

In today's Ireland, the answer to Yeats's question may well be that we need a reinvigorated Europe, one that can provide a continued framework for our national advancement in the years ahead. In my view, this requires that we join with our fellow EU members in agreeing to reform the EU by means of the Lisbon Treaty. The agreement to retain our commissioner and the provision of legal guarantees on taxation, ethical issues and our traditional policy of neutrality represent a genuine effort to address the concerns that arose last year.

I recognize that there are those who have questions about our future and the future of the Union as a whole. They want to know where we fit in the overall scheme of things; how the Lisbon Treaty will benefit them and what this all means for Ireland. The Lisbon Treaty will not settle these questions for once and for all. It is not a revolutionary document. But what it does is this: it provides a fair, balanced and transparent framework in which all of us – the people, parliamentarians and governments – can tackle the major 21st century challenges.

In a changing world, the Lisbon Treaty gives us the tools we need to tackle the challenges which are beyond the scope of individual states, large or small. The Lisbon Treaty is the first Treaty to refer to climate change as part of the Union's competence on environmental issues. This reference was included at the request of the Irish government and it gives the Union a specific basis for promoting environmental action against climate change. We cannot expect to enjoy economic growth and peace and security, if we do not deal with the challenges and opportunities that climate change present us. The European Union is without question the world's leading advocate of urgent action to combat climate change. We need to focus on more knowledge-intensive green technology jobs.

As the American columnist Thomas Friedman put it in his book, *Hot, Flat and Crowded*:

It is in our self-interest that Ireland be engaged and involved in shaping and directing a European Union reformed and improved by the terms of the Lisbon Treaty; a European Union that can better protect Irish interests in a volatile world.

> Green is not simply a new form of generating electric power. It is a new form of generating national power – period. It is not just about lighting up our house; it is about lighting up our future.

It is in our self-interest that Ireland be engaged and involved in shaping and directing a European Union reformed and improved by the terms of the Lisbon Treaty; a European Union that can better protect Irish interests in a volatile world. It is in our self-interest that we send an emphatic message that will serve to eliminate the doubts that linger in the boardrooms of the multinational corporations that have underpinned our economic development. That message needs to be clear and unambiguous: Ireland intends to remain a committed member of the European Union and will do what is necessary to remain the most attractive base from which to do business in the EU. It is in the self interest of each and every one of us to do whatever we can to keep jobs in Ireland.

We Need Europe More Than Ever

Lucinda Creighton TD
Fine Gael Spokesperson, European Affairs

Born and raised in Claremorris, Co. Mayo. Completed primary and secondary education in Convent of Mercy, Claremorris. MA in International Relations, DCU (2001). Studied Law at TCD and graduated with an LLB in 2002. Qualified as Attorney at Law for the State of New York. Attended Kings Inns. Called to Irish Bar in 2005. Completed professional training as Barrister. Elected to represent the Pembroke Ward on Dublin City Council. In 2007, elected to Dáil Éireann. Member of Fine Gael Executive Council, Young Fine Gael National Executive, Joint Oireachtas Committee on European Scrutiny. Full time Member of Dáil Éireann.

Does Ireland Need Europe? The question posed is almost perfunctory. Ireland not only needs Europe, but is in many ways dependent on Europe and in particular on the European Union. When Ireland joined the European Communities in 1973, the Irish people recognized an enormous opportunity. We saw that as a relatively new independent State, we were still largely cowering in the shadow of our nearest neighbour. We saw that our best opportunity to assert our independence and our sovereignty was through engagement with other sovereign nations, in a way by-passing, or leap-frogging, the one nation from whom we wished to assert our freedom.

And what freedom we gained; the freedom to move away from almost total reliance on the United Kingdom for our economic well being; the freedom to develop our own unique sovereignty, by breaking the ancient reliance on one nation, by forging new relations with many others – new relations on our terms and as equal partners. What a sense of self confidence and self belief Ireland has gained during those 36 years since 1973.

Over the years, the EU, and in particular the common market, has provided a framework through which Irish business has thrived. Ireland has gained confidence and independence by accessing extensive consumer markets. The EU opened up huge opportunities for Ireland's economy to thrive. New markets

> The EU opened up huge opportunities for Ireland's economy to thrive. New markets opened up to us, which have seen the Irish economy benefit beyond all expectation.

opened up to us, which have seen the Irish economy benefit beyond all expectation.

Ireland has also, very significantly, been a major beneficiary of European funds since our accession to the EEC in 1973. Receipts from the EU budget during that period amount to a staggering €60 billion in total, or 3.3 per cent of GDP. We have received billions of euro in structural funds, which have built roads and railways all over the country, stimulating further growth and improving Ireland's currency as an international hub. It is estimated that over a million jobs have been created in Ireland since 1973. While there have been frustrations, dealing with the bureaucracy and strict requirements of the EU system, overall it has benefited our country immensely.

Of course the European project has not been perfect. I would be the first to concede that there have been problems, glitches and disappointments along the way. But let us be realistic. This is an unprecedented project. Never before have so many independent nation states pooled their sovereignty and worked together in so many fields – political, economic and social or at so many levels – supranational, inter-governmental, national, regional and local. This is not comparable to the full blown federation of the US, nor with the loose co-operation of the African Union. The European model is unique and in many ways evolving all of the time. In a way it is an uncharted process, unlike any that has gone before. It requires of us, the people of Ireland and the people of Europe, a generosity of spirit, in addition to a political understanding, to recognize that sharing sovereignty is an act of benevolence, but also a very strategic act of self-interest.

Ireland's interest will undoubtedly be served by continued engagement with the European Union, but I am calling for a different form of engagement to that which we have carved out in the past 36 years. Ireland has changed dramatically in that period. We joined the EC as something of a poor relation. Our average income was then 60 per cent of the EU average. We have been so called 'net beneficiaries' since we joined. In other words we have been taking constant handouts from our EU partners for 36 years. The time has now come for a seismic shift in Ireland's attitude to the European Union. We need to understand that it is not simply about what we can

It is time for a national reflection on just how we engage with Europe from this point on. It is clear to me that Europe is a project of the future. The question for Ireland is whether we wish to invest in our own future.

take. It is time for a national reflection on just how we engage with Europe from this point on. It is clear to me that Europe is a project of the future. The question for Ireland is whether we wish to invest in our own future.

Ireland is on its knees economically, and it is through no fault of the European Union. In fact, since the real depth of our recession was understood last summer, the European hand-out machine has been in overdrive, with the ECB lending more per capita to the Irish than to any other member state, including all of the new central and eastern European members. A total of €39 billion to be precise has been loaned to Irish retail banks. Without the ECB, it is inconceivable that some of our key banking institutions would be standing today. Bailouts and handouts have been key to Ireland's interest and engagement in the European project since we joined. But it is high time that we moved beyond this short-sighted approach. We need to see Europe as a spring-board for Ireland as a global player, as a tool to project Ireland into that all-important global economy.

The Irish need to become key players in shaping the European economy. We need to start looking at the potential that exists and play our part in shaping the Europe of the future, for the benefit of the Ireland of the future. Take the single market for example. Its potential is huge. Some people erroneously believe that the single market is something that happened back in Maastricht in 1992. That was merely the birth of the venture, which is largely incomplete. In fact the best is yet to come. Over the coming years there will be huge advances in the single market, in terms of growth and competitiveness. We in Ireland can either choose to play a role in shaping these advances, or we can sit on the fringes, sullen-faced, waiting for more and more handouts from our frustrated partners. I know which option I prefer. I want Ireland to be a constructive player, rather than a caustic spectator.

One of the criticisms of the European Union, is that it has been slow to react to challenges which present on the world stage. This criticism has been particularly vocalized in relation to the economic crisis late last year. There is a deep irony in this. On the one hand, every member state is hankering for the days of yore, where they could behave as whimsically and irresponsibly as they liked, without a thought for the implications for other sovereign countries. On the other hand, they want the rules and institutional structures in place to respond rapidly to the many

We in Ireland can either choose to play a role in shaping these advances, or we can sit on the fringes, sullen-faced, waiting for more and more handouts from our frustrated partners. I know which option I prefer.

challenges that we face. It is time that we realize we cannot continue with the sort of institutional paralysis that exists in Europe. Member states will need to engage in greater levels of decision making at EU level, especially in the economic sphere, in order to prevent parochial, national, and sectoral interests grinding the EU to a halt. In my view, Ireland should be in the vanguard of this.

I think that now is the time for Ireland, emboldened by our recent economic experience, to start trying to shape the European policies and structures that will equip us for a new and inevitable phase of globalization. The first step should be a radical reform of the so-called Lisbon strategy. This is the programme for jobs and innovation in the EU which was established ten years ago and reviewed in 2007. Despite the noble aspirations of this plan, and the massive funds and efforts exerted in trying to implement it, most European citizens have never even heard of it. If you ask 99.9 per cent of Irish citizens whether they are aware of the Lisbon strategy, they are likely to stare blankly. They may well think that it is a not very popular treaty which they will have to vote on this October! On the other hand, most Irish people have probably heard of the Obama proposals for economic stimulation pushed through Congress last spring. There is a fundamental problem with communication in the EU. One simple measure would be to cease naming strategies and Treaties on the basis of the city in which they are signed. While this may flatter the ego of the President or Prime Minster of the day, it does nothing to relate the objective of such a strategy or plan to the ordinary people of Europe.

So first, the task should be to re-brand the Lisbon strategy as the European Jobs Plan or the European Economic Recovery Plan – something straight-forward and comprehensible. Second, the focus of such a plan needs to be two-fold. There should be an internal focus (as already exists) on structural reforms within the EU, aimed at adapting the EU to globalization, but with an added emphasis on the knowledge economy, sustainable growth and in particular strengthened economic governance, to prevent the type of regulatory failures we have seen in recent years. There should also be a new external focus to such an economic plan, looking at policies such as trade and competition, environmental

There is a fundamental problem with communication in the EU. One simple measure would be to cease naming strategies and Treaties on the basis of the city in which they are signed.

diplomacy, energy security and immigration, designed to shape globalization beneficial for two reasons. First, it would allow the EU to develop. Such a two-pronged approach would be its capacity to reform structures internally in order to meet the current demands and the challenges of globalization. Second, it would provide a new emphasis on shaping the global economy, thus enabling the EU to have a strengthened role in defining the global economy as it evolves. Ireland has the potential to play a vital role in promoting such an ambitious economic strategy at EU level. I believe we would enhance both our standing in Europe, and our national self-interest by adopting such a constructive, persuasive role.

Ireland should also look at promoting some bold and pragmatic Europe-wide solutions to the Europe-wide recession. Our inability to coordinate fiscal policy at European level is both good and bad. One might say we get the best of both worlds. Obviously, in Ireland we are intent on retaining our autonomy in relation to taxation. This is a positive as it ensures competition between Member States and can act as an incentive for foreign direct investors to choose a small country such as ours. However, it can lead to delayed coordination and a failure by the EU to act in a concerted fashion at times of crisis. The institutional structures are simply not there. However, why not advocate greater co-ordination on measures that do not impinge on the national interest. Why not identify some 'big bang' measures, which could benefit all member states and would have the added advantage of resonating with all citizens of the European Union. One such measure could be the introduction of a voluntary coordinated cut in VAT rates of 1 per cent across all 27 EU member states. This would be a coordinated budgetary stimulus which could have the temporary effect at least of increasing demand for goods and services across the EU. By virtue of its temporary nature, it would bring spending forward, given that there would be an expectation of a subsequent return to the original higher VAT rates. This would have positive stimulus effects across the entire European Union and would be a popular, tangible measure that the citizens of Europe might well relate to and approve of.

Ireland is on its knees. By the end of this year almost half a million people will be unemployed. Ireland not only needs Europe, but Europe is our lifeline. We cannot afford to continue to

Ireland should also look at promoting some bold and pragmatic Europe-wide solutions to the Europe-wide recession.

Ireland not only needs Europe, but Europe is our lifeline. We cannot afford to continue to entertain the type of begrudging attitude that has crept into our engagement with Europe.

entertain the type of begrudging attitude that has crept into our engagement with Europe. We need to realize *our* future is in shaping and moulding the Europe of the future. It is apt that this is the 20th anniversary of the fall of the Berlin Wall. The collapse of the Berlin wall liberated millions of people, who had for so long yearned for the freedom and autonomy enjoyed by the people of the West. Now is not the time to reconstruct an iron curtain around this island of ours. We need the support, friendship and the cooperation of our European neighbours, now more than ever. This is the only way in which we will truly be free.

Rejecting Lisbon is not Rejecting Europe

Patricia McKenna
Chairperson, People's Movement, former MEP

Became the first Green Party candidate in Ireland elected to European Parliament. Elected at the 1994 election and re-elected at the 1999 election but lost seat at the 2004 election. Former teacher, active in People's Movement which successfully campaigned for the rejection of the Treaty of Lisbon in 2008. Victorious in Supreme Court in 1995, in which she argued it was unconstitutional for Government of Ireland to spend taxpayers' money promoting only one side of the argument in referendum campaigns. Strong advocate of Irish neutrality and the Shell to Sea campaign. Ran as Green Party candidate in 2007 General Election for Dublin Central constituency. Resigned from Green Party in 2009.

The approach being pursued by supporters, since Irish citizens rejected the Lisbon Treaty in a democratic vote, is to use psychological scare tactics to try to persuade people to accept the Treaty. The current and unprecedented economic crisis, brought on by a number of factors, most notably the type of economic approach enshrined in Lisbon and the economic mismanagement by our own politicians, was going to happen regardless of whether we accepted or rejected Lisbon. Scaremongering, which implies that our economic crisis is even partly due to our rejection of Lisbon or that it will get worse unless we vote Yes, does no service to the debate.

This economic argument, which is basically the sole argument of the Yes side, will as the debate continues, be exposed as one of the weakest reasons to support the Lisbon Treaty. It is clear that the very deregulated economic model upon which Lisbon is based is responsible for the international financial collapse. So why adopt a treaty that is founded on a failed economic approach and enshrine that failed approach into the treaties of the new EU established by the Lisbon Treaty?

It is regrettable that our own political representatives who are paid to serve us have dishonestly presented our rejection of the

It is clear that the very deregulated economic model upon which Lisbon is based is responsible for the international financial collapse. So why adopt a treaty that is founded on a failed economic approach and enshrine that failed approach into the treaties of the new EU established by the Lisbon Treaty?

Lisbon Treaty as anti-Europe. They speak of Ireland not being at the heart of Europe' but are, by their own words, trying to remove us from that very heart with terms such as 'isolation' and 'disengagement'. They refuse to state the legal reality that, regardless of whether we accept or reject the Lisbon Treaty, we will still be full members of the EU and that there is no mechanism whereby we can be isolated or cut off from the EU in any way. That is legally impossible under the current treaties. In fact this approach by our own political establishment is the most damaging of all and verges on a treasonous approach to their own nation's interests.

The impression being given that our rejection of Lisbon will damage our prospects for inward investment is yet another scare tactic that has no basis in reality. Take, for example, our nearest neighbour, Britain. The fact that Britain is recognized as the most Eurosceptic member state in the EU has not stopped investors there nor has it affected the beginnings of economic recovery. Furthermore, Norway and Switzerland both rejected membership of the EU and despite not being at 'the heart of Europe' these are two of Europe's wealthiest nations. While I am not advocating non-membership of the EU it is important to point out that survival outside is not impossible even if it is here not the issue.

In fact, as Brian Lenihan recently acknowledged, membership of the monetary union allied to an influx of cheap labour from Eastern Europe played a key part in engineering our economic collapse. It is completely disingenuous and utterly reprehensible then to present self-serving economic arguments for supporting a political treaty especially coming from many of the same political elite responsible for the current mess.

To date, those who want to reverse the democratic decision of the Irish people on Lisbon are relying on a background of emotional reactions and fear factors concerning the economy. They keep peddling the message – the EU as our lifejacket, look what happened to Iceland, etc. but I firmly believe that with a balanced and reasoned debate people will realize they have done the right thing by rejecting Lisbon, particularly from an economic perspective. Considering our current economic situation, where Ireland will be far behind other EU

To date, those who want to reverse the democratic decision of the Irish people on Lisbon are relying on a background of emotional reactions and fear factors concerning the economy.

member states in achieving economic recovery, is it wise to accept proposals that give more power and strength to the EU's Big States while reducing our own? At present EU laws are made by a simple majority of Member States (14 out of 27), so long as between them they have a qualified majority of 255 votes out of 345. Under this 'Nice Treaty' system the Big States have 29 votes each and Ireland has 7, one quarter of each Big State. Under Lisbon, future EU laws would be made by 55 per cent of Member States, i.e., 15 out of 27, so long as they have 65 per cent of the total EU population between them. By basing EU law-making primarily on *population size*, the Lisbon Treaty would double Germany's relative voting strength on the EU Council of Ministers from its present 8 per cent of the total votes to 17 per cent on a population basis, and increases France's, Britain's and Italy's by half, from 8 per cent to 12 per cent – while over halving Ireland's vote from 2 per cent to 0.8 per cent (Art. 16, TFEU). How does having 0.8 per cent of a vote in making EU laws put us 'at the heart of Europe'? Taoiseach Brian Cowen's 'guarantees' do not explain how having half as much influence in the EU as Ireland has today would induce other Member States to listen to our concerns on unemployment and help to resolve the economic crisis in the interest of Irish companies, workers and farmers.

Is it prudent, especially in the current climate of unemployment and threats to wages and working conditions, to copperfasten the Laval and related judgments of the EU Court of Justice, which put the competition rules of the EU market above the rights of trade unions to enforce pay standards higher than the minimum wage for migrant workers? At the same time Lisbon would give the EU full control of immigration policy (Art. 79, TFEU). This combination threatens the pay and working conditions of many Irish people and provides opportunities for the exploitation of non-Irish people. A Protocol in a new Treaty different from Lisbon would be needed to set aside the recent Laval, Rüffert and other EU Court judgments, but the EU Prime Ministers have refused to do that and Ireland, despite having an opportunity to bargain, did not push for this or any other change or Protocol.

Should we endorse a treaty that will allow the post-Lisbon EU to impose Europe-wide taxes directly on us for the first time without need of further Treaties or referendums (Art.311, TFEU)? This could be any kind of tax – income tax, sales tax, and

Taoiseach Brian Cowen's 'guarantees' do not explain how having half as much influence in the EU as Ireland has today would induce other Member States to listen to our concerns on unemployment and help to resolve the economic crisis in the interest of Irish companies, workers and farmers.

property tax – so long as EU Governments unanimously agreed it. If Lisbon were to be ratified, Government Ministers would have every incentive to agree to give the EU much increased 'own resources' by introducing its own taxes to finance the many new functions the EU would obtain under the Treaty.

During the last referendum very little attention was paid to the fact that the European Union could be financed from its own resources under the heading of the 'union's resources'. The European Union would provide itself with the means necessary to attain its objectives and carry through its policies, and it could also establish new categories of 'own resources.' Though these measures require unanimity in the Council and would not enter into force until they are 'approved by the Member States in accordance with their respective constitutional requirements,' it is clear that it opens the way for an EU taxation system, which would make the EU budget wholly independent of its member-states.

Article 269 of the Treaty on the Functioning of the European Union (TFEU) would allow the EU Council of Ministers to finance the attainment of the new European Union's very wide objectives by means of 'new categories of own resources.' These could include virtually any kind of tax – income tax, sales tax, company tax, property tax, and carbon tax – as long as it was unanimously agreed and approved by the member-states in accordance with their respective Constitutional requirements, which in Ireland's case, if the Lisbon Treaty is ratified, would mean majority Dáil approval. The Lisbon Treaty would therefore give permission to the Taoiseach and Government to agree to various EU taxes in the future, without having to come back to the Irish people in a referendum. It is unlikely that the EU prime ministers and presidents would resist for very long the possibility of using its own tax resources to run the new European Union.

Article 93 (TFEU) of the Lisbon Treaty proposes an important amendment to Article 113 of the Consolidated EU Treaties, which at present makes harmonized company taxlaws across the EU a mandatory requirement, although that must be done by unanimity. This amendment states that such harmonization must take place if it is necessary 'to avoid

The Lisbon Treaty would therefore give permission to the Taoiseach and Government to agree to various EU taxes in the future, without having to come back to the Irish people in a referendum.

distortion of competition', allowing a country or business firm to take a case before the EU Court of Justice alleging that, for example, Ireland's 12.5 per cent rate of company tax constitutes a 'distortion of competition' as compared with Germany's 30 per cent rate. It would then be open to the Court to apply the EU's internal market rules on competition matters where majority voting applies to issues of company taxation. The Court could then require Member States to harmonize their company taxes over a specified period of time, although Governments would still decide the actual rates. Lisbon would therefore open a clear way around the present unanimity requirement for matters of company taxes.

That national differences in company taxes constitute 'distortions of competition' would undoubtedly be the main argument after Lisbon for harmonizing indirect taxes on companies, an issue that is especially sensitive in Ireland. The mandatory 'shall adopt' makes it clear that there would be an obligation on member-states to harmonize company taxes, even though there is now a requirement of unanimity, and some states, including Ireland, are against any change. If the Lisbon Treaty were to be ratified the general escalator clause or 'simplified revision procedure' would be the practical way around the unanimity problem on taxes. At present there could be no shift towards qualified majority voting on indirect taxation, because the Constitution of Ireland would have to be changed to permit it. But if we ratify the Lisbon Treaty the Constitution would be changed, so that only the Taoiseach of the day would stand in the way of the European Council moving to harmonize taxes on companies – at least as far as Ireland is concerned. At present the Irish people have a veto on EU indirect taxes. After Lisbon, it would be the Taoiseach alone who would exercise this veto, or the Dáil majority that he and his Government would control. The veto that the Irish people at present have on EU company taxes would be replaced by reliance on the Taoiseach's determination to say No indefinitely.

With the Lisbon Treaty neo-liberalism would become EU economic policy.

The Lisbon Treaty does not bode well for those campaigning for a different type of economic approach that puts people, the environment and the interests of the poorer and exploited peoples of this world before profit and greed. With the Lisbon Treaty neo-liberalism would become EU economic policy.

I firmly believe that the Treaty should be rejected so that

another Europe is possible. There are democracy movements all over the EU hoping that we will say No again as this will provide an opportunity for the peoples of the EU to have their say. One German slogan which I find powerful – 'EUROPE – not without the People', says exactly what is happening and we have a chance to speak for all the people denied a vote on this treaty.

A No Vote Would Impact on Investment

Ruairí Quinn TD

Labour Spokesperson, Education & Science and former Leader,
Labour Party

Born in Dublin and educated at Blackrock College, UCD (B.Arch.) and Athens Centre of Ekistics (HCE). A former architect and town planner, was first elected to Dáil Éireann for Dublin South-East in 1977. Minister for State at the Dept. of the Environment (1982-3), Minister for Labour (1983-7), Minister for the Public Service (1986-7), Minister for Enterprise and Employment (1993-4), Minister for Finance (1994-7) and Deputy Leader of the Labour Party (1989-97), was elected Leader in November 1997 and stood down in August 2002. In 2005, published his memoirs, Straight Left: A Journey in Politics.

The heads of State of Government of the European Union met in Berlin on 24 and 25 March 2007 for celebrations to mark the 50th anniversary of the signing of the Treaty of Rome. The Declaration, issued by the leaders, including then Taoiseach Bertie Ahern, TD, addressed the Union's history and its achievements and its future aspirations and challenges. The Declaration concluded:

> With European unification, a dream of earlier generations has become a reality. Our history reminds us that we must protect this for the good of future generations. For that reason we must always renew the political shape of Europe in keeping with the times. That is why, fifty years after the signing of the Treaties of Rome, we are united in our aim of placing the European Union on a renewed common basis before the European Parliament elections in 2009. For we know, Europe is our common future.

The rejection by Ireland in the June 2008 Lisbon Treaty referendum, meant that this pledge could not be met within the timetable of the European elections held in June 2009. The Irish electorate will now be presented with a second opportunity to ratify the Lisbon Treaty on 2 October 2009.

The Irish government, in consultation with other political parties in the Oireachtas, examined the results of the 2008 referendum and explored the reasons why a large number of Irish people voted against the Lisbon Treaty. The concerns and fears

The Irish negotiators have secured undertakings and guarantees from our European partners, in respect of those matters, some of which are not contained within the terms of the Treaty and others which are related to the Treaty.

which were revealed in that study have been addressed. The Irish negotiators have secured undertakings and guarantees from our European partners in respect of those matters, some of which are not contained within the terms of the Treaty and others of which are related to the Treaty. These will be respected and secured for the Irish electorate following the ratification of the Lisbon Treaty.

The economic consequences for Ireland of a rejection of the Lisbon Treaty would be enormous. Ireland would no longer be seen as a reliable or enthusiastic supporter of the European Project. Unique among the twenty seven member states of the Union, we would be perceived as highly Euro sceptic having voted No on three occasions in recent times by way of referendum. The European Project of the renewal of the political shape of the European Union, which was called for in the Berlin Declaration, would be permanently frustrated. The eight years of constitutional and political negotiation would have been brought to a stalemate.

The effective loss of involvement in decision making in the European Union would be the most important consequence of a No vote.

While it is clear that the political momentum of Europe would pick itself up and start afresh it is not clear what Ireland's role would be in such a situation. However, the economic consequences for Ireland would start to have their effect immediately after the No vote was declared. For a start, our current full membership of the Union would be challenged and questioned by our twenty-six partners and discussions would take place regarding some form of external association, similar perhaps to that enjoyed by Norway. We would remain within the European Economic Area but would have little or no say in the decisions that would shape the development of the European Union. The effective loss of involvement in decision making in the European Union would be the most important consequence of a No vote.

International institutions, in which representatives of the Irish people participate very effectively, ensure a favourable hearing for Irish interests and guarantee a ready flow of information back to Ireland. While small in size Ireland has participated, effectively, in the EU decision making process, protecting its own interests and contributing to the development of a vibrant and successful EU economy. The loss of these rights and influence will undoubtedly prove negative.

To a limited extent, Ireland might be able to change regulations covering certain policy areas, such as workers rights. This could affect competitiveness as well as living standards. However, it seems more likely that Ireland would be bound by EU Single Market standards as a member of the EEA. Under these circumstances, Ireland would have no influence on how standards and regulations were developed in the future and would have to implement whatever was decided by the EU. There would be limited access to information on what was pending in areas affecting Irish interests. This could affect all areas of the economy, such as financial and professional services, air transport, and so forth.

The next most important short-term impact of a second No to Lisbon would be increased uncertainty for all players in the Irish economy. This would be especially important for investors, both foreign and domestic. Whatever the constitutional outcome of a second No vote, this uncertainty would impact negatively on investment and the longer it continued the bigger the problem would grow.

In the longer term, the biggest impact would stem from the loss of influence on the future course of policy developments as they affected the EU economy and hence the EEA of which Ireland would be part. It is not possible to quantify this impact but the experience of the last thirty-five years (e.g., the CAP, regional policy, state aids) shows how important this can be. Even if some of the economic effects might be theoretically small, the importance of confidence and public perception could greatly magnify their effects in practice. In the event of a shift of EU membership to participation in the EEA, the many individual consequences would be much more than a sum of the parts. The impact on confidence in Ireland will be significant.

The history of Ireland's post-independence experience from 1921 to 1961 is not a happy story. Alone amongst all of the countries of what was then Western Europe, Ireland's post-independence experience was an economic and social catastrophe. The experiment in self-sufficiency and Sinn Féin economics had to be abandoned. The opening up of the Irish economy and our participation in the European Project was seen as the only way forward. The struggle for Ireland to move from the economic failures of our self-imposed isolation into participation within the then European Economic Community

It was not until we joined the European Union and decided to share significant aspects of our national sovereignty with our European partners that we fully realized our potential as a sovereign nation. That deliberate act of participation, repeated in successive referenda, has been the basis for our economic prosperity and social progress.

has been described, in detail, by Denis Maher who was a senior civil servant involved in those negotiations. The title of his book *The Tortuous Path*, tells its own story.

Since January 1973 Ireland has been a full and committed member of the European Union. We have been enthusiastic participants in all of its major policy initiatives with the exception of the Schengen area travel arrangements. But even our lack of participation in this agreement was because of the refusal of our neighbour, Britain, to participate in the Schengen Agreement. It was not until we joined the European Union and decided to share significant aspects of our national sovereignty with our European partners that we fully realized our potential as a sovereign nation. That deliberate act of participation, repeated in successive referenda, has been the basis for our economic prosperity and social progress. I would say our success in peacefully resolving the historic conflict between Ireland and Britain over the issue of Northern Ireland was in part due to our membership of the European Union.

The consequences of a second No to Lisbon would be to inevitably start the retreat from those frontiers of success into an uncertain future. We would begin that journey as a small economically weak nation isolated on the periphery of Europe at a time when the world is facing unprecedented global challenges.

Ruairí Quinn TD

Fiach Mac Conghail

Mary Cloake

Dr Finbarr Bradley

Dr Martin Mansergh TD

Noel Whelan SC

Frank Flannery

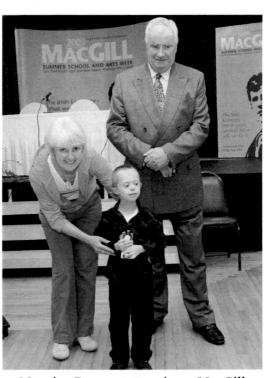

Maurice Regan presenting a MacGill
award to a young poet

Ann Conaghan and Connie McKelvey do
the Donegal mazurka

Michael Gallagher

John and Pat Hume

Mary Claire O'Donnell receiving a
bouquet from Louise McKenna

Myrtle McClay and Charles Byrne

Conal Shovlin seeking advice
from the law

Mark Little

Minister Mary Coughlan TD
and Dr Joe Mulholland

Chapter 11

THE ECONOMY, CULTURE AND CREATIVITY

**CREATIVITY CAN INFORM AND ENHANCE
INNOVATION**
Fiach Mac Conghail
Director, the Abbey Theatre

**THE ARTS – PART OF THE FABRIC OF OUR
ECONOMY**
Mary Cloake
Director, the Arts Council

**CULTURAL DISTINCTIVENESS AS COMPETITIVE
ADVANTAGE**
Finbarr Bradley
Former Professor, DCU, NUI Maynooth and UCD

VALUING ART– IN GOOD TIMES AND BAD
Martin Mansergh TD
*Minister of State at Dept. of Arts, Sport & Tourism and Dept. of
Finance*

Creativity Can Inform and Enhance Innovation

Fiach Mac Conghail
Director, the Abbey Theatre

Worked as theatre, film and visual arts producer. Personal assistant to Noel Pearson during his tenure as artistic director from 1989-91. Was stage manager and administrator at Dublin's Gaiety Theatre and spent seven years as artistic director of Project Arts Centre. Served as Ireland's cultural director at Expo 2000 in Hanover, managed redevelopment of Irish College in Paris as cultural centre and was cultural programme commissioner during Ireland's EU presidency.

As Director of the Abbey Theatre over the last four years, I have been continually mindful of the idea and the legacy of the Irish Republic and how the Abbey can and should still engage with it. Four years ago, this was seen as almost an old-fashioned notion and I then started to use the word 'citizen' which raised even more eye brows. I have committed the Abbey Theatre to supporting the role and place of the citizen in the Republic and to ensuring that art and politics engage with each other in Irish society.

However, I found institutional resistance to this in many quarters and of course, at the height of the 'Celtic Tiger' boom time, discussion of nation, state, language, culture, creativity and the arts were so commodified as to be parcels of saleable goods for the axis between Boston and Berlin. The Abbey Theatre is Ireland's national theatre and existed prior to independence and the formation of the Irish Republic. Without going into detail, the Abbey had to fight and argue for the moniker of 'National Theatre'. Sometimes, this was done out of inaction by the Abbey itself and particularly during the 1950s and 1960s in particular it wielded its monopolistic power to the detriment of playwrights and theatre artists and of course audiences. Quite rightly, the growth of the independent theatre sector arose out of this situation and we now have the work of Field Day, Druid, The Passion Machine, Project Arts Centre and other companies to celebrate.

The economic crisis we are experiencing now should not be about settling old scores or exercising prejudices but is a brilliant opportunity to reassess the cultural, social, political and economic value of our republic and of our culture.

Culture and creativity is not an optional extra but an elemental part of our society and is what distinguishes us from Ireland Inc. We are a Republic and not a corporation ...

This does not mean that the role of the national theatre is redundant – far from it. As we know, a lot of companies are built around an individual artist or writer, be that Garry Hynes at Druid or Michael Colgan at the Gate. The Abbey has a different and more national responsibility and that is to constantly interrogate and engage with Irish society. When I became Director of the national theatre, I promised that one of the primary aims of the Abbey would be to re-engage with Irish society and its politics and community. The Abbey had been remiss about this in the past. I felt that my responsibility was to the artist as citizen and to the audience as community. It was not a fashionable thing to do four years ago but I strongly believe that the act of putting on a play at the Abbey Theatre is a political act. We developed a series of public events and fora and we placed the work of Friel, Murphy, Shakespeare, Shepard, O'Rowe and Barry in a context where, over time and incrementally, the Abbey has been in a position to support and provide an imaginative, cultural and political service to our citizens. We have had opposition to this re-emergence of the role of the Abbey as Ireland's national theatre, not least from board members of the Arts Council and some of our colleagues within the theatre community. Yet whether I or they like it or not, the Abbey has a responsibility to continue to fulfil the ambition of its founders, Yeats, Gregory and Synge. The economic crisis we are experiencing now should not be about settling old scores or exercising prejudices but is a brilliant opportunity to reassess the cultural, social, political and economic value of our republic and of our culture.

Whatever we might think of the Report of the Special Group on Public Service Numbers and Expenditure Programmes ('An Bord Snip Nua'), I ask the Minister to keep the arts portfolio at the cabinet table as a part of a Senior Ministry. The nation was founded by patriots, men and women, who were thinkers, poets, artists and part time soldiers and throughout the emerging years of the Republic, the link between our politicians, policy makers and artists was very strong. Our Proclamation itself is a work of real vision and imagination and was inspired and written by our poets and patriots. We only need to mention Senator W.B. Yeats and Senator Brian Friel as two examples of how we respected and listened to the voice of artists in formulating policy in the political sphere. There was a tradition and knowledge and an understanding in our nation–building programme shared between the left and right-brain-thinking citizens of Ireland. Something happened to that relationship between the artist and the state; between culture and politics, between creativity and economics. Since the era of Lemass, Whitaker and Kinsella to today, culture and creativity have been marginalized from the consciousness and process of policy making. We became more interested in the framework of partnership and agreements than the content of imagination and big picture. I witnessed ugly scenes where tourism officials were demanding arts events be tailored for increasing bed nights rather than trusting the artist to engage with the citizen, where the bed nights would be filled anyway. A meanness and narrow mindedness appeared whereby the pursuit of new ideas and innovation was not considered unless it was for short term financial gain.

Where do they think a culture of innovation, creativity and the bedrock of the smart economy will emerge, if our young citizens cannot assimilate a poem or view a painting or see a play?

Every artist I know is an active citizen who votes and has made a commitment to enrich our society. Yet, with every bad economic situation, the arts are pitted against teachers, nurses and hospital closures. It is not an <u>either or scenario</u> but a requirement for policy makers and politicians to provide an overview of society and to involve all of us in the solution. Culture and creativity is not an optional extra but an elemental part of our society and is what distinguishes us from Ireland Inc. We are a Republic and not a corporation and it is right that artists should contribute to the rebuilding of our society over the next 5-10 years. The sad joke about the recent appointment of the Task Force on the Smart Economy under the auspices of the Department of An Taoiseach is that not one artist, architect, urban designer or philosopher is included in this. Where does the Task force think innovation, content and the creative industries come from?

A schism has occurred in Ireland unlike France, UK, or US. Can we name more than a handful of Oireachtas members who have expressed a public affiliation to the arts? Minister Martin Mansergh is an exception to this. Tom Murphy, in his brilliant play *The Last Day of a Reluctant Tyrant,* wrote the obituary of the Celtic Tiger and reminded us that the 'greasy till' moved from the shop to the bank. He put it all down to the lack of imagination and inquisitiveness or awe. What one of the characters said, which is so apt is: 'Once the people lost the sense of awe, they turned to property and religion'. This is a devastating indictment of the economic and social history of Ireland. We had the attempt by short-sighted politicians to control the education system and concentrate on IT skills one year, on science the next, and yet downgrade the teaching of languages, history and art. Where do they think a culture of innovation, creativity and the bedrock of the smart economy will emerge, if our young citizens cannot assimilate a poem, view a painting, or see a play? How will our left and right brain collude and collide so that our citizens become innovators and not consumers?

Creativity can inform and enhance innovation. There was a report published in June of this year by the European Commission called *The Impact of Culture on Creativity* which explores how culture can nurture innovation and go beyond artistic achievement to create a positive impact on the economy. The Abbey recently published an economic impact study, which illustrated that over a three year period (2006-2008), the arts contributed €118 million to the Irish economy. **The exchange of knowledge should not be considered as a financial exchange in itself. A society is more than an economy. Arts and culture are not about fixing social ills, or attracting tourism, although these are positive spin-offs**, but we can learn from artists and playwrights so that long term and strategic thinking can be inculcated into the problem solving of our policy makers and politicians. The impulse at the moment is to take short term measures, what Michael Cronin calls the 'tyranny of the moment'. The Department of Finance and the Irish Government have to move beyond the unsustainable attention deficit disorder of financial and political fixers. The citizen has to reassert himself and herself. The McCarthy report is waiting to be implemented as Government policy. We in the arts world well understand what cutbacks do; they are done indiscriminately and without a view of the holistic health of society. This is what the proclamation promised and this is what we are looking for: a new ideology or vision from our politicians which is not about being on animal farm, and the survival of the fittest. We want to regain control of the act of citizenship through our culture and creativity and not through NAMA.

I will finish with an excerpt from Michael Cronin's recent

essay in the *Journal of Music in Ireland* (JMI):

> Our problem is that current models of governance and economic activity are overwhelmingly skewed towards short-term benefits and gains so we find ourselves constantly unable to adequately address the major economic and political issues of our time. We also, as a consequence, devalue arts practices in our schools, on our media and in our public sphere. Instead of the culture of *Me, right now*! we ought to be moving to a culture of *All of us, all of the time*. This means that planning practices would be about preserving options for the future, our culture would honour and reward long-term responsible behaviour and our arts policies would favour ambitious sustainable projects over the ephemeral glitz of vox pop. The one thing we know about the future is that we are in it together. Thinking long-term means engaging the collective good of the species over the self-interest of individual members. Thinking long-term also involves the kind of joined-up thinking that sees a structural link between what might seem like the peripheral issue of arts funding and the headline topic of the survival of the planet. The greatest challenge for Irish society in the years ahead is how we answer the question put by one of the architects of the Clock of the Long Now, Stewart Brand, 'How do we make long-term thinking automatic and common instead of difficult and rare?' One answer is to look to, not away from, the arts.[59]

The Arts
Part of the Fabric of Our Economy

Mary Cloake
Director, the Arts Council

Born in Co. Wexford, educated at DCU (MA) and TCD (BA Mod.). Joined Arts Council in 1993 as Regional Development Officer and appointed Development Director in 1997. Director since 2004. Formerly, worked as Arts Officer for Dundalk Urban District Council. Member of RTÉ's Audience Council and in 2006 was member of the Bloomsday 100 Committee. She is Arts Council representative on the Council of National Cultural Institutions (CNCI). In February 2005, appointed to board of Culture Ireland, agency set up to promote Irish arts overseas.

This asset is already part of the fabric of our economy: the arts play an important part in cultural tourism; in attracting foreign direct investment; in the retention of a creative and imaginative labour force; and in creating an environment conducive to research and innovation.

For many people it might seem, reflecting on the last decade, that in the pursuit of an 'economy' we lost sight of the 'society' which is the higher goal. One of my Arts Council colleagues says that the Celtic Tiger bore out for many people their experience that truly 'It's a jungle out there'. The current economic situation presents us with an opportunity to take stock and to reassess our values as a nation. Our challenge now will be to integrate social and community values into the rebuilt economy. Simply looking for a short-term solution to get us back to where we were three years ago would repeat some of the mistakes of earlier approaches to economic development. A more considered approach is required where more nuanced and humane definitions of 'wealth' and 'profit' guide us. I want to highlight two ways in which the arts are fundamental to the task in hand. Firstly, the type of reflection we need at this time as a society has always been part of the core business of art and artists. Secondly, the arts as an intrinsic element in social and community structures can play a key role in reconstructing society. This is the case even in simple pragmatic terms as we seek new and sustainable directions in economic policy.

There is a long tradition in human society of looking to artists for inspiration at times of political, economic or social upheaval. We know this well in Ireland, where artistic ferment provided a vision for the foundation of the state. One of the long-standing and important functions of art is to reflect, comment on, criticize and celebrate society. In this way the arts provide insights and enable us to envisage new directions, attitudes, approaches and opportunities for ourselves as a society. The historian Kevin Whelan says:

> The task of art can not be just a critique [...]: it must also be a repertoire of alternative possibilities.[60]

Imagining a new future, or a number of possible new futures, based on honest scrutiny of ourselves, in all our strengths and weaknesses, is the first and arguably the most important way in which artists can help us now.

The second involves looking at the particular artistic strengths of Ireland. We have consistently been represented among the best artists in the world, especially in the fields of literature, music, theatre and film. The garnering of Emmys, Tonys, Bookers, Oscars and Nobels is only the most obvious and PR-friendly manifestations of a cultural fact with a significant economic reality attaching to it. A combination of four interdependent factors – native ability, learned tradition, community endorsement, and strategic investment by the state – has led to achievements and endorsements both at home and on the international stage that constitute a very real cultural asset.

This asset is already part of the fabric of our economy: the arts play an important part in cultural tourism; in attracting foreign direct investment; in the retention of a creative and imaginative labour force; and in creating an environment conducive to research and innovation.

Cultural tourism is founded on Ireland's artistic reputation. It is a very significant industry, worth an estimated €5.1 billion to the economy annually. In County Donegal alone, the recent Donegal Cultural Compass report has found that arts and cultural enterprises attracted approximately 380,000 visitors in the 2007/2008 tourist season.[61] Fáilte Ireland's own research on attractions indicates that of approximately 4,000 tourism offerings cited by visitors as reasons for choosing Ireland as a destination, almost 50 per cent were arts-related. The Irish Film Board has also found that half of all visitors to Ireland from the US cited seeing Ireland in a film as contributing to their decision to make a visit.

A thriving artistic life is one of the qualities which attract

To generate and support the kind of workforce which is good for the *Smart Economy and* indeed for our society in general, we require creative and flexible thinking, the kind of responsive awareness and acute forms of perception which the arts foster.

Foreign Direct Investment (FDI) into Ireland. It has been well documented that the recreational and amenity environment for employees is a highly influential factor in the decisions global corporations make about their location. FDI is a priority for the Government in its economic recovery programme. It seeks to make Ireland what it calls

> the destination of choice for European and overseas entrepreneurs.[62]

Furthermore, a rich artistic environment is crucial to create, attract and retain a labour force to drive development in industries which require both technological sophistication and a consistent cycle of imaginative renewal. To generate and support the kind of workforce which is good for the *Smart Economy* and indeed for our society in general, we require creative and flexible thinking, the kind of responsive awareness and acute forms of perception which the arts foster.

Artistic intellectual property arguably remains one of the highest value-added sectors in the world economy.

If we are to maintain economic growth into the long term, I would suggest that we also need to ensure that the arts are embedded into our education policy. While the arts have no monopoly on creative thinking, it is unlikely that an education policy which tends to view the arts as peripheral will generate a workforce geared to create the conditions for economic prosperity. The value of an arts education for the wider quality of life of the population at large is also an important issue.[63]

Considerable attention has been given to how a cultural and creative environment supports visibly and less visibly the atmosphere of research and innovation. The arts are an important factor here contributing to a culture characterized by the ceaseless experiment and innovation that is the hallmark of good arts practice.

The Government's *Smart Economy* document has as a recurring theme; the need not only for research and development but also for the commercialization of those ideas and pilots. In relation to such forms of research dis-semination, the Arts Council already plays a pivotal role in the funding it distributes annually on projects, awards, bursaries and commissions. This is our main contribution to cultural R&D and it is critical that it be maintained.

These are all significant economic contributions made indirectly by the arts. It is also important not to overlook the potential of the arts themselves and their related industries, as a foundation stone for new economic development. This potential is highlighted when we consider two themes that have emerged in recent debates on the economy. The first is that competitive advantage can be gained from that which makes Ireland distinctive: features of place, culture and society which other economies will find difficult to replicate.[64] The second is that 'high value-added' sectors are likely to provide more sustainable growth in the long term.

Ireland's distinguishing features include: the fact that we speak English but that it is not our first language; that we are in Europe but also an island on its outward edges; that we have a small population as a country but a vast population as a race; that we can absorb international cultural influences and render them, renewed, as our own. These and other cultural realities allow both global and local perspectives and possibilities. The arts are critical to making, maintaining and communicating this distinctiveness which has been, and will be, fundamental to our national recovery.

With new policies and a re-ordering of the world economy, Ireland has an opportunity to specialize in enterprises that are 'high value-added', where there is a substantial difference between the cost of producing a good or a service and the price at which it can be sold. In traditional industries such as agriculture and manufacturing the difference between costs and sale price has been reduced over the past twenty years because of competition from low-wage economies. In areas where there is a significant intellectual contribution to making the product, margins have remained high. Artistic intellectual property arguably remains one of the highest value-added sectors in the world economy.

The arts offer rich possibilities in contributing to economic recovery. In this context, it was disappointing to read An Bord Snip Nua's evaluation of the arts because of the exclusive emphasis on public expenditure and cost, as exemplified by the following excerpts from the report:

In the voluntary and community sphere, the embedded practice of the arts shapes the distinctive cultural character of Ireland, and can also create jobs and generate income.

- Given the size of the country, it is not financially feasible to provide for a full range of arts activities in every local area

- cultural projects are not affordable given current budgetary constraints ...
- the allocation of grants for overseas activity to Irish artists or arts organizations ... cannot be sustained given other public expenditure priorities ...
- (in) the context of other more pressing spending priorities ... given the level of international competition in this market space, there is no objective economic case for subventing the Irish Film Industry.[65]

In this milieu of the family, the community and the local network, it can been seen that the arts are also crucial to the building blocks of social and environmental capital that have been identified by the government as prerequisites for the *Smart Economy*.

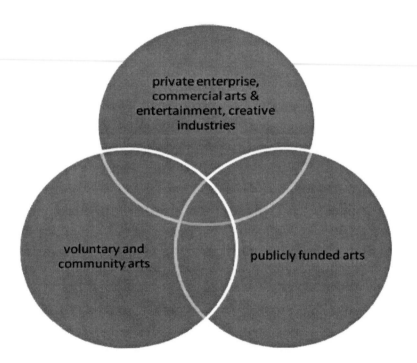

Figure 1

The fact is that the publicly-funded arts are part of a wider creative economy and ecology which includes, at the commercial end, the entertainment and creative industries that contribute substantially to sustaining employment and economic growth (Figure 1). This economic activity is not limited to large corporations: there is also a commercial element in the work of individual artists. The artist, John McHugh, has observed:

> Artists work as sole traders, micro-enterprises trading on the basis of commissions, independent sales and related activities.[66]

This is supported in the recent Visual Artists Ireland publication in which the author Noel Kelly reports that 62 per cent of all artists are registered as self-employed.[67]

In the voluntary and community sphere, the embedded practice of the arts shapes the distinctive cultural character of Ireland, and can also create jobs and generate income. Fintan Vallely describes the way in which a 'seemingly quiet music session of a dozen people' is the centre of circles of involvement, artistically, socially and economically. The circle will broaden to involve upwards of fifty people through family structures 'with music consciousness and most often considerable financial investment in teaching, travel and instruments.' He goes on to describe other ways in which the 'tally of direct and indirect involved persons is brought up to a hundred or more'. He summarizes the effect as follows:

> The impact and the cross-awareness of what appears to be a small event is considerable, and in this way the cumulative awareness of music culture and tradition are established and maintained – and accrue value. Such is art in the community – quite invisible, but with an ongoing ripple-effect and economic reality.

At the same time, Vallely maintains that traditional music exists within, and indeed actively contributes to, a global commercial music industry.[68] He describes various ways in which the practice of traditional music can have 'outlets' in the commercial sphere.

As is evident from the diversity of production described over in Figure 2, the traditional music sector, widely defined, is a significant employer and sustains further employment in related industries. Vallely highlights the employment impact of *Riverdance,* which is credited as having 'fed many hundreds of mouths among musicians since 1995'.[69]

- tourism
- album and literature sales by touring players internationally
- the indigenous Irish entertainment industry and its associated supply, catering, public relations, logistics and organizations
- international recognition of Ireland as a venue for music performance of all kinds
- education – instrumental and dance teaching and academic teaching and research
- print, audio and visual media publishing
- radio and television performance
- live performance at home and abroad

Figure 2: Outlets for Traditional Music (Vallely)

The size and employment effect of the arts-related sectors has been traditionally underestimated. This phenomenon is described by Elizabeth Currid in her study of creative industries in New York: *The Warhol Economy*. Grouped together, New York's creative industries, including fashion, design and the arts, rank among the top three sectors for employment, along with medicine and the financial services sector. In Ireland, although comprehensive up-to-date figures are not yet available, it is estimated that more than 50,000 people in the workforce earn their living either directly or indirectly from the arts and the creative industries. This compares with 70,000 in the ICT sector, generally considered to be one of the lynchpins of our economic development.

Despite this, we actually employ relatively fewer people in the creative sector – 2.5 per cent of the Irish labour force – than in London, where one in seven jobs is in the creative sector, or New England, where the figure is one in 25, or New Zealand, where it is one in 28. Based on the figures for New Zealand, there could be potential to stimulate the creation of up to 10,000 jobs in the creative sector here in Ireland. Clearly the arts and the creative and cultural industries which arise from them offer serious potential to stimulate employment, growth and recovery.

To conclude with a final observation: I would like to invite you to consider the arts not only for their economic contribution, but as forms of reflection, experience and anticipation which bring value to our lives and are an invaluable source of enlightenment. In gathering here in Glenties to consider our conference theme: *The Irish Economy – What went wrong? How will we fix it?*, we might usefully heed the words of Seamus Heaney in his poem 'The Mud Vision':

> As cameras raked
> The site from every angle, experts
> Began their *post factum* jabber and all of us
> Crowded in tight for the big explanations.
> Just like that, we forgot that the vision was ours,
> Our one chance to know the incomparable
> And dive to a future.[70]

In diving to our future, we must make sure that we hold on to the vision.

Cultural Distinctiveness as Competitive Advantage

Finbarr Bradley
Former Professor, DCU, NUI Maynooth and UCD

Educated at North Monastery, Cork, UCC (electrical engineering), Syracuse University (MBA) and New York University (PhD). Manages innovation learning communities in several Irish and international companies. As professor of finance at DCU, developed key graduate programme for IFSC executives. Set up innovative Centre, Fiontar and Irish-medium degree in finance, computing and languages. Former professor in the Economics Department at NUI Maynooth and visiting professor at Smurfit Business School, UCD. Taught at University of Michigan, Fordham University and Helsinki School of Economics. Co-authored book, Capitalising on Culture, Competing on Difference *[Blackhall Publishing, 2008] which focuses on innovation, learning and sense of place in a globalizing Ireland.*

IT companies spend more on the symbolic or design-driven aspects of their products than technical development, an insight missed by the Government's recent *Smart Economy* document.

Paradigm Shift

The world is undergoing a paradigm shift from an industrial or manufacturing age of goods to a learning, innovation or network age dominated by intangible services. An industrial enterprise is wedded to rationality and control rather than emotions, feelings, empathy and relationships, characteristics of a learning organization. Fostering meaning, delivering experiences and nurturing identity replicate the role that selling physical goods played in the industrial economy.

Scientific knowledge operates in the area of information and rationality while literature and the arts are in the provinces of understanding and wisdom. Understanding lies beyond intelligence; it is about conceiving, anticipating, valuing and judging. Wisdom is informed by purpose, ethics, memory of the past, and projection into the future. While information is mechanistic and abundant, wisdom is holistic, conceptual and scarce. Meaning emerges from rootedness, from a strong sense of place founded on memory, tradition and belonging. Value rises as meaning deepens, as knowledge moves from information to understanding and wisdom illustrated in digital media by content, patient tacit knowledge in healthcare, originality in crafts, local expertise in food recipes and traditional practices in farming.

The quality of knowledge depends on a point-of-view or cultural perspective, and is now more important in business than ever. IT companies spend more on the symbolic or design-driven aspects of their products than technical development, an insight missed by the Government's recent *Smart Economy* document. In innovation, while research or information relayed by computers does matter, it is meanings, experiences, and identities that matter most. Policies that recognize the nature and feelings of a people provide a powerful advantage. Ireland's distinct cultural resources, if used properly to mediate between the local and global, could provide this country with an inimitable competitive advantage.

Sustainable Competitive Advantage

The value system used in economics is extraordinarily crude with little role for imagination or mystery. Some economists see rootedness as antithetical to innovation with erosion of a sense of place often cited as an indicator of confidence and independence. Yet an emerging paradox is that in a world of global markets and high-speed communications, location and culture are becoming *more*, not *less* important. Advantage lies in *difference* captured by special places and shared values. As Harvard's Michael Porter argues, enduring competitive advantage lies increasingly in the local.[71] The more complex and dynamic the global economy becomes, the more this is likely to hold true.

Sustainable competitive advantage comes from resources unique or difficult to imitate. Tangible resources (such as money and technology) are *necessary* but *not sufficient*. Intangibles such as human, cultural and social resources, founded on capabilities and relationships, are *essential*. Tacit resources such as imagination, intuition, inspiration, ingenuity, sense-of-self, self-assurance, self-confidence and self-knowledge are crucial. Such resources are least susceptible to imitation, most valuable, and

Tangible resources (such as money and technology) are *necessary* but *not sufficient*. Intangibles such as human, cultural and social resources, founded on capabilities and relationships, are *essential*.

rooted in the social and economic fabric of local relationships

Being distinctive, thinking differently and having different information enable a community to be creative and innovative. Innovative places provide an integrated eco-system where all forms of creativity – artistic and cultural, technological and economic – take root and flourish. A place that succeeds emphasizes culture, attracting and keeping creative people through the qualities of a diverse, authentic and unique community. This in turn attracts enterprise, reversing the traditional direction of development. Unlike the past where reducing business costs or clustering companies in industrial estates was key, a unique innovating milieu that fosters resourcefulness now ensure a country, region or city's long-term competitiveness.[72]

Back to the Future

Contemporary Ireland is badly in need of the driving vision that characterized the Irish Revival, an exhilarating mix of cultural renaissance, idealism and self-reliance, encom-passing a range of innovative initiatives in commerce, agriculture, theatre, literature, sport and language all relating to a common theme: an awakening interest in Irish identity, broadly defined. The notion that cultural self-belief is fundamental to economic development was its vital informing principle, but as P.J. Mathews of UCD points out, the Revival is often portrayed as a purely mystical affair characterized by nostalgia and obsessive anti-modern traditionalism.[73]

The Gaelic League, the Co-operative Movement, the GAA, the Abbey Theatre and various Natural History societies attracted an eclectic array of individuals involved in projects across a wide spectrum, with a sense of identity and national purpose bounding them in a common enterprise. Co-operative organizers, sceptical farmers, idealistic patriots, language enthusiasts and literati of all stripes contributed to the exciting mosaic of the time. This vision was never articulated as one seamless manifesto, yet there existed certain common characteristics across all organizations.

Foremost was self-reliance or *character* and the notion

that the responsibility for development resided in Irish, not foreign hands. Shared identity and sense of place were pre-requisites to the development of character and imperative for innovativeness. Horace Plunkett saw a commercial ethos, moral courage and thrift as core elements in his vision of the Co-operative Movement. Character was also at the core of the Gaelic League, the intellectual and industrial movement that fostered use of the Irish language and supported native literature and arts. Central to its philosophy was an insistence that the Irish personality could not reach its full potential except within a cultural milieu proper to it. It held that creative personalities cannot be produced without an integrated community having a unique and continuing experience of its own.

Accepted that we now are in a completely different political and technological context it is essential to recapture the spirit and excitement of the Revival. The diversity that constitutes Irishness is a potential source of enrichment through cross-fertilization, both north and south of the border. While a once-thriving scientific culture was in decline by the time of the Revival, natural history was vibrant, especially in the Northeast. Much of this work was stimulated by the same motivation as the Revival: an explosive interest in things Irish and a patriotic urge to provide an identity for Ireland while rejecting models imposed from outside.

Distinctiveness & Innovation

David Landes of Harvard concludes in a groundbreaking book, *The Wealth and Poverty of Nations*:

> if we learn anything from the history of economic development, it is that culture makes all the difference.[74]

Culture is a core pillar of France, whose approach to cultural nationalism independent Ireland was meant to be based on. Italy also illustrates the importance of culture and meaning as a competitive strength. Italian design is impossible to imitate, a heritage of arts and crafts resources developed over generations, a critical innovative resource. Nordic countries long recognized cultural rejuvenation as essential for national self-reliance with rootedness providing a quality aspirational work ethic and empowered innovative community. Danish education is deeply influenced by the 19th century Grundtvig folk high-school concept which communicates a deep purpose, awakening pride in national

Italian design is impossible to imitate, a heritage of arts and crafts resources developed over generations, a critical innovative resource. Nordic countries long recognized cultural rejuvenation as essential for national self-reliance with rootedness providing a quality aspirational work ethic and empowered innovative community.

culture while refusing to devalue others, and love of learning that continues long after a student is finished with formal study. In Finland, a country Ireland is often urged to emulate, dynamic integration in the global economy, strong national sentiment, a unique language and closeness to nature, represent important sources of meaning. Irish commentators focus on that country's huge R&D spend but do not appreciate that strong affirmation of its culture is the key and might similarly be a driver of innovation at home.

Ireland's distinctive cultural resources have the potential to develop an economy full of innovative, creative and entrepreneurial vitality. The promotion campaign of IDA Ireland, *The Irish Mind*, sells potential investors an image of a creative, imaginative and agile Irish mindset. The theme brands Ireland as a place particularly suited for creative and innovative ventures, yet still rooted in distinctiveness. It offers the intriguing speculation that the centuries-old Irish genius for creative communication, the basis of literature, provided the catalyst that makes it one of today's leading software producers. The Irish psyche, IDA Ireland maintains, has an innate creativity, manifested in literature and music, a curiosity in others, seeking to build relationships, tolerance for ambiguity and ability to handle this better than most other people.

Ireland's heritage provides the ideal base for creativity. Ruptured roots, a historical tragedy, now offers the benefit of double vision, a crucial source for creative endeavour. Different traditions lead to diversity in meanings, *Idir Dhá Chultúr* as Declan Kiberd puts it. This *Divided Mind*, poet Thomas Kinsella's expression, can be seen in the work of artists like Robert Ballagh and Louis le Brocquy. The conventional practice of separating the artist and thinker, imagination and reason, runs counter to the distinctive nature of the Irish mind. This combines both the artistic and analytic, the emotional and rational, disorder and order, what one writer named '*chaordic*'.[75]

Balancing science and technology with a tradition of metaphors, narrative, stories and mythology, offers a huge competitive advantage. Fostering the scientific mind of separability and rationality along with the spiritual is key.

> **This country has natural advantages for the learning age but these will only be realized if the artistic is combined with the scientific, interpreted through the prism of Irish culture and tradition.**

Irish mythology, for instance, which is not linear but has a meandering interconnectedness, is ideal for an emerging sustainable age where, as I argued earlier, conversation, interpretation, empathy, meaning and relationships are the most critical innovation resources. However, Ireland's current innovation policy focuses on scientific research based on objectivity, denying the legitimacy of the subjective world of feeling, ignoring our distinct and most valuable resource, a sense of connection and the imaginal life.[76] Innovation is really about stories and the Irish are the world's great story-tellers.

The scientific mind simplifies and narrows experiences into manageable principles whereas the arts emphasize complexity – crucial if imagination, intuition, inspiration and innovation are to flourish. This country has natural advantages for the learning age but these will only be realized if the artistic is combined with the scientific, interpreted through the prism of Irish culture and tradition. The Irish language can be an especially potent resource for nurturing sensitivity to difference, meaning and aesthetic qualities. We squander such self-knowledge at our peril.

No nation can be truly innovative if people do not know who they are, where they come from, and where they are trying to go.

While T.K. Whitaker and Seán Lemass were responsible for transforming the Irish economy and embracing the world, a strong cultural perspective was at the core of their vision. Few commentaries stress this and it is ignored by today's policy-makers. To quote Whitaker:

> English does not carry all our traditions, all the emotions and aspirations we have experienced as a people ... if as a result of indifference, the Irish language were allowed to die, the loss would be irreparable. ...We would have cut ourselves off from an invaluable heritage and made ourselves even more vulnerable than we are already to absorption in an amorphous Anglo-American culture.[77]

Conclusion

This argument is no exercise in dreamy nostalgia, or an attempt to turn back the clock to some perceived pure and idyllic golden age. It is a thesis light years away from Éamon de Valera's notion of 'frugal self-sufficiency' yet shares a similar appreciation of the value of indigenous resources. Far from representing dead artefacts that are anti-modern and non-economic, cultural resources represent dynamic and unique sources of competitive advantage.

The idea that a strong identity is opposed to materialism, the profit motive, technological innovation and modernism reflects an unfortunate legacy of the elites who governed this State over its first decades. In the space of eighty odd years, we have moved from one extreme to another: from a place where culture featured prominently in the national vision to its opposite, where science, rationality and markets dominate. We must harness the positive elements of both. Our special circumstances present great opportunities for empathic relationships with countries who like ours suffered the humiliation of colonization.

No nation can be truly innovative if people do not know who they are, where they come from, and where they are trying to go. Prospering in a multicultural world requires individuals that understand their own culture. Grounded this way, they appreciate diversity and the cultural values of others with whom they must co-operate. While remaining open to outside influences, they learn to identify difference and appreciate distinctiveness. They absorb different ideas, yet are not dominated by globalized cultural influences. This generates an innovative mind frame. Radical, yet realistic, changes in education and enterprise policy, are needed to grasp opportunities that, while rooted in place, could create an Ireland globally competitive and self-reliant, utterly unique while eminently cosmopolitan, anchored by meaning, comprising people of all traditions sharing a communal commitment to place.

Valuing Art – In Good Times and Bad

Martin Mansergh TD
Minister of State at Dept. of Arts, Sport & Tourism and Dept. of Finance

Educated at King's School, Canterbury and Christchurch, Oxford (MA and DPhil). Entered civil service in 1974. First Secretary, Department of Foreign Affairs (1974-81). Appointed Special Advisor to Taoiseach Charles J. Haughey in 1982. Joined Fianna Fáil Party in 1981. Nominated to Seanad in 2004. Publications include The Spirit of the Nation: The Collected Speeches of Charles J. Haughey 1957-1986, Parnell and the Leadership of Nationalist Ireland and Ireland and the Challenge of European Integration.

There is currently an exhibition in the Hunt Museum of the work of Seán Keating, the artist of the Irish Revolution – his *Men of the South* painting of Seán Moylan and his comrades hangs in my office. Keating was also someone who depicted the building up of the new State, notably in his pictures of the Shannon Scheme at Ardnacrusha. In an article written in 1924, he captured the sober pessimism of his time and of ours:

> We ignore our national assets, and proclaim our bankruptcy on the housetops.

There is a danger in times like these that we focus almost exclusively on the negatives, the retrenchments that have undoubtedly to be carried out, to keep ourselves afloat, rather than the possibilities we have of expanding creativity. As the Government document *Building Ireland's Smart Economy* stated last Christmas:

> the arts, cultural and creative industries are key economic contributors.

As I was opening another exhibition, entitled *Beware the Jabberwock*, of animal prints from the Renaissance onwards in the antiquarian book collection of Marsh's Library, I came across in the catalogue part of a Lewis Carroll verse which, read in full, also has some application to present times:

There is a danger in times like these that we focus almost exclusively on the negatives, the retrenchments that have undoubtedly to be carried out, to keep ourselves afloat, rather than the possibilities we have of expanding creativity.

> He thought he saw a Banker's Clerk
> Descending from a bus:
> He looked again, and found it was
> A Hippopotamus.
> 'If this should stay to dine,' he said,
> 'There won't be much for us!'

That sums up pretty well people's fears about available resources being swallowed up by the banking mess, though it is the Government's job through NAMA and otherwise to minimize that risk, with legislation due to be published shortly.

We have come out of a period that has seen a considerable blossoming of the arts, which have been better resourced in recent times than they had ever been previously. With money relatively more abundant, new or better performance facilities have been built, and the vision of greater community participation in the arts around the country has gone some distance towards being fulfilled. We have the infrastructure which can revive and encourage touring, whether by art exhibitions or companies of performers.

I do not propose to go into at any length what went wrong, except to say that as a society we became over-confident, and practically everyone in a position to speak with some authority, Government, Central Bank and IMF included, completely underestimated the risks, imagining that we had, at least fiscally, a considerable margin of safety, and that the safest investments were property and banks. Whether alternative prescriptions then of higher taxes, higher public spending and less public saving would have yielded any substantially better outcomes is to be doubted. While some may have been more prescient than others, and we can all point selectively to things we expressed some concern about, almost no one foresaw in full what was coming. There was an impatience with restraints on making money, with any close regulation, either domestically or at EU level, strongly resisted – the reason no doubt last time round for the multi-millionaires against the Lisbon Treaty. The invincibility and superiority of the market was with many an article of faith. Today, both indigenous and multinational organizations can barely cope with the flood of casualties from the sharpest economic contraction in 80 years. In the words of the Comte de Ségur, commenting on the failure of the privileged class to anticipate the French Revolution:

> a carpet of flowers covered the abyss, which might not have opened up to anything like the extent experienced but for worldwide factors compounding the domestic ones.

Fifty and certainly one hundred years ago, we were an infinitely poorer country. Yet the principal justification for our independence, for more than half a century preceding it and for a least a generation subsequent to it, was Ireland's cultural distinctiveness. Indeed, Article 1 of the Constitution, unaltered in 1998, affirms not only the right of the Irish nation to self-determination, but also the right *to develop its life, political, economic and cultural, in accordance with its own genius and traditions.* These traditions, still being upheld today, go back some thousands of years to the passage graves of Brú na Bóinne with their stone decorations, examples of which I saw last Friday while visiting the cairns of Loughcrew in North-West County Meath. Today in the 21st century, we would amplify, in both a domestic and global context, cultural distinctiveness by linking it to the concept of cultural diversity.

There is no doubt that over the past one hundred years we have, culturally speaking, in certain genres, punched far above our weight. Ireland's culture and heritage are a major attraction to visitors, being a reason why about half of them come to Ireland, with visits to sites and attendances at performances accounting for much of their activity here. Culture and heritage also provide significant employment, some of it seasonal, estimated as being up to 64,000 people. Even if making a creative living in the arts world is difficult and challenging, though in another sense infinitely rewarding, it is an old fallacy to think that those who work in the arts are somehow of less value or priority to society than those who work in the fields, the factories or the offices. The greatest economist of the 20th century, John Maynard Keynes, married to ballerina Lydia Lopokova, founded the Arts Theatre in Cambridge in 1936, which began with a performance by the Vic-Wells, a ballet company, which he also co-founded, directed by Cork-born Ninette de Valois. Keynes became first chairman of the British Arts Council in 1946, a model for our own formed in 1951.

Ireland's culture and heritage are a major attraction to visitors, being a reason why about half of them come to Ireland, with visits to sites and attendances at performances accounting for much of their activity here.

Culture and heritage are also a significant employer, some of it seasonal, estimated as being up to 64,000 people.

The Empress Maria Theresa of Austria let herself down badly when she strongly advised one of her Archduke sons, who was considering recruiting Mozart to his household, against employing composers and 'useless' people like that. Much more admirable was the message from Pope Urban VIII on the day of his election in 1623 to Bernini, famous sculptor and future architect of the Vatican:

> It is your great good luck, Cavalieri, to see Maffeo Barberini Pope, but we are even luckier in that the Cavalieri Bernini lives at the time of our Pontificate.

In the bicentenary year of Haydn's death, it is worth recalling what Tim Blanning has written in *The Triumph of Music*:

> At the beginning of his career Haydn became famous because he was the Kapellmeister for the *Esterházys*; by the time he died, the Esterházys were famous because their Kapellmeister was Haydn.

Ars longa, vita brevis. Few things from past ages and civilization survive better than their art. The art of our time and of this country will be one of our more enduring legacies to future generations. They will be puzzled, if we do not value it as much through harder times also.

We need to keep to the fore a positive vision of how the arts play an integral role in the development of our country, and an understanding of how they can be used, not only as an asset in their own right, but as an enhancement to many other forms of activity.

Of course, in the current difficult situation, the chill winds of reduced personal incomes and reduced Government support are being experienced by those working in the arts, as in every other sphere, with undoubtedly more to come. I would like to commend all those in the arts community for the resourcefulness with which they have coped with difficulties to date. The Government's aim in the arts has been as far as possible to maintain activity and employment, even if some capital programmes, such as ACCESS III, have had to be put for the time being on the back burner. We must not, however, fall into the trap of becoming purely defensive. We need to keep to the fore a positive vision of how the arts play an integral role in the development of our country, and an understanding of how they can be used, not only as an asset in their own right, but as an enhancement to many other forms of activity.

They should be part of every child's education. Many companies and groups actively value young talent. Every so often we see performers whom an Italian cultural phrase book would describe as '*un giovane astro nascente. Sarà bravo, vero?*' At the other end of the age spectrum, painting groups can give a new purpose, meaning and richness to life amongst older people. My house in Tipperary is covered with paintings, mostly of the West of Ireland, by my mother, when she was in her 70s, broadly of the school of Kenneth Webb. She was also a friend of Hilda van Stockum.

Things we somehow managed to afford when we were poor ought to be sustainable, even at a reduced level, in the current turbulence.

In the past year, I have opened many exhibitions of work by young or established artists, but also by amateur art groups. The Office of Public Works sometimes sponsors a local arts exhibition, from which it can purchase pictures for new buildings. OPW are putting many of our heritage buildings, where suitable, at the disposition of festivals, helping them to keep down their costs, as well as providing them with venues that people are attracted to, but also giving them a greater sense of public ownership of historic properties belonging to the State. We have a touring exhibition of our own, the *Art of the State* exhibition, the State in this instance being both the Republic and Northern Ireland, which I will be opening in Portstewart in early September and Clonmel in October, this year featuring portraits.

The artistic retreat at Annaghmakerrig in Co. Monaghan, which is maintained by OPW, is managed jointly by the two Arts Councils, North and South, and I had dinner there with the NI Arts Council earlier this year, from which good ideas flowed, some of them since being implemented.

Culturally, there are no borders. *Kulturkampf* is as redundant as armed struggle, even though an older Ernie O'Malley once inverted Hermann Goering by saying, '*when I hear talk of guns, I reach for my culture.*' National cultures are receptive to other influences, and themselves contribute something that can be appreciated far away. There are overwhelming cultural reasons, in addition to the political and economic ones, for continuing to belong as a fully committed member to the European Union, and not becoming, in the apt words of David O'Sullivan speaking earlier this week, 'a non-playing member.' The Director of the Irish College in Paris, Sheila Pratschke, was in with me earlier this week, and I would be sorry if the type of exchanges that were fostered, when I joined the Department of Foreign Affairs thirty-five years ago, by the Cultural Relations Committee, and latterly

Culture Ireland, were to fall a victim of current financial circumstances. Things we somehow managed to afford when we were poor ought to be sustainable, even at a reduced level, in the current turbulence.

In 1773, some years before the French Revolution, the Controller-General of Finances, a tough-minded cleric called the Abbé Terray, who was trying to pull the State's dilapidated finances together, wanted to demolish one of the most famous royal châteaux of the Loire at Chambord, as an economy measure. Luckily, the intention was never carried through. Any reorganizations and rationalizations that we have to carry through should be proportionate, and recognize, respect and appreciate the component identities and contributions of valuable institutions, and ensure that they are not written off wholesale.

Any reorganizations and rationalizations that we have to carry through should be proportionate, and recognize, respect and appreciate the component identities and contributions of valuable institutions, and ensure that they are not written off wholesale.

In the thirty-five years I have been, in one form or another, a public servant, the arts, like science and a number of other policy sectors, have been part of a variety of departmental configurations. Charles Haughey took a particular interest in the arts and did much for them, but his successors gave them a department of their own. They are important enough to need to be represented directly at the government table, naturally grouped with a selection of related responsibilities.

A younger party colleague informed me in the lift a few months ago that 'there are no votes in the arts', compared presumably to mass sporting events. I would be tempted to respond, 'Why not art for art's sake?' but, recognizing that that might not be allowed me, I would be confident that we could find the same economic justifications which other countries and cities can find for properly supporting their cultural activities. I am looking forward to seeing *The Rivals* in the Abbey Theatre on Tuesday, and may I impart with the same confidence as Mrs Malaprop that, despite having to make hard choices on diminished arts funding, the Government will not turn out to be:

as headstrong as an allegory on the banks of the Nile.

Chapter 12

A NEW POLITICAL LANDSCAPE?

**THE STATE OF THE ECONOMY IS THE
DETERMINING FACTOR**
Noel Whelan SC
Barrister and Political Commentator

NEW MORE RADICAL FINE GAEL IS EMERGING
Frank Flannery
Director of Organization, Fine Gael

The State of the Economy is the Determining Factor

Noel Whelan
Barrister and Political Commentator

Born in Wexford and educated at UCD (Politics & History) and Kings Inns (Law). Formerly, political adviser at Fianna Fáil HQ and Special Adviser at the Dept. of An Taoiseach. Practises as a barrister on the Dublin and South East circuits and writes a weekly political column for The Irish Times. Has published a number of books including Politics, Elections and the Law (2001) and the Tallyman series of election guides, the most recent of which was The Tallyman's Campaign Handbook – Election 2007. A frequent contributor to radio and television news and current affairs programmes.

We 'political analysts' are often asked at the height of election campaigns to predict the outcome. However, since we are not psychics, we can do no such thing. I am always more comfortable when I am asked to look back and assess the recent past rather than when I am being pressurized into predicting the future, even the near future. I am particularly comfortable being asked to assess what happened in an election some eight weeks or so ago. There has been time to dissect the results data and reflect on their implications in a calmer atmosphere than that which usually prevails over the results' weekend.

In my view, the three sets of elections held last month *did not* represent a historic *transformation* in Irish politics which some have found it to be or which some hope it was. The results of the election *did*, however, alter the political landscape to this extent:

- A large block of support has left Fianna Fáil and moved primarily to Fine Gael (and to a lesser extent to Labour in Dublin).
- This shift in support has left Fine Gael by far the largest party in *local* government.

Whether or not this shift will endure as a lasting change in the political landscape, even in the medium term, remains to be seen. My guess is that it will.

Whether or not this shift will endure as a lasting change in the political landscape, even in the medium term, remains to be seen.

My guess is that it will. Although the reversal which Fianna Fáil suffered in the 2004 local and European elections did not undermine their capacity to secure re-election to government in 2007, this time things are different because:

- The scale of the shift in support away from Fianna Fáil is much larger.
- The economic uncertainty in which this shift occurred will persist.
- The 2009 election results reveal underlying weaknesses in Fianna Fáil's organisation and electoral capacity.

Put simply, the party's position is vulnerable and particularly vulnerable in Dublin.

2009 Local Election Results

Let us look first at what happened in the three sets of elections held in June starting with the local elections. Our focus here will be on the county and city council elections only. In all, there are 883 seats available in city and county councils, but only 130 of these are in areas covered by the four Dublin county councils. This meant that although Fianna Fáil's vote fell more sharply in Dublin than the rest of the country, the fall in seat numbers measured nationally was not as dramatic because although Dublin has about 28 per cent of the population and about a quarter of the electors, it elects only 15 per cent of the county and city councillors.

Speaking at the MacGill Summer School in 2004 I pointed out that the results of that year's local and European elections represented Fianna Fáil's worst electoral performance in history. This time it was even worse. Fine Gael won almost 128,000 more votes than Fianna Fáil and now has 122 seats more than Fianna Fáil (340 versus 218) on the city and county councils. After the 1999 local elections Fianna Fáil had 105 more seats on these councils than Fine Gael. That gap narrowed considerably to only 8 seats after the 2004 election but has now widened again but in Fine Gael's favour.

Fine Gael won almost 128,000 more votes than Fianna Fáil and now has 122 seats more than Fianna Fáil (340 versus 218) on the city and county councils.

2009 European Election Results

What is significant in the results of the European elections is the fact that the gap between Fine Gael and Fianna Fáil is more than 92,000 votes in Fine Gael's favour. Apart from that, the iconic event was the loss of their seat in the Dublin constituency, which leaves them without an MEP in the capital. The party's vote in the capital in the European elections fell more than 7 per cent. In the South constituency their vote actually fell more than 13 per cent, whereas their vote was relatively stable in East and down only 2 per cent in North and West, which was not bad considering their incumbent MEP announced his retirement just four weeks before polling. After the 2009 European Elections, Fine Gael is still the largest party in Ireland's European Parliament delegation although its numbers have been reduced from 5 to 4, Labour and Fianna Fáil have equally sized representations, namely, 3 MEPs each, the Socialist Party has elected its first ever MEP in Joe Higgins and there is now only one independent MEP.

2009 By-Election Results

The most striking thing about the results of the Dublin Central by election is again the drop in Fianna Fáil support. Fianna Fáil in government has always suffered a significant fall off in support in by-elections. In a study of all by-elections from the early 1980s to 2006, Dr Adrian Kavanagh of NUI Maynooth put the average drop in Fianna Fáil's support in by-elections, when measured against the previous general election, as being in the order of 8 per cent. The drop suffered by Fianna Fáil in the 2009 Dublin Central by-election was four times Kavanagh's average. Fianna Fáil support levels in Dublin Central in recent elections were a peculiarity because of the appeal of Bertie Ahern in his home base but of course the party's by-election candidate was his brother Maurice. 12,734 people in Dublin Central voted for a Fianna Fáil candidate called Ahern in 2007 but only 3,770 voted for a Fianna Fáil candidate called Ahern in the 2009 by election (29 per cent).

George Lee's runaway victory was the story in the Dublin South by-election. He almost doubled the Fine Gael vote achieved in the 2007 general election. Dublin South is, in fact, the most volatile of constituencies which always has a multiplier on the national media,but this was an incredible performance.

12,734 people in Dublin Central voted for a Fianna Fáil candidate called Ahern in 2007 but only 3,770 voted for a Fianna Fáil candidate called Ahern in the 2009 by-election (29 per cent).

Turnout

In assessing the significance of the fall in Fianna Fáil's support in the 2009 elections one has also appreciate that the turnout was relatively high and was at a level akin to that we usually see in general elections. The turnout in the 2004 local and European elections was truly historic. It was a full 9 per cent points higher than the 1999 elections reversing a three and a half decade trend of declining voter turnout. While it is difficult to be certain about comparative turnouts in Ireland (because of the despicable state of our electoral register until recently) this year saw the high level of turn out maintained for the local and European elections.

Reasons for Fall in Fianna Fáil Support

In 2009 a significant national, if not international political issue came to dominate the local elections- the economic crisis, in all its shapes and forms. The state of the economy and the public's placing of responsibility for it at the Government's doorstep was the determining factor in this election: it's the economy stupid!

In June 2008 Fianna Fáil's 42 per cent opinion poll rating was the highest it had been in years and Brian Cowen was the most popular party leader. Since then, however, Fianna Fáil's vote as measured in opinion polls has halved, the Taoiseach's rating has more than halved and the Government's satisfaction rating has collapsed. While the results of the 2009 elections did not show a fall in Fianna Fáil's vote to the extent reflected in the poll it was still a steep fall and it occurred for the same reason.

The massive drop in Fianna Fáil's support reflected in the Irish Times/TNS MRBI poll in November 2008 could be explained by the electorate's trauma in coming to terms with the scale of the new economic realities. However, the fact that the party's support dropped by a further 5 per cent in the March TNS/MRBI poll and this drop has been partially reflected in these elections suggests to me that different factors may be at play. It is precisely because the public appreciate how bad things are economically that the Govern-

The party's unpopularity flows not just from the difficult measures the Government is now taking but from the fact that much of the electorate is placing blame for the mess which necessitates those measures at Fianna Fáil's door.

ment's ratings have fallen so severely. The fall in the opinion poll and the fall of Fianna Fáil's support in the 2009 elections is about accountability – the public is visiting responsibility for the economic crisis on Fianna Fáil. The party's unpopularity flows not just from the difficult measures the Government is now taking but from the fact that much of the electorate is placing blame for the mess which necessitates those measures at Fianna Fáil's door. With harsher steps still having to be taken by the government in next autumn's budget there is little prospect of an improvement in Fianna Fáil's fortunes in the coming months.

Weaknesses in Fianna Fáil Organisation and Electoral Capacity

Finally, I will make some brief observations on the internal weaknesses within Fianna Fáil which, in my view, the bad results in this election revealed. In many ways, Fianna Fáil's urban and Dublin problem, apparent particularly in the 1991 election, was temporarily resolved, or masked, by the fact that Bertie Ahern became party leader. The strength of the Ahern brand and appeal more than compensated for the weakness of the Fianna Fáil brand in urban areas and Dublin. The boom times of the 1990s and early 21st century also masked the difficulties which the party faced because of declining loyalties among the electorate. In addition, the party side-stepped its organizational difficulty by relying on professionally paid people for electioneering and on individual candidate campaigns for Dáil contests. This endangered the party's base and party insiders acknowledged that there were signs of this effect in the bad results in the 2004 local and European elections.

The party's success in the 2007 general election and the fact that within the party that electoral achievement was seen as one which the party itself delivered through hard work and organisation skill in many ways blinded the party to the enduring organisation difficulties which persisted. Since the 2007 Election the party's energy has been sapped, firstly by the enduring tribunal controversies which ultimately compelled Bertie Ahern to resign and then by the economic crisis.

Many within the higher echelons of the party itself, at both parliamentary party and national executive level, cite mistakes

> Since the 2007 Election the party's energy has been sapped, firstly by the enduring tribunal controversies which ultimately compelled Bertie Ahern to resign and then by the economic crisis.

The party needs now, however, to find a means of renewing itself while simultaneously being in government if it is to be able even to contain the electoral onslaught that appears to await it.

which the party made in its candidate selection process for recent elections. In many local electoral areas Fianna Fáil abandoned the traditional method of selecting candidates at a local convention of party delegates. Candidates were instead selected through an interview process overseen by party headquarters. The Fianna Fáil national executive has long had the power to approve candidates and regularly used this power to set the number of candidates to be selected by convention and to add candidates if the line-up selected locally was not perceived to be strong enough.

Since the 1990s the national executive has played an increasingly significant and more direct role in candidate selection for Dáil elections through a committee. In the lead-in to the 1997 and 2002 elections this committee of leading national party politicians and strategists supervised candidate selection in almost all Dáil constituencies. The committee carried out relatively sophisticated polling in key marginal constituencies, often testing several potential candidates and canvassing local opinion within and outside the party on their strengths. Where necessary, prominent local figures outside the party were approached to stand. Having identified its ideal line-up, the committee set about persuading the local organization and strong-arming deputies to deliver it at convention. Where this was not possible conventions were held but allowed to select one candidate short of the desired line-up and the committee itself recommended an additional name to the national executive. All of this was done carefully by a committee of respected party strategists and politicians and with at least some regard to the need for local organization buy-in. It also proved relatively successful, with almost all candidates so selected in 2007 being elected. In contrast, the national party's involvement in candidate selection for these local elections appears to have been shambolic. Candidate interviews were conducted by panels which often did not include a politician or even a national executive member. Candidate-selection issues certainly do not explain the scale of the Fianna Fáil setback but in this initial phase they were the biggest talking point within the party.

It is interesting that all the major revitalization programmes in Fianna Fáil have been done when the party in is opposition: Lemass's programme of revitalization in the late 1940s and mid 1950s, Lynch's reforms from 1973-77 and the Ahern reorganization of 1996-7. The party needs now, however, to find a means of renewing itself while simultaneously being in government if it is to be able, even to contain the electoral onslaught that appears to await it. If not, Fianna Fáil is likely to get a lengthy opportunity to revitalize itself in opposition.

New More Radical Fine Gael is Emerging

Frank Flannery
Director of Organization, Fine Gael

Born in Co. Galway and educated at St. Clement's College, Limerick, NUIG and UCD where he took an MBA. Joined Rehab Group in 1973 and became Group Chief Executive in 1981. Held position until he stood down in 2006. Established Rehab Lotteries in Ireland and Charity Lotteries in the UK. Has served on RTÉ Authority, National Rehabilitation Board and St. Luke's and St. Anne's Hospitals' Boards. Former Chairman of Disability Federation of Ireland. Has been involved with Fine Gael since 1977. Member of Strategy Group (1981-2) and so-called National Handlers up to 1987. Trustee of the Party, member of Executive Council and former Director of Elections.

I hope you will forgive me if I start with a little history. As we all know, the great mother ship from which our two main political parties were launched was the Sinn Féin Party that emerged from the elections of December 1918. However, the political landscape that we currently enjoy, if that is the right word, only began to emerge in June 1922. In one of the most important General Elections ever fought in this country, the Pro-Treaty Sinn Féin Party defeated the Anti-Treaty Sinn Féin Party, by 59 seats to 35. Labour, making its first foray into electoral politics, won only 16 seats.

The 1922 election set a pattern for Irish politics, which has broadly endured to this day.

The 1922 election set a pattern for Irish politics, which has broadly endured to this day. Pro-Treaty Sinn Féin morphed into Cumann na nGaedheal, which then became Fine Gael. Anti-Treaty Sinn Féin split into Fianna Fáil and a rump Sinn Féin party. Labour was, for many decades, the odd man out with no direct connection to Sinn Féin, owing its origin to the Labour movement. However, that is no longer the case following its merger with Democratic Left in 1999, a party that was previously known as Official Sinn Féin. In other words, we can probably regard the Labour Party today as an associate member of the Old Sinn Féin Club.

The three party system or as it is sometimes described, the two and a half party system, established in 1922, has broadly remained in place ever since. Nor is there any sign, as far as I can see, that this system is under any threat. Nearly 70 per cent of the electorate voted for the three main parties in the local polls, while the remaining 30 per cent of the vote was split between modern Sinn Féin, the Greens and Independents.

Fine Gael was established in 1933, one year after Cumann na nGaedhael suffered its first election defeat to Fianna Fáil in 1932. It was the result of a merger between Cumann na nGaedhael, the Army Comrades Association and the National Centre Party, a party with strong connections with the old Irish Parliamentary Party. Although most analyses of this period have tended to focus on the inclusion of the Blueshirts in the formation of Fine Gael, I believe that the merger with the Centre Party was actually much more significant. By allying itself with elements of the old Irish Parliamentary Party in 1933, the new Fine Gael Party effectively distanced itself from its more radical Republican inheritance. Fianna Fáil, of course, mercilessly exploited this development. It very successfully tagged Fine Gael as the 'West Brit' party, the Establishment party, the party of the status quo

The incorporation of the Centre Party into Fine Gael also allowed Fianna Fáil to argue that its opponent was the party of the Lawyer and the Big Farmer, whereas it presented itself as the party of the small farmer and the man in the street. Fianna Fáil's very successful branding of Fine Gael, and Fine Gael's inability or unwillingness to resist this branding, is one of the chief reasons why Fine Gael has spent so much of its history in opposition. It would be wrong, however, to suggest that Fine Gael's lack of electoral success was simply an issue of poor branding. Fianna Fáil was and remains one of the great democratic parties of the world, and an election machine par excellence. Any party, regardless of its brand, would have found it very difficult to compete with it.

However, things may finally be changing. Although it is far too soon to be certain, I think we may be at an inflection point where the continuing dominance of Fianna Fáil can no longer be taken

Although most analyses of this period have tended to focus on the inclusion of the Blueshirts in the formation of Fine Gael, I believe that the merger with the Centre Party was actually much more significant.

for granted. If we look at the polls from June 2008 to May 2009, they show the following key developments:

- Support for Fianna Fáil has halved from 47 per cent to 24 per cent
- Support for Fine Gael has risen from 20 per cent to 34 per cent
- Support for Labour went from 10 per cent to 17 per cent, peaking at 21 per cent in February 2009.

Fianna Fáil was and remains one of the great democratic parties of the world, and an election machine par excellence. Any party, regardless of its brand, would have found it very difficult to compete with it.

If we look at the Local and European elections two things stand out. First, although Labour did well, it did not achieve the political breakthrough it has always craved – and that opinion polls indicated might be possible. Second, it was Fine Gael that achieved a historic breakthrough. For the first time in its history, it is the biggest party in the State and by a large margin. Labour's lack of a breakthrough reflects a very uneven geographical performance. The party did well in the East. They are now the largest party in three out of the four local authorities in Dublin (City Council, Fingal and Dún Laoghaire), and are in second place in South Dublin. However, Labour did poorly in the West and managed to get only 4 per cent of the farmers' vote nationally.

The most striking aspect of the local elections was the fact that Fine Gael, for the first time since 1927, outperformed Fianna Fáil in a national election. If we look at the Lansdowne exit poll data, it is clear that Fine Gael scored consistently ahead of Fianna Fáil and Labour in every demographic, socio economic and age group. Its highest performance was 63 per cent among farmers but it lead in all groupings and; its lowest was 29 per cent in the 18 to 24 age group and in the C2DE socio-demographic group which for Fine Gael is a very high level in these segments. Fianna Fáil's highest vote was 27 per cent in the 50+ age group and its lowest was in the 25 to 34 age band where it gained only 20 percent of the vote.

While all of this is very positive for Fine Gael, it leaves open the question of whether 2009 represents a real breakthrough for Fine Gael, or is just a temporary blip before normal service resumes. There are three arguments that can be made in favour of the temporary blip thesis. We are in the the middle of the worst recession in modern times and a

Government party is always going to do badly in mid-term elections. The locals are not a true test of the electorate's mood. Fine Gael was riding high in the early 1980s, only to come crashing down a few years later. There is a very good chance that history will repeat itself and that Fianna Fáil will come roaring back. Let me discuss each of these points in turn.

First, there is no doubt that any party in Government right now would be under pressure. However, it is also clear from various pieces of research that the electorate holds this particular Government directly responsible for the economic crisis we now face. The electorate has not bought the argument that Ireland is just one economy among many that is suffering from a global recession. There is a general understanding that Ireland is, as the recent IMF report points out, suffering the worst recession of all of the advanced economies. Moreover, all of the economic commentary right now is suggesting that we are still a very long way from an economic recovery let alone feeling its beneficial effects.

Second, I think there is little doubt that the local elections were a credible test of public opinion. The electorate were clearly voting on national rather than local issues. This is supported by the fact that the local results were broadly in line with the national polls. Indeed, Garret FitzGerald has argued that, because of Fianna Fáil's traditional strength in local government, the local results probably underestimate the full extent of the national shift away from Fianna Fáil. I think it is important to remember, in this context, that Fianna Fáil has always seen control of local government as the key to national success. This control, in the words of Lemass, 'cemented Fianna Fáil into the political structures of the country'. In 2009, that cement was well and truly smashed.

Finally, there is the legitimate issue that Fine Gael has, as at times in its past, failed to take full advantage of electoral opportunities. Historically, we have suffered from a sense of inferiority, which has seriously hindered our ability to win. This time, however, it is different. I have been around Fine Gael since 1977 and I can clearly see the emergence of a winner's mentality in the party. That historical sense of inferiority, while not completely gone, is almost gone. More importantly, the party is finally getting a clear image of what it wants to be. I think there is a desire in Fine Gael to re-capture some of the vision and idealism

The most striking aspect of the local elections was the fact that Fine Gael, for the first time since 1927, outperformed Fianna Fáil in a national election.

that motivated the founding generation of this State. There is also a growing understanding in the party that the economic crisis obligates us to reinvent the way we run our economy and govern our country. Put simply, I think a new, more radical Fine Gael is emerging.

But where does all of this leave Fianna Fáil? I think it is now Fianna Fáil rather than Fine Gael that has to start asking some serious questions about itself and its role in Irish society. One of the party's key advantages in the past was its claim that Fianna Fáil wasn't just a political party, but a national movement Fine Gael was the party of the privileged, while Fianna Fáil was the party for everyone, the party that was in touch with mood and soul of the nation. I just do not see how Fianna Fáil can continue to credibly make those claims. How can a party which has repeatledly portrayed as the friend of the bankers and the developers, now present itself as the party of the people? How can a party that has abandoned the austerity and probity of its founders, claim that it is in touch with the needs and desires of ordinary people?

In the past, Fianna Fáil could rely on the fierce loyalty of its voters. If the local elections told us nothing else, they told us that Fianna Fáil can no long rely on that blind loyalty. Those days are well and truly gone. In the past, Fianna Fáil could also rely on their leaders being a strong electoral asset. Elections were normally built around the leader. This may not be the case with Brian Cowen. Brian Cowen is, as Ruairí Quinn has noted, the most tribal Fianna Fáil leader since de Valera. However, he may lack the charisma and vision of de Valera. Brian Cowen has pointed to Lemass as his political hero. But he may lack Lemass's optimism and can-do approach to politics and Government.

In the past, Fianna Fáil was able to present the public with a strong vision of the Ireland it wanted to create. These days, the party simply does not 'do' vision. Instead of the language of hope and aspiration, we hear the voice of the technocrat. Is it possible that 2007 was for Fianna Fáil what 1992 was for the British Conservatives – the election they needed to lose? By winning that election, have they seriously compromised their long-term future? Am I saying that Fianna Fáil is down and out? Absolutely not! I am certainly not writing any obitu-

However, it is also clear from various pieces of research that the electorate holds this particular Government directly responsible for the economic crisis we now face.

I think there is a desire in Fine Gael to re-capture some of the vision and idealism that motivated the founding generation of this State.

ary for Fianna Fáil today. But I do believe that Fianna Fáil faces a series of challenges without parallel in its history.As a result, Fine Gael has an historic opportunity to position itself as the natural party of Government.

To paraphrase the old slogan: 'Fianna Fáil's difficulty is Fine Gael's opportunity.' But on the other hand – and finally – all political parties and the entire system now faces perhaps its greatest challenge ever, to deliver a safe future for our citizens. How each of them responds to this challenge, will also, no doubt, have a significance on the shape of the political landscape. Now we must also look to the past, the 1950s, 1970s and the 1980s, what was done well and badly in past recessions. The philosopher Santana probably said it best: 'Those who cannot remember the past are condemned to repeat it.'

There is also a growing understanding in the party that the economic crisis obligates us to reinvent the way we run our economy and govern our country.

References

Official Opening [Michael McLoone]

1 Ireland's Five Part Crisis: An Integrated National Response, National Economic & Social Development Office (NESC), No. 118, March 2009.

Chapter 1 [Rowena A. Pecchenino]

2 I would like to thank Jim O'Leary and Finbarr Bradley for their comments and guidance. Without their assistance I could not have written this paper. All errors or interpretations are, of course, mine alone.

3 John Paul II, Homily, Phoenix Park, 1979; http://www.vatican.va/holy_father/john_paul_ii/homilies/1979/documents/hf_jp ii_hom_19790929_irlanda-dublino_en.html

4 R. O'Donnell, 'Reinventing Ireland: From Sovereignty to Partnership', Jean Monnet Inaugural Lecture UCD, 29 April 1999.

5 B. Nolan, 'Trends in Income Inequality in Ireland', Public Lecture, 14 March 2006.

6 T. Inglis, Moral Monopoly: The Rise and Fall of the Catholic Church in Modern Ireland (Dublin: UCD Press, 2nd revised ed., 1998).

7 H. E. Scharrer, 'Ireland Out of Step', *Intereconomics,* 36(2), 2001, pp. 57-58.

8 J. FitzGerald, 'The Macro-Economic Implications of Changes in Public Service Pay Rates', *Quarterly Economic Commentary,* Winter 2002, pp. 43-58; F. Ruane and R. Lyons, 'Wage Determination in the Irish Economy', *Quarterly Economic Commentary,* Winter 2002, pp. 59-76; J. O'Leary, 'Benchmarking the Benchmarkers', *Quarterly Economic Commentary,* Winter 2002, pp. 77-91.

9 National Competitiveness Council, Overview of Ireland's Productivity Performance, 1980-2005, 2006.

10 'Hear that Hissing Sound?', *The Economist,* 8 December 2005; J. Malzubris, 'Ireland's housing market: bubble trouble', *ECFIN Country* Crisis, *Focus,* 5(9), 2008, pp. 1-7.

11 IMF, Country Report, No. 07/325, September 2007.

12 OECD, Economic Surveys – Ireland 2008, April 2008.

Chapter 1 [Karl Whelan]

13 Patrick Honohan and Brendan Walsh, 'Catching up with the Leaders: The Irish Hare', Brookings Papers on Economic Activity, Part 1, 2002, pp. 1-57.

Chapter 1 [Fridrik M. Baldursson]

14 Patrick Honohan (2009), *Euro Membership and Bank Stability Friends or Foes? Lessons from Ireland,* available at http://www.tcd.ie/Economics/staff/phonohan/.

15 Kaarlo Jännäri, Report on Banking Regulation and Supervision in Iceland: Past, Present *and Future,* 2009, available at http://eng.forsaetisraduneyti.is/news-and -articles/nr/3581.

Chapter 2 [David Murphy]

16 Karl Marx, *Das Kapital*, Ch. 10, 1867.

Chapter 3 [Peter Bacon]

[17] Adele Bergin, Thomas Conefey, John FitzGerald and Ide Kearney, 'Macroeconomic Context for a Sustainable Recovery', ESRI, March 2009.
[18] Annual Competitiveness Report 2008: Volume Two: Ireland's Competitiveness Challenge, January 2009.
[19] Retail Related Import & Distribution Study, Competition Authority Dublin, July 2009.

Chapter 5 [Michael O'Sullivan]

[20] Karl Marx and Friedrich Engels, *Ireland and the Irish Question* (Moscow: Progress Publishers, 1986).
[21] P. Pettit, Republicanism: A Theory of Freedom and Government (Oxford: Oxford University Press, 1997).

Chapter 6 [Annette Hughes]

[22] The average GNP forecast for the Irish economy in DKM's November 2008 edition of the *Economy Watch* was 2.1 per cent for 2009. This was based on 15 forecasts made over the previous three months. Available at www.dkm.ie
[23] Calculated by the Central Bank of Ireland. The *nominal* measure isolates the effect on competitiveness of exchange rate movements and takes a weighted average of the bilateral exchange rates with 56 trading partners. The consumer price deflated HCI (*real HCI*) takes into account changes in domestic inflation relative to price changes in the 56 trading partners along with exchange rate developments. The index deflated by producer prices covers 36 trading partners due to more limited data.
[24] Getting Fit Again: The Short Term Priorities to Restore Competitiveness, National Competitiveness Council, Forfás, June 2009.
[25] Figure taken from the Report of the Special Group on Public Service Numbers and Expenditure Programmes, July 2009, vol. 1, p.1.
[26] National Employment Survey, CSO, Annual earnings were reported to be 32 per cent higher in the public sector, 2008.
[27] Report of the Independent Review of Credit Availability – Review of Lending to SMEs, Mazars, June 2009.
[28] IBEC, Survey of Credit Conditions, November 2008.
[29] NCC Statement on the Costs of Doing Business 2009 (work in progress, unpublished).

Chapter 6 [David Begg]

[30] Adair Turner, *Just Capital – The Liberal Economy* (London: MacMillan, 2001), p. 41.
[31] Paul Krugman, *Pop Internationalism* (Cambridge, MA: MIT Press, 1997).
[32] Seán Ó Riain, The Politics of High-Tech Growth – Development Network States in the Global Economy (Cambridge: Cambridge University Press, 2004), p. 234.
[33] ibid., p. 242.

Chapter 6 [Brendan Tuohy]

[34] R. Fanning, *The Irish Department of Finance, 1922-1958* (Dublin: Institute of Public Administration, 1976), p. 24.

35 Institute of Public Administration, *The Devlin Report: A Summary* (Dublin: Institute of Public Administration, 1970), p. 3.
36 PA Consulting Group, 'Evaluation of the Strategic Management Initiative', Dublin, 2002, Department of An Taoiseach (http://www.onegov.ie/eng/Publications/Evaluation_of_SMI.pdf).
37 Office of the Comptroller and Auditor General, 'Improving Performance: Public Service Case Studies', Dublin, 2007.
38 OECD, 'Public Management Review: Ireland – Towards an Integrated Public Service', Dublin, 2008.
39 Report of the Task Force on the Public Service, 'Transforming Public Services: Citizen-Centred – Performance Focused', Dublin, 2008.
40 Government Statement on Transforming Public Services, Dublin, 2008.
41 Department of Finance, 'The Report of the Special Group on Public Services Numbers and Expenditure', Dublin, 2009.

Chapter 7 [Don Thornhill]

42 This is an abridged version of an earlier draft paper made available at the MacGill Summer School in July 2009. The earlier draft can be downloaded from www.competitiveness.ie or can be obtained by emailing the author at dthornhill@eircom.net.
43 **Disclaimer:** The National Competiveness Council (NCC) which I currently chair has recently published a policy paper on education which I refer to in the paper. Nonetheless, except where otherwise attributed, the views and opinions expressed in this paper are my own and should not be attributed to any of the organisations with which I am associated including the National Competitiveness Council. Any errors are my responsibility.
44 NCC Statement on Education and Training, 9 March 2009 – see http://www.competitiveness.ie/media/ncc090309_statement_on_education.pdf
45 See OECD, PISA Database 2006; www.pisa.oecd.org/document/2/0,3343,en_32252351_32236191_39718850_1_1_1_1.0 00html. Discussed in more detail in the earlier draft of this paper.
46 EUROSTAT, Structural Indicators, see http://epp.eurostat.ec.europa.eu/portal/page/portal structural_indicators/indicators/social_ cohesion
47 OECD, Education at a Glance, 2008; see https://www.oecd.int/olisweb/portal/site/olisnet/menuitem.cc9285ff2a6fd9900444078 2643c066a0/
48 Emperica, Benchmarking Access and Use of ICT in European Schools, 2006 see http://ec.europa.eu/information_society/eeurope/i2010/benchmarking/index_en.htm
49 Source: OECD, Education at a Glance 2008. Table B2.2. Data discussed in the earlier draft of this paper.
50 NCC Statement on Education and Training, p. 6.
51 Report of the Special Group on Public Service Numbers and Expenditure Programmes, July 2009; see www.finance.gov.ie
52 For more detail see a provocative blog post by Ronan Lyons on teacher salaries http://www.ronanlyons.com/2009/04/20/tackling-the-thorny-issue-of-teachers-pay/
53 Purchasing power parities are used to compare living standards in different countries.

They indicate the appropriate exchange rate to use when expressing incomes and prices in different countries in a common currency. PPP is the exchange rate that equates the price of a basket of identical traded goods and services in the countries being compared.

54 The importance of this has since been reduced.

55 Report of the Special Group on Public Service Numbers and Expenditure Programmes, July 2009; see www.finance.gov.ie ,Volume II, pp. 58-60.

56 These include securing sufficient enrolments, complying with national curricular requirements, employing qualified teachers and adhering to other national regulations and policy requirements.

57 These issues are discussed in more detail in the earlier draft of this paper accessible at www.competitiveness.ie or available from the author at dthornhill@eircom.net

58 Where is the wealth of nations? World Bank, 2006; http://siteresources.worldbank.org/INTEE/214578-1110886258964/20748034/All.pdf

Chapter 11 [Fiach Mac Conghail]

59 Michael Cronin, 'The Long Now', *The Journal of Music in Ireland*, November-December 2008, p.14.

Chapter 11 [Mary Cloake]

60 Kevin Whelan, *Between filiation and affiliation: the space of art* (Dublin: The Arts Council 2008).

61 *Donegal Cultural Compass* (Donegal: Donegal County Enterprise Board, 2009).

62 Smart Economy Policy Document.

63 See www.artscouncil.ie for publications discussing this issue.

64 Finbarr Bradley and James J. Kennelly, Capitalising on Culture, Competing on Difference (Dublin: Blackhall Publishing, 2009).

65 Report of The Special Group on Public Service Numbers and Expenditure Programmes (Dublin: Government Publications, 2009).

66 John McHugh, unpublished document, July 2009.

67 Noel Kelly, Economic Conditions of Visual Artists in Ireland (Dublin: VAI, 2009).

68 Fintan Vallely, 'The Arts, the State and the Wealth of Nations: Case Studies of Ireland and Scotland. Session 4. Traditional/Folk Music. Paper for *The Arts The State and the Wealth of Nations Conference*, Trinity College Dublin, 23/24 April 2009.

69 ibid.

70 Seamus Heaney, The Mud Vision, New Selected Poems 1966-1987 (London: Faber and Faber, 1990).

Chapter 11 [Finbarr Bradley]

71 M.E. Porter, *The Competitive Advantage of Nations* (New York: Free Press, 1990).

72 R. Florida, *The Rise of the Creative Class* (New York: Basic Books, 2004).

73 P.J. Mathews, *Revival: The Abbey Theatre, Sinn Féin, The Gaelic League and the Co-operative Movement* (Notre Dame: University of Notre Dame Press, 2003).

74 D. Landes, *The Wealth and Poverty of Nations* (London: Little, Brown and Co., 1998), p. 516.

75 D. Hock, *One from Many: VISA and the Rise of the Chaordic Organization* (San Francisco, CA: Berrett-Koehler Publishers, 2005).

76 P. O'Connor, Beyond the Mist: What Irish Mythology Can Teach Us About Ourselves (London: Orion, 2000).

77 T.K. Whitaker, *Interests* (Dublin: Institute of Public Administration, 1983), p. 239.